D1877986

Treasure of Ambedkar Series 01

The Evolution of Provincial Finance in British India

A Study in the Provincial Decentralisation of Imperial Finance

Treasure of Ambedkar Series 01

The Evolution of Provincial Finance in British India

A Study in the Provincial Decentralisation of Imperial Finance

Dr B.R. Ambedkar

KALPAZ

© Reserved
All rights reserved. No part of this work may be reproduced, stored, adapted, or transmitted in any form or by any means, electronic, mechanical, photocopying, micro-filming recording or otherwise, or translated in any language, without the prior written permission of the copyright owner and the publisher. The book is sold subject to the condition that it shall not, by way of trade or otherwise, be lent, resold, hired out, or otherwise circulated without the prior publisher's written consent in any form of binding or cover other than that in which it is published.

The views and opinions expressed in this book are author(s) own and the facts reported by them have been verified to the extent possible, and the publishers are not in any way liable for the same.

Treasure of Ambedkar Series 01

The Evolution of Provincial Finance in British India

ISBN: 978-93-5128-267-9

First Published 1924
Reprint **2017**, in India by
Kalpaz Publications
C-30, Satyawati Nagar,
Delhi – 110052
E-mail: kalpaz@hotmail.com
Ph.: 9212142040

Printed at: G. Print Process, Delhi

PREFACE

For a long time to come students will be saved the conventional humiliation of making an apology for presenting a study of Indian Finance or Economics. But it will, on the other hand, be necessary, I fear, for an equally long period, for them to tender an apology for the shortcomings of their respective investigations. Even when the treatment of a subject is analytical, a good analytical study often requires an historical setting. Unfortunately no spade-work has been done in the field of Indian Finance. Consequently the difficulties which beset a pioneer in that field are immense. There is occasionally the difficulty owing to the antecedents of some point not having been quite completely elucidated. Often there is the apprehension of some error having crept in, and, when there is hardly anyone to save the student from it, there is nothing but to smart under a sense of irritating affliction. Not very seldom does it happen that a pioneer student is jubilant over his find of material bearing on his subject, but it is not without a long and wearisome search that he is able to sift the grain from the chaff. Again, sources sometimes prove false guides, so that a perusal of them only ends in a considerable waste of time and energy.

Precisely these have been the difficulties besetting the present task. There are no books to prepare the student for his work and hardly any savant to lighten his labour or set him on the proper track. Notwithstanding such odds, an attempt is made to make this study thorough without being too detailed. This has rendered the undertaking quite a laborious one. But I do not wish to speak of the labour that is involved, nor do I wish to astonish the reader with what might appear to be a formidable list of books and documents consulted in the preparation of this monograph. What I am anxious to speak of are its shortcomings. There are indeed many of them which a well-versed critic may spot out. It is my hope that they are not of such a character as seriously to impair the value which this monograph may otherwise be said to possess. My regrets are with regard to only a few of them. I have specified a date as to when Local Decentralization of Finance commenced in India ; but I feel that that date may not be the earliest and that there may be a date earlier than that one given by me. I wish I had settled that point finally. But that would have been a task analogous to that of searching for a needle in a haystack, and it is doubtful whether the value of that result would have been commensurate with that labour. Besides, although I am not confident of my date, my feeling is that later researches may after all confirm my statement. Another matter which I have not dealt with, but which I would have liked to have dealt with, was the inter-relation of Provincial and Local Finance. This I had originally planned to do, but left pursuing it because I found that the chief subject I was dealing with, namely, the Provincial Decentralization of Imperial Finance, began to be overlaid by facts and arguments not germane to that topic. These shortcomings will, however, be removed by a supplementary monograph on Local Finance in British India, which is well under way and which I hope to publish before long. Occasional repetitions may also be pointed out as a defect of this monograph. That they should be avoided is all very well. But where economy in the words of explanation are likely to obscure, repetitions such as are unavoidable must be justified, for the interests of clarification should always outweigh the tedium they involve.

I cannot conclude this preface without thanking Mr. Robinson, the Financial Secretary at the India Office, for many valuable suggestions and for the loan of many important documents bearing on the subject. I am also thankful to Prof. Cannan, of the University of London, who has read the rough draft of a small part of the manuscript. My debt to Prof. Seligman, my teacher at Columbia University, is of course immense: for from him I learned my first lessons in the theory of Public Finance. I am obliged to my friend Mr. C. S. Deolé for assistance afforded in the dreary task of reading the proofs.

FOREWORD

The problem discussed by Mr. Ambedkar in his excellent dissertation is one that is arousing a growing interest in all parts of the world. From the very beginning we find fiscal burdens imposed by both central and local governments. As soon as there was a political organization, the conduct of war on the one hand and the provision of local protection and convenience on the other called for expenditures on the part of both state and local authorities. It was only at a later period that there was interpolated between the local and the central political organizations the intermediate form which Mr. Ambedkar calls the provincial government. The names applied to these various classes of expenditure differ with the authorities themselves. In India we speak of local, provincial, and imperial expenditure; in Germany, of local, state, and imperial expenditure; in the United States and Switzerland, of local, state, and federal expenditure; in Australia, of local, state, and commonwealth expenditure; in South Africa and Canada, of local, provincial, and federal expenditure; and in France, of local, departmental, and general expenditure. In some cases, as in the British Empire, there is being developed a still more comprehensive class of expenditures, borne by the empire at large.

The character and importance of these various classes of expenditure and the relations between them are undergoing a continual change, due to an alteration in the functions of government. This is itself largely due to a change in the general economic conditions, resulting in a gradual modification either of political structure or of administrative activity. In some countries, as in Canada, Argentine and Brazil, the provinces are really a creation of the central government; in other countries, as in the United States, Germany, and Switzerland, the federal government is the creation of the originally sovereign states. In some countries the intermediate (provincial or state) government is suffering a loss of importance as compared with the local or central governments; in other countries, the reverse is true.

With the increasing pressure of taxation and the development under modern democracies of augmented governmental functions, the problem of the equitable distribution of burden among these various forms of government is becoming more or less acute. What Mr. Ambedkar calls assignments, assigned revenue, and shared revenue, is symptomatic of the choice of methods in all countries. One of three fundamental plans must be pursued. Either the central or the provincial government may be maintained by the other, according to the relative degree of strength: in former times, in the United States, and in Germany the states were supposed to support the central government, either wholly or in large measure; in modern times, in Canada and Australia, the reverse is true. Or, secondly, distinct revenues may be allocated to the separate governments: until recently the federal government in the United States, Germany, and Switzerland was supported primarily by indirect taxes; the state governments by direct taxes. Or, thirdly, the revenues may be collected by one government and a portion of the proceeds allotted to the other: there are many instances of a state or provincial tax being shared with the federal government, and still more examples of a federal or central tax being shared with the state or provincial government. In the United States at present the proper disposition of the inheritance tax as between state and federal government is fast becoming a burning question; in Germany the fiscal relations of state and federal government are in the forefront of political discussion.

The value of Mr. Ambedkar's contribution to this discussion lies in the objective recitation of the facts and the impartial analysis of the interesting development that has taken place in his native country. The lessons are applicable to other countries as well; nowhere, to my knowledge, has such a detailed study of the underlying principles been made.

It is true that only half of the picture is presented. For the situation has everywhere been complicated by the entrance of the local authorities into the field; and by their claims to fiscal consideration as compared with both state (provincial) and general (federal) demands. In the United States, for instance, the now widely debated problem of financing the schools is largely dependent for its solution on the proper answer to be given to the question of fiscal interrelations. To this question Mr. Ambedkar proposes to devote himself in a subsequent study. If he succeeds in illumining that situation as successfully as he here deals with the initial problem, he will lay us all under still deeper obligations.

EDWIN R. A. SELIGMAN

COLUMBIA UNIVERSITY, NEW YORK
October, 1924

CONTENTS

INTRODUCTION

DEFINITION AND OUTLINE OF THE SUBJECT

A STUDENT of Indian Finance has two chief sources of information and guidance open to him. One is the Annual Budget Statement, and the other is the annual volume of Finance and Revenue Accounts. Though separately issued, the two are really companion volumes inasmuch as the Financial Statement forms, so to speak, an exhaustive explanatory memorandum of the annual financial transactions, the details of which are recorded in the volume of Finance and Revenue Accounts.

Helpful as these sources are, they are not without their puzzles. A reference to the latest volume of Finance and Revenue Accounts will show that the accounts therein are classified under four different categories :—(1) Imperial, (2) Provincial, (3) Incorporated Local, and (4) Excluded Local. But this is by no means uniformly so. For instance, a volume of the same series before 1870 will not be found to contain the accounts called "Provincial," nor will the accounts styled "Local" be found in any volume prior to 1863. Similarly, any volume of the Financial Statements before 1870 will be found to divide the financial transactions covered therein into—Imperial and Local only. But a volume of the same series after 1908 curiously enough groups the accounts not under Imperial and Local but under (1) Imperial, and (2) Provincial, while the Financial Statements after 1921 cover only the Imperial Transactions. Nothing is more confusing to a beginner than the entrance of the new, and the exit of the old, categories of accounts.[1] The natural question that he will ask is, how did these different categories evolve, and how are they related to one another ?

In the present study an endeavour is made to explain the rise and growth of one of them, namely, the "Provincial." But in order that there may be no difficulty in following the argument it is deemed advisable to preface this study with an outline defining its subject-matter and indicating the inter-relations of the parts into which it is divided. To facilitate a thorough understanding of the subject the study is divided into four parts, *each* one dealing with the Origin, Development and Organization of Provincial Finance and the final form in which it

[1] It is surprising that the category of accounts, called "Excluded Local," which is to be found in the volume of Finance and Revenue Accounts, never appears in the Financial Statement. The author has not been able to trace the reason for its exclusion. In the *Madras Manual* (Vol. I, Chapter V, pp. 467–9) it is argued that the ground for the exclusion is technical and consists in the circumstance that the Excluded Funds are not collected by the ordinary revenue collecting agency of the Central Government and are not subject to its interference. Another technical ground may also be found in a ruling given in the third edition of the Civil Account Code (p. 137), according to which Funds were called Excluded, i.e. from the Financial Statement, because they were not required to be lodged in the Government Treasury. But a ruling on the same point given in the seventh and latest edition (p. 122) of the same seems to imply that every public fund must of necessity be lodged in a Government Treasury. The more probable explanation is that given in the *Moral and Material Progress Report* for 1882–3 (Part I, p. 107), where it is said that these funds have no place in General Finance because they "consist chiefly of special trusts and endowments."

was cast by the constitutional changes of 1919. In Part I a somewhat thorny, untrodden and yet necessary ground has been covered in order to give a complete idea of the origin of Provincial Finance. While due homage is paid to the adage which requires students of the present to study the past, nothing more than the past of the present has been dealt with. In Chapter I, Part I, an attempt is made to present a picture of the system of Finance as it existed before the inauguration of the Provincial Finance and to state the causes that called for a change in its organization. In Chapter II a rival system of Finance proposed during the period of reconstruction is brought to light and shown why it failed of general acceptance. Chapter III is devoted to the discussion of a plan which was a compromise between the existing system and its rival, and the circumstances which forced its reception.

Having explained the Origin in Part I, the Development of Provincial Finance is made the subject of Part II. How far the arrangement followed in Part I is helpful must in the absence of anything to compare with it be left to the opinion of the reader. In regard to Part II, however, it is to be noted that the arrangement is different from what is adopted in the only fragmentary sketch published on the subject of Provincial Finance in 1887 by the late Justice Ranade. As will be seen from a perusal of Part II, one of the features of Provincial Finance was that the revenues and charges incorporated into the Provincial Budgets were revised every fifth year. Justice Ranade in his pamphlet, which simply covers the ground traversed in Part II of this study, and that too up to 1882 only, has taken this feature as a norm by which to mark off the different stages in the growth of Provincial Finance from one to another. Consequently, each quinquennial period to him becomes a stage, and in his hands the history of Provincial Finance falls into as many stages as the quinquenniums into which it can be divided. It may, however, be submitted that if every revision had changed the fundamentals of Provincial Finance, such an arrangement would not have been illogical. But as a matter of fact, Provincial Finance did not change its hue at every revision. What the revisions did was to temper the wind to the shorn lamb. If the history of the development of Provincial Finance is to be divided into stages according to the changes in the fundamental basis thereof, then emphasis has to be laid on features altogether different in character. Writers on the theory of Public Finance seem to conceive the subject as though it were primarily a matter of equity in taxation and economy in expenditure. But to a Chancellor of the Exchequer finance is eminently practical with a problem to solve, namely, how to bring about an equilibrium in the Budget. If we scan the history of Provincial Finance in British India with a view to discover the method of meeting the problem of equilibrium in Provincial Budgets and the changes introduced in it from time to time, we shall find that Provincial Finance has evolved through three distinct stages, each with its own mode of supply, namely, Assignments, Assigned Revenues, and Shared Revenues. Consequently, instead of following the mechanical plan of Justice Ranade, it is believed to be more logical and instructive to divide the stages in the growth of Provincial Finance according to the method of supply to the Provincial Governments adopted by the Government of India. Consequently, Part II, which deals with the Development of Provincial Finance, is divided into three Chapters: (1) Budget by Assignment, (2) Budget by Assigned Revenues, and (3) Budget by Shared Revenues.

This discussion of the Origin and Development of Provincial Finance is followed in Part III by an examination of its Organization. Chapter VII in Part III is devoted to the analysis of the hitherto neglected rules of limitations on the financial powers of Provincial Governments primarily to bring out the fact that Provincial Finance was not independent in its organization. The analysis of the true position of Provincial Finance is, however, reserved for Chapter VIII, in which the conclusion is fortified by a reference to the character of these limitations, that, notwithstanding the high-sounding appellation of Provincial Finance, there were neither provincial revenues nor provincial services as separate from Imperial revenues and Imperial services, so that instead of being federal in its organization the system remained essentially imperial. Chapter IX discusses how far it was possible to enlarge the scope of Provincial Finance without jeopardy to the constitutional responsibilities of the Government of India under the old law.

Part IV is a discussion of the changes introduced into the mechanism of Provincial Finance by the Reforms Act of 1919. Chapter X of this Part is devoted to the analysis of the causes which led to these changes. In Chapter XI a full description of the changes effected by the new law is given, while Chapter XII forms a critique of the new regime.

In view of the fact that students of Indian Finance ordinarily content themselves with the phrase "Decentralization of Finance," to indicate Provincial Finance, a word of explanation in justification of what may rather be called the too cumbersome title of this study. No student of Indian Finance, who is sufficiently acquainted with the branching off of the system in different directions, will fail to mark the inadequacy of the phrase Decentralization of Finance to mean Provincial Finance. If there were in the Indian system only the Provincial Decentralization there would have been no necessity to labour for a new title. As a matter of fact, the starting points of decentralization are by no means the same, and the systems evolved through it are quite different in character. For instance, the centre of decentralization and the systems evolved by the policy of decentralization brought into operation in 1855 were different from the centre and the systems evolved therefrom by the policy of decentralization initiated in 1870. Again, the centre which is gradually being decentralized since 1892, be it noted, is different from those affected by the decentralization of 1855 or 1870. To put it more clearly, the decentralization of 1855 was the decentralization of *Indian* Finance resulting in—

(I) the separation of Local from Imperial Finance.

The decentralization of 1870 was the decentralization of *Imperial* Finance resulting in—

(II) the separation of Provincial from Imperial Finance.

And the decentralization commencing from 1882 is the decentralization of *Provincial* Finance resulting in—

(III) the separation of Local from Provincial Finance.

Obviously then, "Decentralization of Finance" far from being indicative of Provincial Finance, is a general name for this variegated and multifarious process of decentralization described above, and it cannot but be confusing to use as a title to the study of one line of decentralization a phrase which can be generically applied to all the three lines of decentralization distinguished above. In order, therefore, that this study may not be taken to pertain to a line of decentralization other than the one it purports to investigate, it has been thought proper to designate it "The Evolution of Provincial Finance in British India" with a sub-title, "A Study in the Provincial Decentralization of Imperial Finance," where the words Provincial and Imperial must be read with the emphasis due to them. How careless the phraseology often is may be instanced by the fact that Justice Ranade's pamphlet referred to above is styled "Decentralization of Provincial Finance." Although it deals with the development of Provincial Finance, it is likely to be passed over by the student, for its title implies that its subject-matter must be the growth of Local Finance. If Justice Ranade had been conscious of the varieties of decentralization, he would have probably realized that the title of his pamphlet was false to its contents.

PART I

PROVINCIAL FINANCE : ITS ORIGIN

CHAPTER I

THE IMPERIAL SYSTEM

ITS GROWTH AND ITS BREAKDOWN

THE Imperial system of Government in India dates from the year 1833.

Of the two chief motives which led Parliament to establish it, one was to replace the existing multiplicity in the systems of justice and police by a uniform system of the same, common as far as possible to the whole of India with its varieties classified and systematized. Under the existing system then prevailing such multiplicity was inevitable, for not only the civil and military government and the ordering and management of the revenues of each of the three Presidencies, Bengal,[1] Madras,[2] and Bombay,[3] were vested in their respective Governors in Council, but each Governor in Council was also empowered to make and issue such rules, ordinances and regulations for the good order and civil government of the territories he individually commanded, provided that they were just and reasonable and not repugnant to the laws of the British realm. To the codes of law promulgated by these authorities must be added the whole body of English Statute law introduced in India so far as it was applicable, by the charter of George I

[1] 13 Geo. III, c. 63, s. 36

[2] 39 and 40 Geo. III, c. 79, s. 11.

[3] 47 Geo. III, Sess. 2, c. 68, s. 3.

in 1726 and such other English Acts subsequent to that date as were expressly extended to particular parts of the country.

The work of administering such a diverse body of laws proved so embarrassing that it was the view of the supreme Court of Calcutta that

> "no one person can pronounce an opinion or form a judgment . . . upon any disputed right of persons, respecting which doubt and confusion may not be raised by those who may choose to call it in question ; for very few of the public or persons in office at home, not even the Law Officers, can be expected to have so comprehensive and clear a view of the Indian system of law, as to know readily and familiarly the bearings of each part of it on the rest." [1]

The other motive was to create a strong central government to deal effectively with the European settlers in the country. It is to be noted that if the native population suffered under the uncertainties of law, the British population lived under the most galling restrictions. The revelations of oppressions by Englishmen practised, in the early days of British rule, contained in the report of the Secret Committee of the House of Commons appointed in 1771 to inquire into the affairs of the East India Company, were followed by very stringent laws governing the entry and residence of private British subjects in India. No British subject of European birth was allowed to reside in India beyond 10 miles from any one of the principal settlements without having previously obtained a special license from the Company or the Governor-General of India or the Governor of the principal settlement in question.[2] The Court of Directors of the Company, subject to revision of the Board of Control,[3] were empowered to refuse such licenses [4] and the Governments in India were strictly enjoined not to sanction the residence of British subjects on their own authorities except under special circumstances [5]

[1] Quoted in Herbert Cowell's *The History of the Constitution of Courts and Legislative Authorities in India*, Calcutta.

[2] 33 Geo. III, c. 52, s. 98.

[3] 53 Geo. III, c. 155, s. 38.

[4] *Ibid.*, s. 33.

[5] *Ibid.*, s. 37.

and were authorized, in cases they deemed proper, to declare licenses otherwise valid as void.[1] Counterfeiting licenses[2] and unlicensed residence[3] were made crimes punishable with fine or imprisonment; and persons who were dismissed from, and who had resigned service, were declared guilty of illicit trade if they lingered beyond the 10-mile limit after their time had expired.[4] Unlicensed British subjects were made liable to be deported,[5] and such as were licensed were required to register themselves in the court of the district in which they resided.[6] Subjected as they were to the regulations of the Local Government[7] they were made amenable to justice in India as well as in Great Britain for all illegal acts done in British India,[8] or in Native States.[9] To render them impotent to cause complications, they were not allowed to lend money to or be concerned in raising any for native princes[10] or foreign companies or foreign European merchants. Similarly to protect the natives from their oppression they were forbidden to lend money to the latter at a rate of interest exceeding 12 per cent. per annum on penalty of forfeiting for every offence treble the value,[11] and they were placed under the jurisdiction of the Justices of the Peace in all cases involving assault or trespass[12] on, and small debts[13] due to, the natives of India. Moreover, every British subject of European birth was required to register in the office of his district the name, etc., of his native stewards, agents, and partners,[14] on penalty of being disentitled to recover or receive any sum or sums of money by reason of the joint concern or to compel an account thereof by any suit in law or equity in any court within the provinces.[15]

The ruling race had long chafed at these restrictions,

[1] 53 Geo. III, c. 155, s. 36.
[2] *Ibid.*, s. 120.
[3] 33 Geo. III, c. 52, s. 131.
[4] *Ibid.*, s. 134.
[5] 53 Geo. III, c. 155, s. 104.
[6] *Ibid.*, s. 108.
[7] *Ibid.*, s. 35.
[8] 24 Geo. III, c. 25, s. 44.
[9] 26 Geo. III, c. 57, s. 67.
[10] 37 Geo. III, c. 142, s. 28.
[11] 13 Geo. III, c. 63, s. 30.
[12] 53 Geo. III, c. 155, s. 105.
[13] *Ibid.*, s. 106.
[14] 21 Geo. III, c. 70, s. 13.
[15] *Ibid.*, s. 16.

under which it was placed, without much avail. They were evidently aimed at keeping out an element dangerous to the stability of the Indian Empire, but, as time went on, and as the Indian Empire was consolidated by successive victories over the native princes, there was raised against these restrictions such a storm of indignant criticism that even those who had acquiesced in their virtue were forced to admit that they had outlived their purpose. While the British Parliament could not help abiding by the sentiments of the time, it refused to disregard the consequences which it thought would inevitably attend upon the free ingress of British subjects of European birth under the then existing system of government. It realized that a harmonious treatment of the immigrants and an effective control over them was absolutely essential. Parliament was afraid that the different governments armed as they were with co-equal and independent powers of legislation and administration by exercising these powers with regard to the immigrants entering their respective territories, with different views and according to inconsistent principles might integrate the whole mass of them into a disaffected body difficult to be dealt with. Besides the necessity of a harmonious treatment based on uniform principles, the fears of Parliament that the ingress of British immigrants would result in the revival of oppression on the natives were not completely allayed. As its recrudescence was felt to be a likely event, Parliament desired to subject them to a strong and uniform central control, so that the offender in one jurisdiction might not be able to find an asylum in another. Thus, whether considered from the standpoint of bringing about uniformity of laws or securing stringency of control over elements subversive of order, the then existing system of government with its divided jurisdiction was ill-suited for the purpose held in view. An all-powerful Central Government legislating for and controlling the affairs of India as a whole was deemed to be the only solution for the emergency. Accordingly there came to be enacted in 1833 that

"the Governor-General in Council (at Fort William in

Bengal) shall have power to make laws and regulations for repealing, amending, or altering any laws or regulations, whatever, now in force or hereafter to be in force in the said territories or any part thereof, and to make laws and regulations for all persons, whether British or native, foreigners or others, and for all Courts of Justice, whether established by His Majesty's Charters or otherwise and the jurisdictions thereof, and for all places and every part of the said territory, and for all servants of the said Company within the dominions of princes and states in alliance with the said Company . . . ;"[1]

A Central government was thus created by vesting the legislative power exclusively in the Governor-General of India in Council. But it could not have been all-powerful had the two Presidencies of Madras and Bombay remained as heretofore invested, by law, with the civil and military government of their respective territories. On the other hand, if Parliament had stopped short of divesting them, there would have ensued the possibility of a conflict between these governing authorities and the sole legislative authority newly created. Being responsible for peace, order and good government, the former could have refused to govern according to laws made by the latter, and all the gain expected to arise from the institution of a central and strong government would have been lost. To eliminate this element of weakness in the Indian polity newly established, Parliament proceeded to divest the presidencies of Bombay and Madras of the high status which they hitherto occupied as *responsible* governments, so that according to the new Constitution

"... the Executive Government of each of the several Presidencies . . . (was to be) *administered* by (not vested in as heretofore) a Governor and three Councillors"[2]

[1] Sec. 43 of 3 and 4 Will. IV, c. 85, an Act for effecting an arrangement with the East India Company, and for the better government of His Majesty's Indian territories.

[2] *Ibid.*, s. 56. By sec. 57 power was given to reduce the number of councillors at the Presidencies or suspend them altogether, leaving the Executive Government at the Presidency to be carried on by a Governor alone. This power was exercised in 1833 by reducing the executive councillors at Bombay and Madras from three to two respectively.

While

"... the Superintendence, Direction, and Control of the whole civil and military government of all the ... territories and Revenues in India (was) vested in a Governor General and Councillors styled the Governor General of India in Council." [1]

Thus came to be established in India the Imperial system of government. It is true that long before its establishment the Government of Bengal [2] had the supreme power, not only of superintending and controlling the government and management of the Presidencies of Madras and Bombay in the matter of commencing hostilities, or declaring or making war against any Indian prince or power, or for negotiating or concluding any treaty of peace or other treaty with them, except in case of emergency, but it also possessed by a later enactment the power of superintendence in all such points as related to the collection or application of revenues, or to the forces employed, or to the civil or military government of the said Presidencies. [3] But it must not be supposed, as is often done, that before 1833 the two Presidencies were in any real sense subordinate to Bengal in their domestic affairs. The fact that Madras and Bombay were required constantly and diligently to transmit to the Government of Bengal true and exact copies of all orders and resolutions and their acts in Council, and were enjoined to pay due obedience to the orders of the Government of Bengal, must not be construed to mean any subordination in their internal affairs. For, barring the extra territorial authority vested in the Government of Bengal, it must be borne in mind that, equally with Bengal, [4] the Governments of Madras and Bombay were *vested* each [5] with the civil and military government and also with the ordering and management of all territorial acquisitions and their revenues. Along with the Government of Bengal they possessed as stated before co-equal and independent powers of legislation within their respective jurisdictions. A truer view

[1] 3 and 4 Will. IV, c. 85, s. 39.
[2] 13 Geo. III, c. 63, s. 9.
[3] 33 Geo. III, c. 52, s. 40.
[4] 13 Geo. III, c. 63, s. 7.
[5] 33 Geo. III, c. 52, s. 24.

therefore seems to be that they forwarded the copies of their proceedings to the Government of Bengal for information rather than for orders. At any rate, such seems to have been the view taken by the Government of Bengal itself, for, though it had the power to issue orders and compel obedience to them it had in practice confined its supervision and control "to pointing out an irregularity and requesting that it be not repeated." More than this was thought inadvisable [1] and it is doubtful [2] whether it would have been constitutional.

The Imperial system of Government was necessarily accompanied by the Imperial system of Finance. Before the inauguration of the Imperial system of Administration the several Presidencies were like separate clocks each with its own mainspring in itself. Each possessed the powers of sovereignty, such as the legislative, the penal, and the taxing powers. They were independent in their finance. Each was responsible for the maintenance of services essential for peace, order and good government within its jurisdiction and was free to find money by altering or levying taxation or borrowing on credit to meet its obligations. For their ways and means they often drew upon the resources of one another, not, however, because their exchequers were not distinct, but because they were parts of a common exchequer belonging to the East India Company. All this was changed by the Act of 1833, which vested the revenues and the government of the different territories in the Governor-General of India in Council. The revenues and the services became by law the revenues and the services of the Government of India. The provinces became the collecting and the spending agencies of the Government of India. They ceased to levy any new taxes

[1] Cf. Min. on the Constitution of the Indian Government by the Governor-General, Lord William Bentinck, dated September 14, 1831. Also Memorandum *re* the same by the Secretary to the Government of Bengal accompanying the despatch of Lord Canning dated December 9, 1859, published in H. of C. Return 307 of 1861.

[2] Cf. the despatch of the Court of Directors to the Government of Bengal No. 44 dated December 10, 1834, *original* draft in the India Office Records.

or to collect the old ones in their own name. In like manner the services they administered became a charge of the Government of India, which distributed among the various provinces sums from the consolidated fund for the maintenance of the services. It was by law provided that without the previous sanction of the Government of India the provinces were not to spend the fund allowed to them in creating any new office or granting any salary, gratuity, or allowance.[1] The public debt was no longer a charge upon the revenues of any particular Presidency alone, nor did there remain any question of primary or secondary liability as between the revenues of the other Presidencies. All the provincial debts became the debts of the Government of India and were charged to the revenues of India as a whole. In short, the financial system which was roughly analogous to the system of separation of sources and contributions from the yield was changed into a system of aggregation of sources and distribution of the yield; for, as observed in a Government Resolution by virtue of the Act of 1833,

"British India, though for the sake of convenience subdivided into Presidencies under separate locally controlled governments, (became) in reality one sole grand Power in dependence on Great Britain, having undivided interests, a single exchequer, and controlled in all essential and general principles by one Government—the Governor General in Council. . . . The entire resources of India (were) applicable to one purpose only, the discharge of its engagements and those connected with its management in England, and to whatever section of British India funds (were) wanting, funds (were) supplied, as a matter of course, without any reference to the particular source from which they were derived." [2]

So comprehensive did the system of Imperial Finance become in time that when in 1858 the Crown took over from the Company the government of India it was found that

[1] 3 and 4 Will. IV, c. 85, s. 59.

[2] Government of India Financial Department Resolution dated November 22, 1843.

"no province had any separate power of legislation, any separate financial resources, or practically any power of creating or modifying any appointments in the public service; and the references to the Government of India which this last restriction involved gave that Government the opportunity of interference with all the details of provincial administration." [1]

Whatever may have been the merits of the Imperial system of Government from the military, political, legislative, or administrative points of view, it is a melancholy fact that as a system of finance it proved unequal to the strain imposed upon it. From its very start it suffered from the fatal disease of financial inadequacy, and it was only occasionally that the efforts of the Finance Ministers were successful in restoring an equilibrium and staving off the hour of crisis. How chronic the deficits were may be seen from the following figures :—[2]

INSUFFICIENCY OF IMPERIAL FINANCES

Year.	Surplus	Deficit	Year	Surplus	Deficit.
	£	£		£	£
1834–35	—	194,477	1846–47	—	971,322
35–36	1,441,513	—	47–48	—	1,911,986
36–37	1,248,224	—	48–49	—	1,473,225
37–38	780,318	—	49–50	354,187	—
38–39	—	381,787	50–51	415,443	—
39–40	—	2,138,713	51–52	531,265	—
40–41	—	1,754,852	52–53	424,257	—
41–42	—	1,771,603	53–54	—	2,044,117
42–43	—	1,346,011	54–55	—	1,707,364
43–44	—	1,440,259	55–56	—	972,791
44–45	—	743,893	56–57	—	143,597
45–46	—	1,496,865	57–58	—	7,864,222

Anyone who ponders upon this pitiable story of Indian Finance as revealed by these deficits can hardly fail to

[1] *Report of the Royal Commission on Decentralization in British India*, p. 24.

[2] From the Financial Statement of British India for 1860–1 by Mr. Wilson. H. of C. Return 33 of 1860, p. 100.

wonder with Disraeli who remarked in the House of Commons that

"able as has ever been the administration of India, considerable and distinguished as have been the men whom that administration had produced, and numerous as have been the great Captains, the clever diplomatists, and able administrators of large districts with whom the Government has abounded, the state of the finances of India has always been involved in perplexity, and India that has produced so many great men, seems never to have produced a Chancellor of the Exchequer." [1]

The causes of this collapse, however, are not far to seek. The inadequacy of Indian Finances is mainly to be ascribed to an unsound fiscal policy. The policy was unsound for various reasons. In matters of state economy it is usual to argue that the expenditure to be incurred should determine the magnitude of revenue to be raised. But experience has shown that this stock maxim has proved ruinous wherever its limitations have failed to receive their due weight. It cannot be too often said that the growing expenditure of the State can only be sustained from the growing wealth of the society. Nor can it be too strongly emphasized that the test of sound finance does not merely consist in being capable of raising the requisite amount of revenue. It must be remembered that the *mode* of raising the revenue is an aspect of the question which is fraught with tremendous consequences for the stability and productivity of the nation. It is too obvious to be denied that a tax system by its unequal incidence may cause social upheavals, just as by its unwise incidence on trade and industry it may impoverish society by setting out of gear its economic mechanism and technique and eventually beggar the State by impairing the productive powers of society. Wisdom therefore requires that those who are entrusted with the financial management of the State should look beyond the more immediate object of raising and spending of money, for the "hows" of finance

[1] *Sir Charles Woods' Administration*, by West, pp. 65–6.

are very important, and can be seldom neglected in practice with impunity. The wealth of society is the only patrimony on which the State can draw, and the State that damages it cannot but end in damning itself. History abounds with instances of States wrecked by the unwise neglect of these evident truths, but if an illustration be wanted in further proof thereof, the system of Imperial Finance established in India is matchless for the purpose.

The land tax was the heaviest impost of the Imperial revenue system in operation. The underlying doctrine of the tax in India has been that it is of the nature of rent paid by the cultivator to the State in virtue of the theory that the land in India has from immemorial times been regarded as the property owned by the State. The cultivator is not the proprietor, but is the occupier of the land. The land is let to him and the State is therefore justified in claiming the whole of the economic rent arising from the land. On this assumption the land tax has been imposed irrespective of the question of necessity or justice.

Besides this legal fiction of State landlordism there was also another economic principle which was taken to be the justification for the enhancement of the land revenue. There is reason to believe that the Physiocratic doctrine of *produit net* had its influence in the management and fixing of the land tax in India. We find high officials in India arguing in the early stages of the revenue management that "whether or not the principle of the French Economists of laying all the taxes on the land be . . . erroneous or otherwise, it is certainly conformable to the prevalent system in India; nor is that theory supported by the French alone, but by respectable authorities in England, who contend that all taxes fall ultimately on the products of the soil, and that in advancing a different doctrine the eminent author of *The Wealth of Nations* is at variance with himself, inasmuch as his previous data lead to that conclusion."[1] Whatever may have been the reasons for augmenting the

[1] For this remarkable controversy, which has escaped even the comprehensive eye of Baden Powell, *see* House of Commons paper 306 of 1812–13.

land tax, few can deny that a heavy consolidated impost on the first exertions of any species of industry absorbing the whole or nearly the whole of its profits is ruinous and impolitic. It becomes an effectual bar to the creation of that produce on which the future exertions might be profitably employed and through the medium of which individual wealth and public revenue may be increased to an almost inconceivable extent. A land tax of this nature was sure to blast the very production of that wealth which industry would have otherwise brought into being. The land tax was so heavy that the system of tax prevailing in India might well have been called a near approach to the single tax system.[1]

While the land tax prevented the prosperity of the agricultural industry the customs taxes hampered the manufactures of the country. There were internal customs and external customs, and both were equally injurious to trade and industry. The internal customs [2] were made

[1] The ratio of the land revenue to the total revenues of India was as given below:—

Year.	Ratio	Year.	Ratio.	Year.	Ratio
1792–3 to 1796–7	50 33	1817–8 to 1821–2	66 17	1842–3 to 1846–7	55 85
1797–8 to 1801–2	42 02	1822–3 to 1826–7	61 83	1847–8 to 1851–2	56 06
1802–3 to 1806–7	31 99	1827–8 to 1831–2	60 90	1852–3 to 1855–6	55·40
1807–8 to 1811–2	31·68	1832–3 to 1836–7	57·00	Average for 64 years	54 07
1812–3 to 1816–7	52 33	1837–8 to 1841–2	59·05		

[2] Mr. Trevelyan, who closely studied the system, was so much horrified by its injurious effects that he wrote "although we now have ocular demonstration of its existence, yet when it has once been abolished the world will find it difficult to believe that such a system could have been tolerated by us for the better part of a century."—*System of Transit and Town Duties in the Bengal Presidency*, p. 6.

up of transit and town duties. For the purposes of transit duties the country was artificially divided into a number of small customs areas. Goods may be manufactured and consumed *ad libitum* within each customs area, but the moment they left their own division they became liable to duty. The injurious effects of this regulation, though concealed, were none the less real. The transit duties held up trade, which in its turn reacted adversely on the manufacturers of the country. Adam Smith has told us how the growth of industry depends upon the extent of the market. Here for the purposes of the transit duties the whole country was cut up into small bits after the manner of squares on a chess board. What wonder is there if trade, and its handmaid, industry, both languished to a serious extent. The adverse effect on the transit duties was also felt in another way. In every country somewhat industrially advanced there is not only a social division of labour, but there is also a territorial division of labour, otherwise called localization of industry. Evidence is not wanting to show that the localization of industry formed a prominent feature of Indian economy.[1] Under it each locality in India specialized in a particular art or industry ; for instance, cotton was grown in one locality, woven in another, and bleached in a third place. But it often happened that these localities were situated in different customs areas, and a raw good might have had to pay the transit duty many a time before it reached its finished stage. To avoid this each locality was obliged to waste its energies along unprofitable lines in order to escape the transit duties.

The town duties, which formed a part of the internal customs, also worked in their effects towards de-urbanization. Commercial entrepôts are admittedly vast instruments of the trade of a country. The opportunity of ready purchase and sale of almost every kind of commodity in any quantity, accumulated capital, extended credit, general information all meet here as in a centre. They support, encourage and give life to commerce and to the trade of a country. But the direct effect of the town duty was to distract and

[1] See M. Martin's *Eastern India*, 3 vols.

drive away trade, for under the system every article which was subject to it had, after the payment of transit duty, to pay on entry, in the town, the town duty and, if it underwent any change of form by manufacture within the town of entry, it could not have been furnished to any neighbouring place without a second impost being paid upon it under the transit duty system, enhanced in proportion to the increase of value it might have acquired from the labour and the skill bestowed upon it. The consequence was that towns dwindled both in trade and industry owing to the reason that merchants ceased to frequent them and that no manufactures of articles subject to the transit duty were capable of being established in them except for their own supply.

It was in this depressed condition that the Indian industries were called upon to meet foreign competitors. But the external customs cannot be said to have protected, much less fostered them. As a rule commercial tariffs are based upon what is called commodity competition. The import tariffs are designed to check by means of higher duties the importation of such foreign commodities as are likely to interfere in the successful manufacture of the same commodities at home and the export tariffs are framed principally with a view to give bounties to such of the home commodities as have a chance of securing a foothold in foreign markets. But the theory of external customs in India had no connection with the theory of commodity competition. In comparison with the policy actually adopted even a protectionist would have preferred to see trade left perfectly free, for the tariff was based on political rather than economic considerations. The Indian Import Tariff varied not with the nature of the imports but with the origin of the imports and the bottom on which they were shipped. Being political in character it was preferential in design and in its framework. It is to be regretted all the more that the preference involved an unmitigated loss to the people and to the government. It was excusable to have admitted into India goods of English origin and shipped on English bottoms at a rate half of what goods of foreign origin and shipped on foreign bottoms were charged with. But nothing can extenuate the sacrifice imposed upon the Indian industries by letting in British goods at lower rates than what the Indian goods had to pay under the internal customs ; and this was done when, be it remembered, England was prohibiting by high tariff the entry of India-made goods and India-built ships ! But while the import tariff made it easy for the foreigners to compete successfully with Indian manufactures burdened as they heavily were by the weight of the internal customs, Indian goods found it considerably difficult to compete in foreign markets under the incubus of export duties which formed one of the most lamentable features of the Indian tariff and which endured long into the nineteenth century.[1] Thus the customs laws internal and external blockaded trade and smothered industry. The comparatively paltry revenues derived from them is the best proof of their ruinous effects.[2]

[1] It is difficult to cite references to every statement made above. The tariff history of India is yet unwritten, but ample evidence bearing on the point will be found in the Parliamentary Committee on Trade in 1821 and the Evidence submitted to the Committees appointed by Parliament to investigate into the affairs of the East India Company in 1813 and 1853. Particular attention is invited to the Report and Evidence of the Committee on East India Produce, 1846.

[2] The following table gives the ratio of the Customs Revenue to the total revenue :—

Year	Ratio	Year	Ratio.	Year.	Ratio
1792–3 to 1796–7	2 38	1817–18 to 1821–2	8 32	1842–3 to 1846–7	6 02
1797–8 to 1801–2	3 10	1822–3 to 1826–7	7 58	1847–8 to 1851–2	5·40
1802–3 to 1806–7	4 16	1827–8 to 1831–2	8 12	1852–3 to 1855–6	5 52
1807–8 to 1811–12	5 04	1832–3 to 1836–7	7·19	Average for 64 years	6 22
1812–13 to 1816–17	6 68	1837–8 to 1841–2	6·76		

Hendricks, *op. cit.*, p. 286.

When these resources failed the Government resorted to some very questionable means of raising revenue.

On an impartial survey of the revenue system as prevailed under the Imperial regime one is constrained to say that justice in taxation was conspicuous by its absence. It was a cruel satire, or at best an idle maxim, for the lancet was directed not where the blood was thickest but to that part of the body politic which on account of its weakness and poverty most meekly bore the pang. The landlords who passed their lives in conspicuous consumption and vicarious leisure on the earnings of the poor tenants, or the many European civil servants who fattened themselves on pay and pickings, were supremely exempted from any contribution towards the maintenance of the Government whose main activities were directed towards the maintenance of pomp and privilege. On the other hand, the salt tax [1]

[1] The percentage ratio of the salt revenue to the total revenue at different times was as follows :—

Year.	Ratio	Year	Ratio	Year	Ratio
1792–3 to 1796–7	14 13	1817–18 to 1821–2	11 25	1842–3 to 1846–7	11 65
1797–8 to 1801–2	12 10	1822–3 to 1826–7	11 87	1847–8 to 1851–2	9 14
1802–3 to 1806–7	11 09	1827–8 to 1831–2	12 03	1852–3 to 1855–6	9 17
1807–8 to 1811–12	11 14	1832–3 to 1836–7	9 72	Average for 64 years	11·07
1812–13 to 1816–17	10·92	1837–8 to 1841–2	12 37		

Hendricks, *op. cit.*, p. 283.

and the Moturpha,[1] and other oppressive taxes[2] continued to harass the industrious poor. It is indeed true that many petty and vexatious taxes prevalent under the native rule were abolished ; there is, however, enough evidence to show that the revenue thus lost was made up by enhancing those that were continued to be levied, particularly the land tax. The latter charge has always been officially denied,[3] but none the less it remains true that the land tax has been consolidated and increased concurrently with, if not consequently upon, the abolition of such other taxes as being raised from the poor cost the Government more than their yield.

Under the injurious revenue system described above, the taxing capacity of the people decayed so that not-

[1] In a petition drawn up by the Madras Native Association to the House of Commons in 1858 it was described as "a tax on trades and occupations embracing weavers, carpenters, all workers in metals, all salesmen whether possessing shops which are also taxed separately, or vending by the road-side, etc., some paying imposts on their tools, others for permission to sell, extending to the most trifling articles of trade, and the cheapest tools the mechanics can employ, the cost of which is frequently exceeded six times over by the Moturpha, under which the use of them is permitted." Quoted by Raghuvaiyangar in his *Progress of the Madras Presidency*, 1893, p. 113.

[2] Dr. Francis Buchanan in his *Journey from Madras*, Vol II, notes that "at Sati-Mangalam in Coimbatore, South India, a new stamp duty of $\frac{3}{4}+\frac{1}{8}$ of a Vir-Raya Fanam, or about $5\frac{1}{4}$*d.*, has been levied on every two pieces of fine cloth ; and of $\frac{3+\frac{3}{4}}{8}$ of a Vir-Raya Fanam, or of about $2\frac{3}{4}$*d.*, on every two pieces of coarse cloth. The weavers in consequence have given up work, and gone in a body to the Collector, to represent their case. The tax is levied in place of a duty of 4 or 5 Fanams a year, that was formerly levied on every loom ; by the weavers it is considered as heavier"—pp. 240–1. He also notes "at Dodara Pallyam which contains 50 houses of weavers, the weavers are quite clamorous about the new stamp duty ; which, they say, will for every loom cost them 20 Fanams in place of 5 which they formerly paid." *Ibid.*, p. 242.

[3] Parliamentary Papers, Vol. V of 1831, Minutes of Evidence on the East India Company's affairs, Q. 3864–66.

withstanding its numerous resources[1] from which it derived its revenues the Imperial Government was unable to make both ends meet. It ought to serve as an object lesson to all financiers to show that when their revenue laws are harmful to the resources of the people they must blame none but themselves for their empty treasury.

[1] The following is a conspectus of the taxes levied :—

Source of Revenue	Amount of Revenue raised in Millions £	Period. No of Years.	Period. Dates.	Locality and Date of Commencement.
Land Revenue	662 308	64	1792–3 to 1855–6	Throughout the period in Bengal, Bombay and Madras since 1834–5 in N.-W.P. and 1849–50 in the Punjab.
Sekyer and Abkary	9 729	20	1836–7 to 1855–6	Throughout the period in Bengal, N.-W.P., Madras and Bombay, and since 1849–50 in Punjab.
Excise .	4 987	,,	,,	Bengal accounts exclusively.
Moturpha	6 455	,,	,,	Madras accounts exclusively.
Salt . .	135 532	64	1792–3 to 1855–6	Bengal since 1792, Madras 1822, Bombay 1822, N.-W.P. 1839.
Opium .	106 707	,,	,,	Bengal since 1792, Bombay since 1820.
Post Office	8 888	,,	,,	Bengal and Madras since 1792, Bombay since 1813, Punjab 1849, N.-W.P. 1835.
Stamps .	16 697	59	1797–8 to 1855–6	Bengal from 1797, Madras from 1813, Bombay from 1819, N.-W.P. from 1834, Punjab from 1849.
Customs Duties *Internal :* 1. Transit 2. Town *External :* 1. Import 2. Export	76·179	64	1792–3 to 1855–6	Bengal, Madras and Bombay from 1792–3, N.-W.P. from 1834–5, Punjab since 1849–50.
Mint Revenue	3·221	,,	,,	Bengal from 1792, Madras and Bombay from 1813.
Tobacco	1·437	18	1836–7 to 1853–4	Madras 1836 on.
Miscellaneous	194 777	64	1792–3 to 1855–6	Same as under land revenue.

Was the money raised by such injurious taxes without reference to their effect on the productive powers of the country spent on such public utilities as were calculated to enrich and elevate the economic life of the tax-paying population? A glance at the following table giving the distribution of the expenditure by decades on the different services will show how the money was spent :—

DISTRIBUTION OF THE EXPENDITURE *

Percentage Ratio of Total Expenditure on	In the Year					
	1809–10	1819–20	1829–30	1839–40	1849–50.	1857.
Military	58 877	64 290	53 754	57 721	51 662	45 55
Interest on debt . .	18 010	12 805	12 124	9 756	10 512	7 19
Civil and Political . .	7 221	8 900	9 575	12 296	8 902	9 62
Judicial	7 525	6 800	7 107	9 565	7 180	9 38
Provincial Police . .	1 991	2 093	1 535	2 062	2 062	
Buildings, Fortifications, etc. . . .	1·639	1 756	2 810	1 428	1 661	—

* "Past, Present and Prospective Financial Condition of British India," by Colonel Sykes, *Journal of the Royal Statistical Society*, 1859, Vol. XXII, p. 457.

Prominent among this array of figures are those on the military expenditure and though they have dwindled in years they have invariably consumed more than one half of the total revenues of the country. But the stupendous figures opposite military do not represent the true burden of that expenditure. To them must be added the figures for the interest charge on debt, for the debt incurred was entirely a war debt. India was all throughout this period a battle-ground between the Country Powers and the East India Company. The two Mahratta Wars, the three Mysore Wars, the two Burmese Wars, the two Afghan Wars, and the Carnatic Wars, not to speak of the numerous other minor engagements, were fought in the interests of adding India to the dominions of the Company and of the Crown. While Parliament claimed that the dominions of the East India Company were the dominions of the Crown it must be borne in mind that it refused to pay a farthing of the purchase money. On the other hand, the entire cost of these wars was borne by India as so much dead weight on her scanty resources. The charges shown separately under buildings and fortifications must also be included in the military expenditure, to which category they really belonged. On making these needful additions we find the unparalleled fact of a country wasting between 52 to 80 per cent. of its precious little money on war services. It may, perhaps, be argued on the other hand that much of the military expenditure, large though it was, went back into the coffers of the Indians themselves as they formed the bulk of the forces employed in the country. The Indians, of course, formed a very large portion of the military,[1] and if the scales of salaries fixed for the European and native forces were equal the result would have been favourable to the natives of the country, though it cannot be said to have excused that huge military expenditure. But the scales of salaries for the Europeans and natives were so grossly unequal[2] that one European drew on an aver-

[1] This may be seen from the following figures :—

STRENGTH OF THE INDIAN ARMY BEFORE THE MUTINY *

	European.	Native.	Total.
Artillery	6,419	9,138	15,557
Sappers	110	3,043	3,153
Cavalry	3,456	30,533	32,989
Infantry	29,760	188,660	218,420
Total	38,745	231,374	270,119

* Report of Major-General Hancock on the Reorganization of the Indian Army, Parliamentary paper of the year 1859, p. 21.

[2] This is indicated by the following table :—

COST OF AN INFANTRY REGIMENT PER MONTH

EUROPEAN.

	Details.			Total.		
	Rs.	As.	Ps.	Rs	As.	Ps.
Officers.						
37 Officers	14,734	14	3	21,779	2	7
Staff and Establishment	4,515	12	4			
Command and other allowances	2,528	8	0			
Men.						
117 N.C.O.s	2,289	4	5	25,999	8	0
950 Privates	11,203	8	4			
Rations, clothing and other charges	12,506	11	3			
Total				47,778	10	7

age more than the salaries of four natives put together. So this expenditure, whether from the standpoint of public utility, or private employment, did not benefit the population which contributed to the revenues of the State.

The civil and political charges which absorbed nearly 10 per cent. of the revenue can hardly be said to be recuperative in their effect. This part of the expenditure again was not shared by the native population which bore its burden. As a result of conquest the natives naturally came to occupy a secondary position; but the conquest had done more than merely degrade their status. It had engendered a certain sense of distrust for the natives in the minds of Englishmen. Conquered and distrusted the natives since the commencement of British rule had come to be excluded from the higher administrative posts of the country.[1] It was to remove this injustice that Parliament in the Act of 1833 provided

"that no native of the said territories, nor any natural-born subject of His Majesty resident therein, shall, by reason only of his religion, place of birth, descent, colour or any of them be disabled from holding any place, office, or employment under the said Company" (sec. 87).

NATIVE

	Details.			Total.		
	Rs.	As.	Ps	Rs.	As.	Ps
Officers.						
26 Europeans	9,861	2	1	13,527	8	7
20 Natives	940	0	0			
Staff and Establishment	1,209	1	4			
Command and other allowances	1,517	5	2			
Men.						
140 N.C.O.s	1,780	0	0	9,606	14	0
1,000 Sepoys	7,000	0	0			
Charges	826	14	0			
Total				23.134	6	7

It is evident from this table that if we deduct the salary of 26 European officers and command and other allowances shown under the heading "Native" which amounts to Rs. 11,378 7. 3. we shall find that 1,104 Europeans drew Rs. 47,778 10. 7. while 1,160 natives drew only Rs. 11,755 15. 4.

[1] Before 1833 the very meagre scale on which they were employed is disclosed by the following figures :*—

But, as a matter of fact, till after the Mutiny not one of the natives was appointed to any office except such as they were eligible for before this Statute was passed, because the Court of Directors in interpreting it advised the Government of India at the very start that by this enactment

"practically . . . no very marked difference of results will be occasioned. The distinction between the situations allotted

Native Civil Servants of the 1st Class attached to the Secretariat of the 3 Presidencies Receiving per Month Salaries of —	Bengal.		Madras		Bombay.		Total.	
	No	Total Salary Drawn	No	Total Salary Drawn	No	Total Salary Drawn	No	Total Salary Drawn
Rs. 500 and upwards	5	2,700	—	—	5	2,500		
Rs 400 „	2	800	—	—	1	400		
Rs 350 „	4	1,400	1	350	1	350		
Rs 300 „	3	900	—	—	2	600		
Rs 250 „	5	1,250	—	—	1	250	89	20,690
From Rs. 250 to 200	17	3,460	5	1,155	1	200		
„ „ 200 „ 150	10	1,590	4	682½	—	—		
„ „ 100 „ 150	5	550	5	525	5	330		
Below Rs. 100 . .	6	470	1	87½	2	140		
Total . .	57	13,120	16	2,800	16	4,770		

* Report of the Civil Finance Committee on Native Establishment at the three Presidencies.—Bengal Financial Consultations dated April 13, 1830, India Office Records. The subordinate establishments of uncovenanted Christian and native servants attached to the several Presidencies were divided by the Committee into four classes, (1) comprehending Head clerks, Registrars, Managers and their assistants, Examiners, Investors, etc., employed under the Secretaries in superintending and conducting the business of the office; (2) Current Business Writers, and permanent Copyists; (3) Sectioners or copyists paid by piece work, and (4) all inferior servants. The Committee found that

Para. 35. The salaries received by the Current Business Writers in Calcutta vary from Rs. 20 to Rs. 300 per mensem, an average for each individual Rs. 104; in Bombay they vary from Rs. 15 to 120, an average Rs. 48; at Madras it is an established rule that the average remuneration to servants of this description in the Secretariat at that Presidency is Rs. 27½, which is distributed at various rates from 10½ to 87½ rupees, according to the claims of the individuals from length of service and utility. . . .

Sectioners in the Secretariat office, Bengal, were paid at the rate of 750 words per rupee; while at the other two Presidencies it was about 1333 words for a rupee.

Para. 51. The present charge for servants attached to the Secretariat in Bengal is Rs. 1,142 per month; at Madras, including mochies (cobblers), Rs. 455; and at Bombay, Rs. 261. In Bengal there were 186 servants; in Madras, 56; and in Bombay, 42.

to the convenanted service and all other situations of any official or public nature will remain generally as at present." [1]

The judicial and police charges, which together absorbed something like 10 per cent. of the total revenue raised, can only be regarded as protective in their character. Thus the bulk of the money raised by injurious taxes was spent in unproductive ways. The agencies of war were cultivated in the name of peace, and they absorbed so much of the total funds that nothing practically was left for the agencies of progress. Education formed no part of the expenditure incurred and useful public works were lamentably few. Railways, canals for navigation or irrigation and other aids to the development of commerce and industry for a long time found no corner in the imperial budget. For a total area of 837,000 square miles there were constructed a few miles of railways, 2,157 miles of land ways, 580 miles of waterways and 80 miles of telegraph. Or speaking in terms of money spent, we find that for the entire period of fifteen years from 1837–8 to 1851–2 the average expenditure of a productive character amounted only to £299,732 a year.[2] There is a principle well known to farmers that constant cropping without manuring ends in the exhaustion of the soil. It is, however, capable of wider application, and had it been observed in the State economy of India the taxing capacity of the country would have grown to the benefit of the treasury and the people. Unfortunately it was lost upon the financiers of India to the detriment of both.

But if the chance of augmenting the resources by judicious taxes and productive expenditure to cover the chronic deficits was forfeited, there was at least the way open for economy in expenditure. As might be supposed, a strong Central Government of the kind established in 1833 was capable of effecting economy wherever possible. As a matter of fact the centralization was of the weakest kind. *De jure* there was an Imperial system of adminis-

[1] Despatch to Bengal No. 44 dated December 10, 1834, para. 107.

[2] *Statistical papers relative to British India.* Edited by Thornton, 1853.

tration, but the *de facto* administration was conducted as though the primary units of executive government were the Provinces and that the Government of India was only a co-ordinating authority. This was obvious from a variety of circumstances. Legislation was, it is true, centred in the Government of India; none the less the laws that were passed by the Government of India were passed *for* the different Provinces as though the initiative in legislation still lay in the Provinces and that the Government of India was only a sanctioning authority. Each Province had its own customs, internal as well as external, a survival of their sovereign status. Each Province continued to have its own Army. Notwithstanding centralization, the account system still remained provincial, sustaining the sense of their financial independence. The work of administration and collection of revenue being still conducted by them, the provinces behaved as though they were the lawful authorities charged with the responsibilities of Government. This spirit of independence bred insubordination, and some of the Provinces, particularly Bombay and Madras, endeavoured to resist the attempts of the Government of India to tax the people under their jurisdiction when the cost of the mutiny compelled it to levy fresh burdens. The point to be borne in mind is that the Act of 1833 made an unfortunate divorce between the legal and administrative responsibility. The Imperial Government were responsible in law but did not administer the country. The Provincial Governments administered the country but had no responsibility in law. This divorce had a fatal effect on the economy in the finances of the country. As was inevitable extravagance in expenditure had become the rule in practice and it was inherent in the Imperial system itself. Economy is begotten of responsibility, and responsibility is obtained where a government has to *find* the resources to meet the charges it desires to incur. Prior to the inauguration of the Imperial system the Provincial Government had the obligation to raise money for the charges included in their budgets. Consequently they had to be economical. But under the Imperial system, while the budgets for the various services were prepared by the provincial authorities, the responsibility for finding the ways and means rested on the Government of India. Formerly they knew the limits of the purse they had to draw upon, but under the Imperial system they

> "had no means of knowing the measure by which their annual demands upon the Government of India ought to be regulated. They had a purse to draw upon of unlimited because of unknown depth. They saw on every side the necessity for improvements, and their constant and justifiable desire was to obtain for their own provinces as large a share as they could persuade the Government of India to give them out of the general revenues of the Empire. They found by experience that the less economy they practised, and the more importunate their demands, the more likely they were to persuade the Government of India of their requirements. In representing these requirements, they felt that they did what was right, and they left to the Government of India, which had taken upon itself, the responsibility of refusing to provide the necessary means." [1]

To these extravagant demands the Government of India had often to yield; for, till very late, it did not possess the machinery to appraise the demands and to control the expenditure on them. It is not usual to expect much efficiency from any Imperial system of administration, much less when it covers not a department, not a province, but a country as big as a continent. Merely from being huge it is slow to move. Much slower would it necessarily be if it were a system as unorganized and unconsolidated as the Indian system was. First of all, the Imperial system in India was without its executive machinery of control. The Act which created it must be said to have grievously erred in uniting into one the Government of Bengal and the Government of India. As a result of this fusion the machinery was overstrained. Its duties as the Government of Bengal left it very little time to attend to its duties as

[1] *The Administration of the Earl of Mayo, as Viceroy and Governor-General of India—a Minute by the Honourable John Strachey*, a member of the Council and late acting Governor-General, dated April 30, 1872. Calcutta Office of the Superintendent of Government Printing, 1872, p. 46.

the Government of India. There was not only a common executive, but there was also a common Secretariat charged with the work of the two Governments. Overworked as the Secretariat was, its efficiency was considerably lowered by the absence of any officer specially charged with the duty of handling the finance of the country till 1843. It was in that year that Lord Ellenborough, the then Viceroy of India, separated the Secretariat of Bengal from that of India,[1] and attached to the latter a distinct office called the Financial Secretary to the Government of India,[2] unencumbered with the details of any other Department of State except that of finance. But while the want of a scrutinizing officer was thus made good by this appointment of a distinct Secretary of Finance, it was not possible for him to enforce economy in expenditure in the absence of a centralized system of audit and account and of an appropriation budget. Notwithstanding the establishment of the Imperial system of finance, the officers of audit and account remained attached to the Secretariats of the various Provincial Governments. They were not accountable to the supreme Government on whom the responsibility for the ordering and the management of the revenues of India had by law devolved. Being attached to the provincial Secretariat the Government of India could issue orders with regard to the accounts and the audits not directly but only through, and with the interpretation of, the Local Government concerned. Secondly, the budget system, though good enough for the purposes of mercantile accounts, that is, record, was useless for the first and elementary purpose of all good State accounts, namely, check. There were indeed three estimates (sketch, regular, and budget) prepared for the purposes of the financial administration of the country showing the amount of money required for the carrying on of each of the different services. But this distribution of public money on the different services was not held to mean appropriation. It was only

[1] Government of India Resolution, Home Department, April 29, 1843.

[2] Government of India Resolution dated January 4, 1843.

treated as cash requirements. Owing to this fact the grants were never carefully prepared nor was the limit set on them observed in practice. As there was no budget of specific votes or sanctions for each of the services the audit and account was simply concerned with noting whether record was kept of all the money that was received and paid through the public treasury. It is evident that in the absence of an appropriation budget the primary object of all State accounts and audit, namely check on the spending authority to abide by the sanction, was never achieved. The Provincial Governments, extravagant in their demands, were also careless in the matter of expenditure. So long as the Government of India remained without an appropriation budget and a centralized system of audit and account, it continued to be only a titular authority in the matter of financial control, and the provinces, though by law the weakest of authorities in financial matters, were really the masters of the situation.

To its inability to curb the extravagant habits of the provincial authorities generated by a financial irresponsibility on the part of the Provincial Governments and inefficiency on the part of the Central Government must be added the general spirit of apathy which marked the Executive Council of the Government of India in matters of finance. While it was true that nothing could be spent from the revenues of India without the specific vote of the Executive Council, it does not appear that the Council from its way of working could have taken any keen interest in promoting economy in expenditure. The Council acted collectively, and there was no distribution of executive work among the different members which composed it. With the exception of the Department of War and Legislation the whole work of the Government was brought before the Governor-General and his Councillors. As a result of its colleetive working

"every case actually passed through the hands of each member of the Council, circulating at a snail's pace in little mahogany boxes from one Councillor's house to another." [1]

[1] W. W. Hunter, *Life of Mayo*, Vol. I, p. 190.

Under such a system nobody was a Chancellor of the Exchequer to urge economy, because everybody was supposed to be one. The result was that finance in being everybody's business suffered from being nobody's business, so that funds were distributed not according to the genuine needs of the services, but according to the relative claims and persistency of the clamour made for them.

Sufficient evidence has been given to show that the collapse of the Imperial system was due to a faulty fiscal system marked by injurious taxes and unproductive and extravagant expenditure. It must not, however, be supposed that this faulty fiscal policy commenced with the inauguration of the Imperial system. On the other hand, it was a heritage which descended to the Imperial system from the past. None the less it is obvious that a timely revision of the fiscal policy and the strengthening of central control would have solidified the foundation of the Imperial system. But a much too long continuance thereof undermined its financial foundations, and as it could get no more money to meet its rising expenditure from a people whom it had beggared, the Imperial system succumbed to the shock of the Mutiny, never to rise again in its original garb.

CHAPTER II

IMPERIALISM *V.* FEDERALISM

As the result of the cost of the Mutiny of 1857 the already precarious condition of the Imperial Finance became so grave that no problem during the succeeding decade can be said to have engrossed the attention of responsible authorities as the one relating to the rehabilitation of that tottering system. Although the controversy as to the proper line of reconstruction to be adopted was long drawn out, the causes of the collapse were so patent that all those who had anything to do with Indian Finance unmistakably laid their finger on one supreme defect in the system whose breakdown they had witnessed, namely, the irresponsible extravagance it engendered in the Provincial Governments. To obviate this evil it was sought on the one hand by some responsible authorities

"to make the Local Governments partners in the great joint stock of Indian Finances, and, so to enlist their interest and animated co-operation with the Government of India, instead of keeping them on the footing of agents and servants, who, having no motive for economy and using the means of their masters, think only of enhancing their own demands by comparisons more or less well founded, with the indulgence conceded to others." [1]

This view gradually led to the formation of a considerable body of well-trained opinion for changing united India into the United States of India,[2] by making the provinces

[1] Minute by H.E. Sir W. R. Mansfield, Commander-in-Chief, dated October 17, 1867. *Papers, etc., on the extension of Financial Powers to Local Governments*, pp. 99–103.

[2] Cf. the Note of Col. R. Strachey dated August 17, 1867, in

into separate and sovereign States. The aim was to substitute a Federal system for the Imperial system and to assimilate the financial position of the Central authority in India to that of the Central authority in the United States. For the consummation of the Federal plan it was urged that the revenues of India should not be dealt with as one income, collected into the Imperial Treasury and thence distributed among the different Provincial Governments. According to the plan each province was to be allowed to keep its revenues and meet its charges from them. The Central Government was to have its own separate resources and, if need be, supplemented by contributions from the provinces as their share of the expenditure of the Central Government based on some equitable standard. Thus under the Federal plan the consolidated Imperial Budget with its formal division between Imperial and Provincial was sought to be replaced by the creation of distinctly separate budgets, Central and Provincial, based on a genuine division of services and allocation of revenues.

Many advantages were claimed in favour of the Federal plan. First it was believed that the separation of the revenues and services would lead the ways and means of the Central as well as of the Provincial Governments to be clearly defined, so that each one of them would be responsible for administering its affairs within the funds allotted to it. Heretofore the Provincial Governments sent up their estimates of revenue and expenditure as returns unconnected with each other, and the task of balancing them was left to be done by the Supreme Government upon the aggregate of the different provincial estimates submitted to it. Under the Federal plan the provincial estimates would have to be balanced accounts of receipts and charges made over to them. Though primary it was not the only advantage which the Federalists claimed for their plan, for it was advanced not only as a measure to set bounds to the extravagant expenditure of the Local Governments

J. F. Finlay's *History of Provincial Financial Arrangements*, List of extracts, p. 3.

by limiting the funds on which they were to draw, but also as a measure for setting bounds to the growing expenditure of the Central Government as well. The Federalists did not conceal the fact that the Central Government, being in a position to draw upon the total resources of India as a whole, was inclined to be extravagant in its own expenditure. They therefore thought that the Federal plan, involving as it did the allocation of revenues and services, would result in enforcing economy on the Central as well as on the Provincial Government.

The Federal plan was not only proposed by its advocates in the interests of economy and responsibility, but also in the interests of plenty. The Federalists denied that India offered few sources of revenue for the growing expenditure of the State. Though the Indian Finance ferry was water-logged, it was their view that there were many sources of taxation with the outpourings of which it could be set afloat. But they argued that these available sources were left untapped, as the Imperial Government, which could tap them, would not do so because of their restricted *locale* ; and Provincial Government, which would like to tap them, because of their restricted *locale* could not do so under the existing constitutional law. But if the Provincial Governments were vested or rather re-vested with the powers of taxation as they would be under the Federal plan, such sources of taxation as were given up for being too regional in character by the Imperial Government would be used by the Provincial Government to the great relief of Indian Finance as a whole.

Not only was Federalism advocated in the interests of economy and plenty, but also in the interests of equity. It was contended that the existing system resulted in an iniquitous treatment of the different provinces. If we take public works of provincial utility and the expenditure incurred upon them in the different provinces as the criterion, the criticism of the Federalists cannot be said to have been unfounded. On the other hand, the following figures go to substantiate a very large part of their arguments :—

OUTLAY ON PUBLIC WORKS

Average for the years 1837–8 to 1845–6.

Province.	Population in thousands.	Area in sq. miles.	Revenues in hundreds of Rs.	Expenditure on Public Works in hundreds of Rs.
Bengal .	40,000,000	1,65,443	10,239,500	1,79,812
N.W.P. .	23,200,000	71,985	5,699,200	1,41,450
Madras .	22,000,000	1,45,000	5,069,500	30,300

Compiled from *Calcutta Review*, 1851, Vol. XVI, p. 466.

Thus the outlay on public works was in Bengal 1¾ per cent.; in North-Western Provinces, 2½ per cent.; and in Madras a little over ½ per cent. of their respective revenues. This favoured treatment of some provinces as against the others was justified by the Imperial Government, which distributed the funds, on the ground that the favoured provinces showed surpluses in their accounts. But the Federalists pointed out these deficits and surpluses ascribed to the different provinces were grossly fictitious. They were the result of a bad system of accounts. The system was bad for the reason that it continued to show the accounts of the financial transactions of the country not according to Heads of Account but according to the provinces in which they occurred as used to be the case before 1833 when there was no common system of finance. With the passing of the Act of 1833 this system of accounts had become quite out of keeping with the spirit and letter of that Act. This would not have mattered very much if the All-India items were separated from the purely provincial items in the General Heads of Account. In the absence of this the evils of the system were aggravated by entering exclusively into the accounts of a province the charges for what was really an All-India Service, so that it continued to show deficits, while others which escaped continued to show surpluses and claim in consequence the favoured treatment given to them. The Presidency of Bombay offered to the

Federalists a case in point. The demands of the Presidency were invariably received with scant courtesy by the Government of India, for in its history Bombay seldom showed any surplus in her accounts. But, if it had been realized that the deficits were caused by the barbarous system of accounts which kept on charging the Presidency with the cost of the Indian Navy, it undoubtedly would have fared better. Such vicious ways of apportionment were not the only evil features of the system of accounts. Under it it was quite common to charge one Presidency with the cost of a service and to credit another with the receipts thereof. How the deficits found in the Madras accounts were inflicted upon it by the erroneous system of accounts may be seen from the following :—

Cost of the Army of Occupation.		Revenues derived from the Occupied Territory.	
Debited to	Amount. Rs.	Credited to	Amount. Rs.
Madras	79,83,000	Bombay . . .	20,00,000
		Bengal	1,04,22,870

Compiled from *ibid.*, p. 475.

Taking into consideration the iniquities involved in such a system of accounts, it is beyond dispute that the advantage claimed by the Federalists for their plan was neither fictitious nor petty. A division of functions between the Federal and Provincial Governments would have in itself been an advantage by comparison with the existing chaos. And, if it did not result in equity, it had at least the merit of opening a way for it.

When however the Federal plan was put before the authorities in the form of a practical proposal, it gave rise to a determined opposition. The challenge was at once taken up by the supporters of the Imperial system who, be it noted, were mostly military men in civil employ. They opened their attack on the Federal plan from two sides, that of practicability and expediency.

Is it possible, asked the Imperialists, to localize the revenues and charges of India as belonging distinctively to one particular province? They insisted that "from the commencement of (the British) power (in India) . . . the interests and affairs of (the) presidencies and the provinces have been interwoven and interlaced—one often overlapping the other, and vice versa—in a manner from which extrication or disentanglement is now impossible, without making changes which would entail inconveniences greater than any entailed by the existing system. . . . The army of Bengal Presidency is quartered not in the rich districts of the Lower Ganges, but mainly in the poorer districts of the Punjab. Thus placed, that army defends virtually the whole Presidency. The Madras army is not kept within that Presidency, but holds, besides the Madras country, the Deccan, the Central Provinces, and British Burma. Similarly the Bombay army holds, besides its own Presidency, the State of Rajputana and of Malwa. The Lower Provinces or Bengal proper are in themselves rich; but besides their own revenues they receive large customs receipts, which belong partly to them, but largely also to the other Divisions of the Bengal Presidency. Even Bengal opium does not entirely belong to Bengal, a large portion being raised in the North-Western Provinces. In Bombay the opium revenue does not, strictly speaking, belong to that Presidency at all, being raised beyond its limits, in the territories which, if included in any Presidency at all, would pertain to that of Bengal. Some of the Salt Duties, both of Madras and of Bombay, are raised on salt destined for consumption in Central India, and, in strictness, should be credited to the Government of India. Instances might be multiplied; but it becomes instantly evident that, if an adjustment of these matters with a view to complete localization of finance were to be attempted, many difficulties, perhaps even disputes, would arise. . . ."[1]

Arguing in the same strain, Lord Lawrence, the then Viceroy of India, wrote:

"Experience has shown that it is convenient that the resources of British India should be considered in the aggregate and not with reference to the particular province in which it is raised. If the rule were otherwise, we must

[1] Note by Sir Richard Temple dated November 7, 1868, *Papers, etc., on the extension of Financial Powers to Local Governments*, pp. 197–208.

enter into the question—what are the revenues which each province may fairly claim? What are the items of expenditure which may justly be charged to each? Is the Punjab, for instance, to be charged for all the British troops located in the hills for sanitary considerations? Is the whole of the force ranged against the North-Western border to be similarly debited? Are the troops quartered in Rajputana to be charged to the Bombay Presidency to which they belong, or in what manner is their cost to be arranged for? On the other hand, we may be asked, why should not Bengal in particular—which, having no foreign neighbours, and a docile and timid population, requires only a minimum garrison—have the benefit of her surplus revenues? Why on the opposite view of the question should not Bengal bear her share of the cost of the troops located in the North-Western Provinces, the Punjab and Central India, which guard her from such invasions as those of the Rohillas, the Mahrattas and the Pindaries of former times? These are all questions which would require solution if each were to have a financial system of its own." [1]

and in his opinion the question was impossible of solution.

But the Imperialists went further than this and argued that, even if it were possible to distinguish and localize the charges and the revenues into provincial and central, it was inexpedient to do so. Under the existing system of finance, they held that

" the Imperial Government, disposing of financial resources of the whole of India, can carry those resources at once where they are most needed. There are objects which have a truly national importance, though they may appear chiefly beneficial to a particular district. There may be evils, necessities and dangers in particular districts, which it is the duty of the supreme Government to correct and remedy at the charge of the whole. The creation or improvement of a part may have a national importance, though the expenditure on it may seem unfairly beneficial to a particular locality. A road, a canal, a railway from a cotton district or a coffee district, or a tea district, may have a vital significance to the whole people and commerce of India; and yet the expenditure on such a work be out

[1] Minute dated November 22, 1867, *op. cit.*, pp. 104–7.

of all proportion to the present revenue of the district which it is destined to develop . . . or the supreme Government may find it necessary to lay out, for moral and social purposes, larger sums on recently conquered, savage, or dissatisfied provinces than the revenues of those provinces seemed to warrant, in order to remove causes of disturbances or dangers, and to force those provinces into some degree of harmony with the long settled, pacified, reclaimed portions of the Empire. . . . The old provinces of the Empire conquer the new provinces. The old are bound in duty to civilize what they conquer. We have no right to annex a country and then throw it on its own resources. Conquest has its own duties as well as its rights."

"I venture to demur," wrote Lord Napier of Merchiston, President of the Council of Madras, "to the policy of those who would restrict the benefits of the supreme Government to its receipts, and who would measure out in a parochial spirit to every province appropriations proportional to its specific returns. On the contrary, it ought to be a satisfaction to the rich to help the poor; to the old to protect the young; to the good to improve the bad; for thus all can co-operate in building up the glorious fabric of a—United India. Such ends can only be attained by a Central Government disposing of the financial resources of a whole Empire"[1]

It is evident that arguments or sermons such as the above by themselves could never have supported the cause of the Imperialists. Notwithstanding the emphasis laid upon the difficulty of separating the revenues and charges into Imperial and Provincial, it must be conceded that the task was by no means so insuperable as the Imperialists made it out to be. The difficulty of apportioning the military charges could have been easily obviated by centralizing the military and making it a charge of the Central Government. On the same basis all those services charged to a particular Presidency or Province, but which from their nature benefited the whole Empire, could have been easily incorporated into the budget of the Central Government.

[1] Cf. his Minute dated February 15, 1868, para. 9, *op. cit.*, pp. 186–90.

Similarly it was possible in practice to allocate the existing sources of revenue between the Central and the Local Governments. The Central Government could have been allowed to retain for its use such sources of revenue the *locale* of which extended beyond the limits of a Presidency or the maximum yield of which depended upon a uniform administration of the same throughout the country. While on the other hand the Provincial Government could have been allowed to appropriate such sources which were restricted in their *locale* or the yield of which depended upon local vigilance. For instance, the customs duties could have been easily made a central resource, not only because their incidence was wider, but because they required a common and uniform policy of legislation and administration. The opium revenue could have been treated as a central source of revenue, and the same treatment could have been granted to the salt revenue. Of course it would have been difficult to effect a separation of the sources of revenue in such a way as would have granted to each of the several Governments concerned resources adequate to meet the charges devolving upon them. A certain adjustment of funds by contributions from the provinces to the Central Government or from the Central Government to the provinces would have been inevitable; neither could it have been possible to obviate the adoption of principles more or less arbitrary in the matter of apportionment of revenues or of charges. But admitting the difficulties and arbitrariness involved in the problem of separating the Imperial Budget into a Central and several Provincial Budgets, it must still be said that it was quite capable of satisfactory solution. Colonel Chesney in response to the challenge thrown out by the Imperialists had made a notable attempt to distinguish the existing heads of charges into Imperial and Provincial. In his Indian Polity he says:

"The items of Imperial expenditure for which contributions would be required consist apparently of—(1) the Home Establishment and charges disbursed by the Secretary of State; (2) interest on Indian debt; (3) Establishments of the Government of India ; (4) Diplomatic establishment ; (5) Army ; (6) Imperial Services—Post Office and Telegraph Department ; (7) interest guaranteed on railway capital ; to which must be added (8) grants in aid to some of the poorer provinces (which do not at present pay their expenses)."

This and other efforts convinced the Imperialists that their argument from practicability was bound to fail. Consequently they shifted their emphasis from the argument from practicability to that from expediency. Expediency furnished a better ground for attacking the Federal plan. Can a Federal Government be as efficient as the Imperial Government ? Can its credit be as high ? Can its prestige be as great as that of the existing Imperial system ? It must be premised that it was fresh in the minds of the people that it was the Imperial system with a strong power of control that had saved the country to the British from the hands of the mutineers of 1857. The survival value of the Imperial system had been proved in the struggle. By a clever manœuvre the Imperialists turned to the authorities and asked them to consider what had sustained the Imperial system throughout the struggle. They did not fail to emphasize the point that it was because the Imperial system of finance had given into the hands of the Imperial Government the control over the management of the revenues and disbursements of the Empire that the latter, in an emergency like the Mutiny, could stimulate every source of income, close every avenue of outlet, and concentrate all its expenditure on the capital object at stake—the energetic prosecution of hostilities. They showed that, without the Imperial system of finance, the Imperial Government would have had to deal with lukewarm, reluctant, hesitating or even hostile partners, perhaps not directly concerned in the struggle or convinced of its necessity, and solicitous for exoneration or delay. Further they made out that the Imperial management of finance was vital not only in heightening the efficiency of government, but also in maintaining the high state of credit. Credit, it was argued, depended upon the magnitude of the revenue, and to disintegrate the revenues was tantamount to lowering the credit. The Federal plan was also accused of abrogating the European tradition which has given prestige a very high place in its code for Asian government. It was inconceivable to the Imperialists that the Central Government could maintain its prestige without centralization in finance, for it was the system of Imperial Finance which, having collected the leading strings in political and administrative matters into the hands of the Imperial Government, enabled that Government to dictate a policy and have it executed to its own satisfaction. But who could uphold the prestige of the Central Government, if it became a pensioner of the Local Governments subordinate to it ?

Looked at from the vantage ground of detachment from the time of the controversy one may wonder what strength there was in the argument from expediency which gave the Imperialists such an easy victory over the Federalists. Federal Governments such as those existing in America, Germany or elsewhere do not lend support to the view that in their working there is bound to be a loss of efficiency, credit, or prestige. Their history has belied all these gloomy forebodings. But it should be remembered that at the time the controversy raged in India, much of the history of Federalism was a blank page, for Federalism was itself in its infancy. People, however, sided with the Imperialists, not because they could not draw upon the history of Federalism for arguments in its favour, but because the events of the time had inclined them to support the Imperial system. The Imperial system had saved India from the hands of the Mutiny of 1857, and when their fears of its repetition were not yet allayed it was too soon to expect them to consent to disrupt a machine that had just then proved its worth in the great contest. Conscious though they were of its defects, people recoiled from any attempt to tamper with it. So strong was the partiality of the people for the Imperial system that, notwithstanding the many defects which to their knowledge detracted from the efficiency of the system, they could give a sympathetic hearing to the Hon'ble Major-General Sir H. M. Durand, who wrote :

". . . I assert confidently that at present there is absolutely no ground whatever for the allegation that the financial control of the Government of India goes to undue lengths in what it attempts, and miscarries miserably. . . . On the contrary, any partial miscarriage of control . . . is no proof whatever that the rules are faulty, but that their relaxation is highly inexpedient, and that more rigid subordination of them should be enforced both by the Government of India and the Home Government. To subvert the financial control of the Central Government because one out of nine administrations has proved rather refractory, is about as sensible a procedure, to my mind, as to annul the articles of War and the powers of the Commander-in-Chief because a regiment should somewhat happen to misbehave. I venture to doubt the statesmanship of ruling either India or armies in this way." [1]

Notwithstanding the victory of the Imperialists, it must be said the Federalists lost a cause which was bound to succeed. For the sentiment of the time, however favourable to the retention of the Imperial system, was powerless to resist the force of events. The Imperial Government had to be extricated from the state of chronic penury in which it had fallen, and if statesmanship did not favour the system of Federal Finance as a means, financiers soon learnt that the system of Imperial Finance was doubtful as an end.

[1] Minute dated October 7, 1867, *vide op. cit.*, pp. 94–7.

CHAPTER III

THE COMPROMISE

IMPERIAL FINANCE WITHOUT IMPERIAL MANAGEMENT

If the Federalists failed to carry the day, they at least led their opponents to improve the system by removing some of the most radical defects from which it suffered. Attention was mainly directed towards revising the revenue laws and improving the machinery of control so that more revenues be obtained and less wastefully spent. With the primary object of making the Imperial system strong and prosperous, serious attempts were made about the close of the rule of the East India Company to do away with the oppressive taxes which had so long retarded the prosperity of the people and consequently of the Government. The internal custom duties were done away with, and the country was not only freed from all restrictions which hampered the growth of trade and industry, but positive encouragement was given to them by introducing the element of protection in the import tariff and trade was facilitated by equalizing the duties on English and foreign shipping. Articles of export were also relieved from the handicap of export duties and efforts were made to improve the cultivation and pressing of cotton, tea and other staples which commanded a great market in Europe and elsewhere.

The administrative machinery was next subjected to revision. Advantage was taken of the Indian Councils Act of 1861 authorizing the Viceroy "to make from time to time rules and orders for the more convenient transaction of business in his Council," to bring legally to an end the system under which the whole Council was supposed to take part collectively in the disposal of all the business of the Government by assigning to each member of the Council the charge of a separate department of administration; the Council was thus virtually converted into a Cabinet of which the Governor-General became the head. In this manner a place for a Chancellor of the Exchequer was created to which was appointed the well-known financier, Mr. James Wilson. The attention of Mr. Wilson was directed first of all to the improvements in the machinery of fiscal administration. The credit of establishing in India a uniform system of accounts, centralization of civil and military audit, and the introduction of an appropriation budget, rightly belongs to him. With the improvement in the revenue laws and the check on waste through improved and efficient administration was combined the policy of retrenchment in expenditure,[1] and the budget and audit rules were

"so framed as to leave to the head of each Local Government or of each branch of administration a much larger (*sic*) discretionary power than . . . heretofore . . . allowed in rearranging the details of expenditure"[2]

if that led to retrenchment. So drastic was the economy practised that, soon after the inauguration of the policy of spreading education throughout the country initiated by the dispatch of the Secretary of State in 1854, a stop was put to any increase of expenditure on education.[3]

But notwithstanding all these efforts at betterment howsoever diligently sustained, they did not improve the finances of India materially; at any rate, Mr. Wilson in his Financial Statement for 1860–1, by way of summing up the financial situation, said:

"we have a deficit in the last three years of £30,547,488; we have a prospective deficit in the next year of £6,500,000; we have already added to our debt £38,410,755."

[1] Cf. Finance Department Resolution No. 126 of November 19, 1860, published in the Appendix to the *Calcutta Gazette* dated November 24, 1860, p. 35.

[2] *Ibid.*, para. 20.

[3] Notifications, *Calcutta Gazette*, August 14, 1858, p. 1642.

To meet this huge deficit Mr. Wilson was obliged to augment the stamp duties, double the external customs, and impose an income tax, hitherto unknown to the people. Even the yield of these "three tremendous taxes" did not help Mr. Samuel Laing, the successor of Mr. Wilson, to a prosperous condition, for he too in his Financial Statement for 1861-2 wanted £500,000 fairly to weather his deficit and get into smooth waters with a small surplus. A few years of financial prosperity intervened. But Mr. Massey, who relieved Mr. Laing in 1866,

"upon a review of the financial condition of the Empire and the increasing demands made upon its resources . . . deemed it expedient to make provision for a permanent addition of a million sterling at the least to the existing revenue." [1]

Why the efforts of these successive Finance Ministers were not crowned with success is to be explained chiefly by the fact that the administrative and public needs of the country had grown beyond measure. After the Mutiny

"thousands of Englishmen, not only soldiers, but Englishmen of almost every class, poured into India. Ten thousand things were demanded which India had not got, but which it was felt must be provided. The country (had to be) covered with railways and telegraphs, roads and bridges. Canals (had to be) made to preserve the people from starvation. Barracks (had to be) built for a great European army, and every sort of sanitary arrangement which would benefit the troops (had to be) carried out. This was not only true in regard to matters of Imperial concern. Demands for improvements similar to those which fell upon the Central Government cropped up in every town and in every district controlled by the Local Government. The demands for improved administration also made themselves effective. The police was in a shameful condition throughout India . . . and the inadequacy of the pay given to native judges and other subordinate officers employed in the posts of importance in the courts was declared by Lord Lawrence

[1] Circular letter to the Local Governments dated February 21, 1866.

when he was Viceroy to be a public scandal. Among more than four thousand of these officers in the Bengal Presidency, the highest paid of all, and these were very few, received £180 a year. The great majority received from £12 to £24 a year, sums less than those earned in many parts of India by common bricklayers and carpenters. All these had to be put on a completely new footing." [1]

While the needs for expenditure were thus growing, economy in expenditure became difficult of achievement. Comparatively easy at first, each successive measure of economy became directly, as well as relatively, more arduous than its predecessor. The growing needs of improvements, hitherto neglected, and the contracting scope for economy, combined to demand an ever-increasing scale of taxation. The dangers of increased taxation by an alien Government of a people not interested in obtaining the amenities of life, much less at the cost of a tax, were uppermost in the minds of the three great financiers who were sent out from England in succession to rehabilitate the finances of India on a sound and stable basis. They realized that unless bounds were set to these demands for improved administration and improved material and moral conditions, the immediate benefits of which were enjoyed more by the European than the native population, taxation howsoever high would be inadequate for financial solvency, besides being dangerous to the political stability of the Empire. Under the existing system of barren uniformity and pedantic centralization their object was thought to be impossible of achievement; for the Local Governments, on which alone the Central Government could depend for economy, rendered at best to that Government not only a cold and languid support in financial vigilance and reform, but too often exhibited a passive resistance, and even countenanced evasions of regulations intended to be conducive to economy. The only way to make Local Governments economical in their

[1] The above is taken with some alterations of a purely literary character from the "Observations on some Questions of Indian Finance," by Sir John Strachey. House of Commons Return 326 of 1874.

ways was to give them the power and responsibility of managing their own affairs. As a matter of administrative experience the financiers had found that while some of the branches of revenue and expenditure were truly Imperial, there was a wide field of both of them which was properly local in character, and ought to have been entrusted to Local Governments. They were convinced that there could be no standard of economy until the requirements of the Local Government were made absolutely dependent upon known means, and nothing they thought would serve to make known to the Local Governments the means available for their outlay than to carve out from the Imperial purse a separate purse of definite magnitude for the use of Local Governments and to throw on them the responsibility of meeting their demands and maintaining an equilibrium in their finance.

Thus they were led to the same conclusion as the Federalists. However, to make the plan acceptable to the Imperialists, they made certain concessions without seriously compromising the working of the plan. The Federal plan required a change in the constitution of the system of government in India. It necessitated a *legal* partition of the revenues and charges of India between the Central and the several Provincial Governments. While all, including the Imperialists, recognized in the Federal plan a powerful measure for enforcing financial responsibility and economy, the chief objection to it arose from the fact that it sought *legally and permanently* to divest the Central Government of the resources of India. The financiers as practical politicians soon found out a way to obviate this defect in the Federal plan. By virtue of their experiences of the working of the British Parliament they found that there was no necessity to resort to a constitutional change. Convention was deemed to be as good as law and, once established, can seldom be altered without disturbance. Separation of charges and revenues between the Central and Provincial Governments was therefore proposed to be made a matter of convention which could be upheld so long as it was profitable for the parties concerned to do so.

This gave all the advantages of the Federal plan without legally divesting the Central Government of its control over the resources of India. In its nature it was a compromise between constitutional Imperialism and constitutional Federalism. It meant Imperial finance without Imperial management. Under the compromise the revenues and charges remained Imperial in their status, but their management was to be provincialized, so that each of the Provincial Governments was given to administer a part of the Imperial charges incurred in its territory within the limits of a part of the Imperial revenues collected within its territory. This was the essence of the new plan. It differed from the Federal plan in retaining to the Imperial Government the supreme controlling, councilling and regulating authority in all matters pertaining to Indian Finance, without its being actually engaged in the details of the administration of a *part* thereof.

In the essence of the plan as described above all the three finance ministers who were called upon to undertake the task of reconstruction had agreed. They differed, however, in the scale on which it was to be carried out. Whether Mr. Wilson had ever elaborated his own skeleton of the plan is doubtful; but that the idea of it had occurred to him seems pretty certain. The Income Tax Act XXXII of 1860, imposed by him

"was meant to consist of two parts—first, a variable tax, originally fixed at 3 per cent. on incomes, which percentage it was intended should be raised or lowered as the general exigencies of the Empire required, and which might if the state of the finance should ever permit, be entirely remitted; and secondly, a permanent tax of 1 per cent., which was to be at the disposal of the local administration, and to be expended on roads, canals, and other reproductive public works, within the area which paid the tax (*vide* sections 190–4 of the Act). This portion of the tax was never intended to be remitted. It was always to be kept up, not only to meet the charges to which it was applicable, but in order to maintain the machinery of the tax so that at any moment of exigency, after a temporary remission the other portion of the tax, applicable in aid of the general finances, might be re-imposed without agitation, discussion, or trouble." [1]

But, as Mr. Wilson did not live long enough to elaborate his ideas into a scheme, it is difficult to say to what extent he intended to work them out in practice.

Mr. Laing, the successor of Mr. Wilson, put it in a much more definite shape. His budget for 1861–2 was for a deficit caused chiefly by the pressing demands of the Local Governments for useful public works, and his sense of financial safety compelled him

"to curtail roads, canals and other useful works of this description, to the allotment on which they (had) been carried on or rather . . . starved, since the Mutiny."

But his anxiety to promote the useful public works, the urgency of which he fully recognized, led him to propose to the Provincial Governments a method of supplementing the scanty Imperial grants made to them. He said to them:

"Take what we are able to give you, and for the residue take certain powers of taxation and raise it yourself . . . for there are certain subjects which can be dealt with far better by local than by Imperial taxation . . ."

His object was to enact local budgets "not merely to meet a temporary difficulty but to inaugurate a permanent improvement," to the relief of the Imperial treasury and the benefit of the Provincial Governments. This scheme involving the management of the public works charges by the Local Government with an allotment from the Imperial revenues supplemented by the power to tax had secured a general approval. But at the time when the scheme was put forward the Local Government was without the requisite machinery for carrying into execution the powers of legislation necessary to impose the taxes proposed to be given to them. The execution of the scheme had therefore to be postponed pending the enactment of local legislative

[1] Minute by Sir B. Frere dated November 25, 1866, para. 30. *Papers, etc., on the extension of the Financial Powers of the Local Governments*, p. 42.

councils then undertaken by Parliament. But, the ensuing years having been years of financial prosperity, the interest in the scheme relaxed and it was consequently dropped *sine die*.

This spell of prosperity, however, proved to be only a passing phase and the stress of returning adversity which beset Mr. Massey compelled him to revive the scheme in a much more enlarged form.[1] He proposed that:

> "In considering the ways and means by which the additional amount (of one million sterling) should be raised . . . the most convenient mode of proceeding would be by a partial transfer of charges of a local character from Imperial to local account."

As the annual produce of local funds applicable to local purposes in India did not much exceed two million sterling, it was proposed to make the moderate addition to this amount of £1,200,000 in round numbers to be raised in rateable proportions in the several Presidencies and Local Governments, and applied in relief of a corresponding amount of charge for local services then borne by the Imperial revenues. The above-mentioned sum of £1,200,000 was arrived at by an assessment of 4 per cent. on the estimated revenues of the several Local Governments (except Burma) for the current year, after excluding customs duties and the income tax.[2] The heads of charges to which the proceeds of the new funds were applicable were (1) education, (2) police, (3) district jails, (4) public works, (5) repairs and maintenance of roads. The list of taxes suggested to provide ways and means included (1) a license tax on trades and professions, (2) a house tax, (3) an octroi duty in towns, and (4) a succession duty on lands which did not pay revenue. The Local Governments were to be left free, subject to the approval of the Government of India in Council, to select the particular tax most suited for being levied in their respective territories so as to yield the full amount re-

[1] Demi-official letter dated February 25, 1866, to the Local Governments. *Papers, etc., on the extension of Financial Powers of Local Governments*, p. 67.

[2] *Ibid.*, para. 8.

quired, after deducting the cost of collection, and spend the proceeds on the services mentioned above, on all or any of them, according to their discretion.

The replies of the Local Governments and administrations addressed in connection with this scheme indicated a general agreement as to the practicability of such a transfer of charges being made and being met by new local taxation, though there was also a general disposition to object to the transfer of charges without a simultaneous transfer of revenue with which to meet the expenditure on them. Under the circumstances the Government of India agreed to reduce the expenditure to be transferred to the Local Governments to £800,000, and to transfer to them the proceeds of the license tax as a means for making adequate provision for the same.[1] The favourable reception accorded to the scheme and the sympathetic criticism to which it was subjected led Mr. Massey to extend and modify it. In his exposition [2] of the new and enlarged scheme Mr. Massey wrote:

"my first object has been to select, for the first series of charges to be transferred to local authorities, those items of expenditure which being least susceptible of control by the Government of India, give as a whole, an amount of such dimensions as will not be difficult to manage, and yet will be of sufficient importance to indicate that the measure is intended to be a reality, and a step towards the more complete transfer of the financial administration to the local government. Taking the civil estimates . . . it seems to me, plainly, the most convenient method of proceeding to transfer a few entire grants or section of grants, in preference to selecting special items from several grants. . . . By adopting the plan . . . no change whatever in the system of accounts will be called for; and the only alteration will be, that certain sections of the grants for various purposes, will be provided in a special manner. The only exception to this rule . . . is in dealing with a head

[1] Circular letter dated September 19, 1867. *Op. cit.*, p. 67.

[2] The new scheme was outlined at the request of Mr. Massey by Col. R. Strachey in Note on the Transfer to Local Governments of the Control over Certain Portions of Public Expenditure, *ibid.*, pp. 51–62.

'Miscellaneous' which . . . is rather an incongruous collection of charges. Among these will be retained, for transfer to local management, all those items which would reasonably be termed local . . . and the residue . . . could easily be classed under some of the other main heads of charge. The most important of the charges which I should propose to transfer is that for 'Jails' subordinate to 'Law and Justice,' which may . . . be taken in lump. The charges for 'Registration' and 'Tulubana' also under 'Law and Justice' follow. These are met from special fees credited under the head of 'Law and Justice.' To set off against these charges, a transfer of the revenue under 'Law and Justice' is also proposed. . . . Under 'Education' the 'Miscellaneous' charges are proposed to be transferred to the corresponding transfer of the revenue credited under 'Education.' Next follows the whole of the charges under 'Medical Services' except the fixed 'Medical Establishments and Chemical Examiners.' The entire charge under 'Stationery and Printing' is also taken. Under 'Police' the charges met by contributions from local sources are transferred, including the Railway Police. Against this is set off the receipts under 'Police.' 'Besides the above it is proposed to transfer a portion of the charges, for the collection of the Land Revenue and of the Income Tax and License Tax, which . . . I have assumed as likely to be levied in future. It has been necessary to assign a sum sufficient to cover the general charges which would be transferred and the propriety of transferring a corresponding portion of the cost of collection seems apparent. Under the designation of charges of collection of the Land Revenue were not included the cost of the Revenue Survey or Settlement as they were exceptional and variable, though the charges under 'Allowances to Village Officers' were included.

* * * * *

"The first and principal transfer of revenue will be a portion of the Land Revenue, which I propose to fix at $\frac{1}{16}$th or one anna in the rupee. The same rate will govern the proportion of the charges for collection transferred. . . .

"The next item of revenue which I assume at one-fourth of the Income Tax and License Tax, which I shall suppose to be raised.[1]

[1] In thus calculating the share Mr. Massey wrote, "The Income

"It is next proposed to transfer the whole of the receipts under the following heads: (1) Law and Justice, (2) Police, (3) Education, (4) Miscellaneous, except items of a financial nature, and also (5) all income under Police Works excepting that derived from Irrigation. The items of expenditure under Public Works proposed to be transferred are (1) Roads, (2) Repairs of Civil Buildings, (3) Miscellaneous works both new and repairs, and (4) Tools and Plant."

The scheme thus enlarged was discussed at length from various points of view. But though it won the approval of cautious critics [1] the scheme was too large for the Imperialists. And as the two greatest of them, Lord Lawrence, the Viceroy of India, and Lord Napier of Merchistoun, Governor of Madras, disapproved of it, it failed to materialize in consequence of their opposition.

But unfortunately for the Imperialists, throughout this decade during which they were stubbornly objecting to any surgical operation on their patient—the Imperial system of Finance—it did not show any sign of convalescence. On the other hand, the delay in the operation aggravated its ills. Notwithstanding the constant enhancement in taxation and the reduction in expenditure, the three Chancellors of the Indian Exchequer sent from England could point to only three years of surplus during the decade between 1860 to 1870. On the other hand, to the embarrassments due to constant deficits was added the bewildering breakdown of the budget system created to bring about order and economy in the public finances of the country. Not to speak of its efficiency as an instrument of economy, the

Tax I have taken at 2 per cent., and I have conceived that it will cease below incomes of 2,000 rupees. The Licence Tax I have supposed to be a trade tax beginning at the existing limit and going upwards to meet the Income Tax."

[1] Sir Stafford Northcote declared—"We must take care that the solidarity of Indian Finance is not shaken, and we must provide safeguards against reckless expenditure. We have a system which has raised the credit of India to the highest pitch, and therefore I should be the last to disturb it, and would be slow and cautious in introducing any change. Nevertheless, I repeat that in the principles of Mr. Massey's suggestions I concur."—*Hansard's Parliamentary Debates*, Vol. 191, April 23, 1868.

budget system under the strain due to excessive centralization proved useless even as an instrument of order. The finances fell into a chaos. Notwithstanding the elaborate circulars and orders issued with regard to the accuracy in the framing of the budget estimates, it was an extraordinary phenomenon which confronted the Finance Ministers when the budgets, which were begun with large estimated surpluses, strangely enough closed with large actual deficits. To what extent the actuals erred from the estimates may be seen from the following table:

DERANGEMENT OF GOVERNMENT FINANCES [1]

Year.	Estimate Deficit—Surplus.	Actual Deficit—Surplus.
	£	£
1866–67	− 66,700	−2,307,700
1867–68	1,628,522	− 923,720
1868–69	1,893,508	−2,542,861
1869–70	48,263	−1,650,000 (est)

From the above table it is clear that the estimates for 1868-9 and for 1869-70, which were based on the revised estimates of 1868-69, were expected to end with an estimated surplus of £1,893,508 and £48,263 respectively. But when the actuals of the year 1868-69 showed that instead of a surplus there was to be a large deficit, Lord Mayo, who was in the meantime appointed to the Viceroyalty of India,

[1] Hunter, W. W., *Life of Mayo*, Vol. II, pp. 7–8.
The figures for actual deficits given in the Table differ from those given by Mr. Chapman, Offg. Secretary to the Government of India, F.D., in his Circular letter of 17–8–1870 to the Government of Bombay communicating to the latter Lord Mayo's scheme. According to Mr. Chapman the figures for deficit (actual) are as follows:—

In 1866–67 the actual deficit was . £2,517,491
„ 1867–68 „ „ . £1,007,695
„ 1868–69 „ „ . £2,774,031

—cf. *Papers, etc., on the extension of Financial Powers of the Local Governments*, p. 243, for the Circular letter referred to.

became convinced that if his budget was recast on the basis of these results, it would close with an actual deficit instead of the estimated surplus. This financial surprise threw his budget into confusion, and to restore order he was obliged to adopt the unusual procedure of addition to taxation and the reduction of expenditure in the midst of the fiscal year.

The following is a synopsis of the measures he adopted :—

	£
I. Additional Taxation.	
(1) Income Tax raised from 1 to 2½ per cent.	320,000
(2) Enhanced Salt Duty (in Madras and Bombay) . . .	180,000
Total . .	500,000
II. Reduction of Expenditure.	
(1) Education	350,000
(2) Public Works	800,000
Total	1,150,000
Estimated Deficit	1,650,000

So grave was the crisis that with all these measures he could do nothing more than close his budget with an estimated deficit of £1,650,000, which would have been inevitable had it not been for certain windfalls such as the recovery of the value of supplies in the Abyssinian War and the adjustment of other large outstanding accounts which enabled him to convert his large deficit into a small surplus. Happy as he was over the immediate results of his efforts, Lord Mayo was convinced that there was something rotten in the system of Imperial Finance and, while anxious not to end it, he courageously set forth to mend it by inaugurating the scheme of Provincial Finance represented by the compromise the growth of which will be the subject-matter of Part II of this study.

PART II

PROVINCIAL FINANCE : ITS DEVELOPMENT

CHAPTER IV

BUDGET BY ASSIGNMENTS

1871–72 TO 1876–77

THE origins which led to the formulation of the scheme of Provincial Budget having been presented in the foregoing part of this study, we may now proceed to examine the constitution of the scheme as it was introduced and the changes which it underwent from time to time.

With his sureness of instinct Lord Mayo traced the financial deficits and surprises to the inefficiency of the Imperial and the irresponsibility of the Provincial Governments, and was led to the conclusion that the inauguration of Provincial Budgets was the only remedy equal to the malady. But it must be recalled that the situation was yet dominated by Imperialistic considerations, and while every one in charge of the affairs was desirous, even anxious, to ease the situation by some means or other, few were willing to do so at the cost of Imperial control. Even Lord Mayo was not without his Imperialistic leanings. But the force of the baffling circumstances compelled him to break through the hitherto prevailing spirit of hesitation and indecision, although the steps he took in determining the constitution of the Provincial Budget were slow and cautious.

The scheme which actually came to be introduced from the financial year 1871-2 was first adumbrated in a confidential circular of the Home Department of the Government of India, dated February 21, 1870. Enlarging upon the policy of retrenchment by which the road grant for 1869-70 fixed in the beginning at £1,236,000 came to be reduced at the close of the year to £1,021,178 and that estimated for 1870-1 at £1,000,000 came to be finally settled at £784,839 supplemented by £29,110 for Miscellaneous Public Improvements, the circular gave the Provincial Governments

> "to understand that the diminution that has been made in the Imperial grant for communications and roads is not a temporary diminution caused by present financial pressure. It is the result of a settled policy, deliberately adopted, independently of temporary considerations, and it is far more probable that in future years the special grant for these purposes will be reduced than that it will be increased. It therefore becomes a matter of very urgent necessity that no time should be lost in providing from local sources the funds necessary for the maintenance of the existing provincial and district roads, and for the construction of the new lines of communications which become every day more necessary."

That local wants should be met by local resources had been the ideal of Indian financiers during the entire period of its reconstruction. But that the view had by that time passed beyond the stage of academic discussion is obvious, for the Circular stated that "the Governor-General in Council had fully resolved that he will insist on full effect being given to this principle" in future. Many of the Local Governments took the sentiments of the Government of India conveyed in the Circular in all the seriousness in which they were meant to be taken and had begun to develop their local resources. In the Bombay Presidency a cess of 6¼ per cent. on the Land Revenue was levied and two-thirds of it was set aside for roads and works of public utility. The Madras Government under an old Act of 1866 levied a cess of one-half of an anna on every rupee of annual rental equal to 3⅛ per cent. on the Land Revenue for purposes of district roads. The Bengal Government had declared its intention to follow the Madras Presidency.

Encouraged by the steps taken by these Local Governments the Circular urged upon other Local Governments and Administrations in Northern India, namely, North-Western Provinces, Punjab, Oudh and Central Provinces, to consider the expediency of increasing their road cesses on the land revenue to 5 per cent. The object of the move evidently was to relieve the Imperial treasury of the road grant, once the Provincial Governments were in possession of adequate local revenues.

In this way the Circular contemplated a very meagre scheme of Provincial Budget, incorporating only the charges on local public improvements and the revenues derived from local resources to meet them. But before it could be set into operation the financial difficulties of the Government of India called for a larger measure of relief. Bad as the position already was, there was little confidence to be placed in the stability of the opium revenue ; and, while there was practised a retrenchment in expenditure, the charges for interest on public debt was found to swell enormously. In the midst of such a precarious situation the Government of India decided to reduce the hitherto prevailing rate of the income tax in order to silence the outcry raised against it by the richer classes. As a possible method of ways and means to meet the additional deficit of £1,000,000 that was expected to arise from the reduction in the income tax rate, the Government of India issued another Confidential Circular, dated August 17, 1870, in which a much wider scope was given to the contemplated scheme of Provincial Budgets. It was stated in this Circular that

> "If the income tax was to be reduced, the ways and means of government must be otherwise recruited . . . preferably . . . through the agency of Local Governments, and by adopting such methods of taxation as are considered most suitable to each province and least burdensome to the people."

The method of throwing the burden on Local Governments consisted in making over to them charges of certain departments of the administration more or less local in character with a net grant on them for 1870–1 reduced by a million sterling.[1] It was proposed to distribute this sum among the various provinces in the proportion which the net provincial grant of each bore to the total net grant and leave them free to make up their respective quota of retrenchment either by redistribution, retrenchment, or taxation.

After the concurrence of the Provincial Governments had been obtained to the plan of the Circular, it was announced by the famous Financial Resolution of December 14, 1870, as being adopted for execution from the commencement of the Financial year 1871–2.

We will now proceed to analyse the constitution of the Provincial Budgets as framed by this Resolution. Taking first the expenditure side of the Provincial Budget, it may be noted that the charges for the following Imperial services were incorporated into it:—

*1. Jails.
2. Registration.
3. Police.
4. Education.
5. Medical services (except Medical establishments).
6. Printing.

[1] Net grant means total expenditure on a service minus the receipts from the service.

* Appendix B of the Resolution gives a schedule of certain works for which separate funds were to be provided from the Imperial Revenue. They were Buildings and Offices of the following Departments:—

Opium (not including the Board of Revenue's office in Calcutta).
Mint and Currency.
Post Office.
Telegraph.
Offices of the Supreme Government.
Viceregal Residences
Imperial Museum
Stamp and Stationery Office } Calcutta.
Treasury Buildings
Bishop's Palace
Godavery Works } Reserved as Imperial for the
Karachi Harbour Improvements } present.
Such Military Roads as have been till the current year provided for from the grant for "Military Works."

7. Roads.
8. Miscellaneous, Public Improvements.
9. Civil Buildings.

To provide the Provincial Governments with funds to meet the above charges incorporated into their budgets the Government of India surrendered to them the receipts which accrued from services handed over to them with an additional assignment from the Imperial fisc to bring about an equilibrium. The receipts surrendered and assignments granted to the Local Governments were as follows :—

Assignments made to Provincial Governments for services incorporated into their Budgets by the Financial Resolution No. 3334 dated December 14, 1870.

Services incorporated into Prov. Budgets.	Imperial Assignments for Services.								
	Oudh.	C P.	Bt Burma	Bengal	N W.P	Punjab	Madras	Bombay	Total.
	£	£	£	£	£	£	£	£	£
Jails. . .	26,922	27,881	32,777	218,210	88,394	58,204	91,983	73,440	617,811
Registration	—	3,509	—	36,609	20,129	11,623	22,970	25,372	120,212
Police . .	103,269	130,607	139,253	555,757	348,135	289,950	350,730	388,703	2,306,409
Education .	26,056	27,864	10,998	234,385	103,528	64,909	90,052	118,271	676,063
Medical services (except Medical establishments)	5,049	11,770	6,460	89,713	27,607	24,935	61,696	74,852	302,532
Printing .	7,609	3,640	3,000	41,732	25,302	14,106	25,840	27,050	148,279
Roads and misc. public improvements	32,900	63,403	63,000	157,800	82,636	84,200	123,880	121,900	729,819
Civil buildings .	20,090	14,406	23,959	111,370	63,341	39,710	58,506	107,500	438,882
Public Works Establishments .	13,777	20,230	22,635	69,984	37,954	32,217	47,421	59,644	303,862
Tools and Plant .	1,060	1,556	1,741	5,383	2,920	2,478	3,648	4,588	23,374
Total .	237,182	304,866	303,923	1,520,943	799,946	622,332	876,726	1,001,320	5,667,243
	Estimated Receipts of the Services.								
Jails . .	1,575	6,000	9,420	110,385	11,154	—	7,300	664	146,498
Registration	—	5,500	—	40,000	35,030	20,694	34,000	30,141	165,356
Police . .	10,586	12,520	18,671	70,363	51,730	41,724	32,350	14,000	251,944
Education .	1,482	—	500	42,012	11,050	5,000	6,900	10,480	77,424
Printing .	1,080	—	—	2,000	2,160	—	1,260	—	6,500
Total .	14,723	24,020	28,591	264,760	111,124	67,418	81,810	55,285	647,731
Grand total of net assignments	222,459	280,846	275,332	1,256,183	688,822	554,914	794,916	946,040	5,019,512

Constructed on the basis of figures given in the Resolution of December 14, 1870.

These would have been the total assignments to the Provincial Governments for meeting the charges on the incorporated services, had it not been for the fact that the Government of India desired to obtain relief by way of retrenchment of the provincial resources to make up for the deficits expected to follow the reduction in the income tax. The relief originally fixed at £1,000,000 was reduced to £350,000, distributed rateably among the various provinces. Taking account of these retrenchments the permanent assignments made to the provinces were as shown below :—

Provinces.	Net Assignments.	Proportion of Retrenchment.	Permanent Assignments.
	£	£	£
Oudh	222,459	15,511	206,948
C.P.	280,846	19,583	261,263
Burma	275,332	19,199	275,332
Bengal	1,256,183	87,591	1,168,592
N.W P.	688,822	48,030	640,792
Punjab	554,914	38,693	516.221
Madras	794,916	55,428	739,488
Bombay	946,040	65,965	880,075
Total	5,019,512	350,000	4,688,711

For conversion into Rupees, £1 equal to Rs 10.

Before the commencement of the time appointed to carry the scheme into practice the Government of India incorporated the following additional services [1] into the Provincial Budgets :—The Charges for Petty Construction and Repair of Buildings in the Civil Department excepting the Opium Department in Bengal, the Salt Department outside the Lower Provinces of Bengal and Medical Services such as (1) Salaries of Medical Officers of Medical Colleges and Central Jails, and of Lunatic Asylums at the Presidency towns ; (2) Extra allowance to Medical Officers for the Medical charge of Lunatic Asylums in the mofussil, and of Colleges, Central Jails, etc., also extra allowances to Medical

[1] Finance Department Resolution No. 1659 of March 20, 1871.

IMPERIAL ASSIGNMENTS FOR 1871—72[1]

	Oudh	C P.	Bt Burma.	Bengal.	N W.P.	Punjab.	Madras.	Bombay.	Total.
	£	£	£	£	£	£	£	£	£
Assignment as per Resolution of December 14, 1870	169,355	205,271	192,488	1,176,406	613,095	463,727	643,271	707,693	4,171,306
Add—									
Official Postage	1,551	5,093	—	4,893	10,840	8,031	4,163	4,311	38,882
Transfer from Medical Services	2,139	1,767	745	6,649	5,624	2,828	7,597	8,500	35,849
Transfer of petty construction and repairs of Civil Buildings	699	1,778	420	6,508	2,555	1,908	1,050	4,050	18,968
Other items net	—	—	—	7,866	1,485	—	—	4,600	13,753
					633,599				4,278,758
Deduct—									
Transfer of Ajmere charges to Government of India	—	—	—	—	28,714	—	—	—	28,714
Total	173,744	213,909	193,653	1,202,124	604,885	476,494	656,081	729,154	4,250,044
Deduct—									
Receipts per budget of 1870–1	14,723	24,020	28,591	260,578	109,992	67,418	81,810	55,285	642,417
Net charge in Civil Department	159,021	189,889	165,062	941,546	494,893	409,076	574,271	673,869	3,607,627
Add budget grant for P.W. as per Res of 14-12-1870, viz.—									
Roads and miscellaneous public improvements	32,900	63,403	63,100	157,800	82,636	84,200	23,880	121,900	729,819
Civil Buildings	20,090	14,406	23,959	111,370	63,341	39,710	58,506	107,500	438,882
P.W. Establishments	13,777	20,230	22,635	69,984	37,954	32,217	47,421	49,644	303,862
Tools and Plants	1,060	1,556	1,741	5,383	2,920	2,478	3,648	4,588	23,374
Total public works	67,827	99,595	111,435	344,537	186,851	158,605	233,455	293,632	1,495,937
Grand total	226,848	289,484	276,497	1,286,083	681,744	567,681	807,726	967,501	5,103,564
Deduct—									
Proportion of £350,000	15,557	19,853	—	88,199	46,753	38,931	55,394	66,351	331,038
Revised permanent assignment	211,291	269,631	276,497	1,197,884	634,991	528,750	752,332	901,150	4,772,526
Or in round numbers	211,300	269,600	276,500	1,197,900	635,000	528,800	752,300	901,200	4,772,600
[2] Add—India	—	—	—	—	—	—	—	—	26,700
								Total	4,799,300

[1] Based on the Fin. Dept. Resolution No. 1660 of March 20, 1871.
[2] The item opposite to "India" in the above table is for the Calcutta University and for Prov. services (not including Public Works) in Coorg, Ajmere and other districts under immediate administration of the Government of India.—Sir Richard Temple's Financial Statement for 1871–2.

Officers for the executive charge of jails, and (3) charges for sub-assistant Surgeons and Apothecaries employed in other than civil medical charge of the sudder stations or districts, and for all other subordinate medical establishments. Side by side with these transfers the Government of India withdrew the Calcutta University from the Provincial to the Imperial Budget.[1] To take account of the revision of charges for Official Postage,[2] and Bengal Police,[3] and the additions and withdrawals of services referred to above, the Imperial assignments to Provincial Governments for the year 1871–2 were further altered so that they stood as shown in the table on the preceding page.

Besides these assignments for the fiscal year 1871–2, the Government of India gave the Local Governments a special donation of £200,000 in the year 1870–1 in order that they "may be able to inaugurate the plan successfully, and to have as it were a fair start." Taking round numbers then, the several Provincial Governments had the following resources [4] at their disposal in the year 1871–2 to meet the expenditure incorporated in their budgets :—

Provincial Budget for	Resources.		Total.
	Receipts surrendered by the Imperial Government.	Assignments from the Imperial Treasury.	
	£	£	£
Oudh	14,700	211,300	226,000
Central Provinces .	24,000	269,600	293,000
Burma	28,600	276,500	305,100
Bengal	264,800	1,197,900	1,462,700
N.W. Provinces .	110,000	635,000	745,000
Punjab	67,400	528,800	596,200
Madras	81,890	752,300	834,100
Bombay	55,300	901,200	956,500

[1] Letter from the Secretary to the Government of India, Finance Department, No. 1683 dated March 21, 1871.

[2] Finance Department Resolution No. 1659 of March 20, 1871.

[3] Finance Department Resolution No. 1587 of March 20, 1871.

[4] Financial Statement of 1871–2.

Having analysed the constitution of the Provincial Budgets and noted the receipts and charges incorporated into them, we will proceed to inquire into the peculiarity which marks their constitution as framed in 1870–1. No method of ascertaining this peculiarity would be more direct in its approach towards the question raised above than to ask ourselves what problem the framers of the Provincial Budgets were presented with and how it was solved. From our knowledge of the history of the controversy that raged over the creation of Provincial Budgets we can say that what items of expenditure to incorporate into Provincial Budgets was no longer a prominent question of the time. Long since it was settled that there were charges in the Imperial Budget of a purely local character. By common consent they were regarded as the most unsatisfactory part of the Imperial Budget. It was admitted on all hands that, knowing nothing about these charges, the Government of India was either obliged to sanction an unnecessary charge which may have been carelessly endorsed by the head of a department having no immediate interest in guarding against the waste of public money, or by a too cautious spirit of random parsimony, or by parsimony regulated only by the state of public revenue, refuse its sanction and check prudent and profitable expenditure. As either procedure was likely to cause mischief, it was commonly agreed that such matters over which the Central Government by its supreme ignorance was powerless to exercise any control, should be transferred from the direct purview of the Imperial Government to the immediate control and responsibility of the Provincial Government. One side of the problem had thus been solved by sheer force of circumstances. The matter on which all attention was mainly concentrated was the problem of providing the Provincial Governments with funds sufficient to meet the charges incorporated into their budgets. It was allowed on all hands to be reasonable that the receipts arising from the incorporated services should be appropriated by the Provincial Governments. Two good reasons were advanced for adopting such a procedure. It is laid down as a canon of good finance that tax administration and tax appropriation should go as far as possible together. On this principle it was but proper to have allowed the Provincial Governments to appropriate the receipts from the services which they administered. But there was also another weighty reason which influenced this decision. The main idea in the inauguration of Provincial Budgets was to interest the Provincial Governments in a judicious and economical management of the finances, and one way of sustaining their interest in the same was to have given them the receipts of the services they managed. The receipts, however, were so small a portion of the total funds necessary to meet the provincialized expenditure that the problem of balancing the Provincial Budgets remained unsolved notwithstanding. Two possible ways of solution were before the Government of India at the time: either to transfer for provincial uses certain sources of Imperial revenue or to give a lump assignment from the Imperial treasury. It was difficult for a time to decide which was the more suitable of the two, for they were not only of unequal merits, but they made different appeals to the different parties concerned. To the Provincial Government assignment of revenues was preferable to fixed assignments as giving greater elasticity to their finances. To the Government of India, on the other hand, assignment of revenues seemed to be fraught with grave consequences. The past and the existing financial condition of India did not warrant the Central Government to alienate the sources of revenue it then possessed with equanimity and safety for the future. On the other hand, its prospective condition looked as precarious as its past, and it therefore desired to retain its control over the sources the mobilization of which alone could enable it to stave off any impending crisis. The second alternative, on the other hand, was just such a one as to give the provinces sufficient funds without the Government of India forfeiting its control over its resources. It must not be forgotten that the Government of India by reason of its constitutional position had the sole authority to manage and appropriate the revenues of India. Any solution for financing the provinces had therefore to be in accord with its interests as conceived by itself. This being the situation the method of assignments was adopted in preference to that of assigned revenues in solving the principal problem that arose in connection with the constitution of provincial budgets.

It is because assignment of funds from the Imperial treasury was adopted as a method of supply to balance the Provincial Budgets that the system instituted in 1871–2 has been characterized in this study as a system of Budget by Assignments.

This principle on which the Provincial Budgets were constructed in 1871–2 endured till 1876–7. The assignment made to the Provincial Governments for the year 1871–2 had been declared to be fixed and recurring. Recurring they were, but fixed they were not ; for, every year, since the start, the Government of India kept on adding to and withdrawing from Provincial Budgets items of charge already incorporated in them. In accordance with these modifications in the incorporated charges the Imperial assignments had to be either reduced or augmented as necessity dictated. The progressive changes in the assignments from 1871–2 to 1876–7 with the specific purposes for which they were granted are entered in the following tables :—

Statement of Imperial Assignments to the Provinces for the year 1871-72

PURPOSE OF THE ASSIGNMENT.	AMOUNT ASSIGNED.	
	Details.	Total.
	Rs.	Rs.
Original Assessment		1,19,79,000
Add :—		
For Cemetery establishments	4,000	
,, Compensation for Agra Brick Factory .	28,000	1,14,000
,, Office and House Rent	82,000	
		1,20,93,000
Deduct :—		
For transportation charges for convicts . .	15,000	
,, fees for licensing cargo-boats . . .	2,600	1,24,690
,, receipts of Public Works Departments .	1,07,000	
		1,19,68,310
Special Grants.		
Add :—		
For Calcutta University	60,000	
,, Midnapore Civil Court Buildings . .	31,680	3,41,680
,, Calcutta Small Causes Court Building .	2,50,000	
		1,23,09,990
Total Assignments for 1871-72 .		1,23,09,990

Statement of Imperial Assignments to the Provinces for the year 1872-73.

PURPOSE OF THE ASSIGNMENT.	AMOUNT ASSIGNED.	
	Details.	Total.
	Rs	Rs
Original Assignment		1,19,79,000
Add :—		
Permanent additions in 1871-2 (as above) .	1,14,000	
For Miscellaneous services	2,67,070	3,88,936
,, books and publications	7,600	
,, ground-rent of Orphan School at Howrah .	266	
		1,23,67,936
Deduct :—		
Permanent deductions in 1871-2 (as above) .	1,24,680	1,30,390
For repairing charges of University . .	5,700	
		1,22,37,546
Special Grants.		
Add :—		
For Burdwan Fever Relief	1,00,000	
Compensation for Sudder Court Buildings .	4,00,000	9,66,670
Capital value of annual rent of Rs. 21,000 for public offices	4,66,670	
		1,32,04,216
Deduct fractions		380
Total Assignments for 1872-3 .		1,32,03,836

Statement of Imperial Assignments to the Provinces for the year 1873–74

Purpose of the Assignment.	Amount Assigned Details.	Amount Assigned Total.
	Rs.	Rs
Permanent Assignment for 1872–3 as above .		1,22,37,546
Add :—		
For payment of Medical Officers in charge of Civil stations	3,85,000	4,85,000
For Land Revenue Sub-divisional establishments	1,00,000	
		1,27,22,546
Deduct :—		
Reduction of rent for public offices . . .	21,000	21,000
		1,27,01,546
Sanctioned for 1873–4		1,27,01,000
Add for :—		
Ground rent for Howrah Orphan School . .	266	18,066
Charges on account of European vagrants .	11,500	
Ground-rent charges	6,300	
Deduct :—		
For pay of medical pupils withdrawn from Provincial to Imperial	5,400	3,90,400
For pay of medical officers in charge of civil stations withdrawn from provincial to imperial .	3,85,000	
		1,23,28,666
Special Grants.		
Add :—		
For rent of Small Cause Court		14,400
Total Assignment .		1,23,43,066

Statement of Imperial Assignments to the Provinces for the year 1874–75

Purpose of the Assignment.	Amount Assigned. Details.	Amount Assigned. Total.
	Rs.	Rs.
Permanent Assignment for 1873–4 as above .		1,23,28,666
Add :—		
Assignment for encouragement of Mohammedan education	50,000	50,000
Sanctioned assignment		1,23,78,000
Add :—		
Grant on account of Model Farm . . .	7,000	8,180
Additional grant for ground-rent . . .	1,180	
		1,23,86,180
Deduct :—		
Reduction of outlay on account of churches and burial grounds	14,314	13,44,580
Reduction on account of Assam transferred .	13,30,000	
For ground-rent Howrah Orphan School . .	266	
Total Assignment sanctioned .		1,10,41,600

Statement of Imperial Assignments to the Provinces for the year 1875-76

Purpose of the Assignment.	Amount Assigned.	
	Details.	Total.
	Rs.	Rs.
Permanent Assignment for 1874-5 as above .		1,10,41,000
Add :—		
Grant for Botanical Gardens	52,500	53,680
,, ,, Ground rents	1,180	
		1,10,94,680
Deduct :—		
Public Works charges on account of the Salt Department	13,683	33,163
Assignments on account of lighthouses and ships withdrawn	1,769	
Assignment on account of Town Improvement Fund of Assam	17,711	
Total Assignment .		1,10,61,517

Statement of Imperial Assignments to the Provinces for the year 1876-77

Purpose of the Assignment.	Amount Assigned.	
	Details.	Total.
	Rs.	Rs.
Original Assignment for 1875-6		1,10,41,000
Add :—		
For ground rents	1 180	53,680
,, Botanical Gardens	52,500	
		1,10,94,680
Deduct —		
Public Works charges for Salt Department .		13,683
		1,10,80,997
Deduct :—		
For Form Store Department . . .	8,034	6,034
Add :—		
For Exhibitions and Fairs	2,000	
Total		1,10,74,963
Assignment as sanctioned		1,10,75,000
Add :—		
Grant on account of Bankee and Ungool Estates	3,271	58,753
Cost of the snake-poison commission, establishments and contingencies	6,000	
Grant on account of census registers . .	49,482	
		1,11,33,753
Deduct :—		
Assignment on account of lighthouses and lightships withdrawn	1,769	22,180
Assignment of Town Improvement Fund, Assam	17,711	
Annual cost of lunatics transferred to Tezpore Lunatic Asylum	2,700	
Total Assignment .		1,11,11,573

This completes the account of the services incorporated from time to time and the assignments made for them by the Imperial exchequer during the period in which the system of budget by assignments remained in force. It now remains to consider whether the system under the assignment plan was a success. What constitutes success is a question which is always open to discussion, for what may seem successful from one point of view may be the reverse of it from another standpoint. A discussion, however, of this aspect of the question cannot be avoided, for it was on the results of one stage that an advance towards the second was made to depend all throughout the expansion of Provincial Finance. As the definition of success varies with the standpoints, we must first ascertain them for the purpose of our investigation. Let us therefore inquire into the possible parties whose standpoints counted in the moulding of Provincial Finance, and without whose satisfactory opinion about the results achieved, a new step in advance could not have been taken. The Government of India and the Provincial Governments were obviously the two principal parties. Naturally their standpoints were different, if not antagonistic. The question prominent in the mind of the Government of India was how big was the gain to the Imperial treasury on the transfer. On the other hand, the Provincial Governments were concerned to know whether the resources offered by the Government of India were adequate enough for their safely accepting the responsibility of managing the incorporated expenditure. It is obvious the Provincial Governments would not undertake the responsibility of managing the Imperial expenditure within a certain assignment unless they were sure that the assignments were adequate. Similarly, the Imperial Government would see no advantage in making the transfer unless the Provincial Governments undertook to manage the expenditure at a sum less than what it cost under the direct management of the Imperial Government. Adequacy to the provinces and gain to the Imperial treasury were therefore the two chief considerations which prevailed in the determination of the continuance and expansion of the scheme. The people of the Provinces may also be conceived of as a third possible party whose concurrence may have been deemed a necessary factor in the situation. What their view-point would have been is not altogether a matter of guess. On the other hand, anyone sufficiently acquainted with the nature of popular demands for political advancement could easily imagine that the most urgent concern of the taxpayers would have been neither the well-being of the Imperial nor that of the Provincial Governments, but the distribution of the money they paid along the different channels of expenditure; and if their approval of the results of the scheme had been made a necessary condition of advance, it is probable that the development of Provincial Finance would have been along different lines.

There was a suggestion even at that time that the people of the country should have some voice in the financial arrangements of the country. In paragraph 19 of its Resolution of December 14, 1870, announcing the scheme of Provisional Finance, the Government laid down that

> "Each Local Government will publish its own Provincial Service Estimates and Accounts in the local Gazette, together with a financial exposition (which should, where possible, be made before the local Legislative Council) analogous to that annually made in the Legislative Council of the Governor-General."

If this suggestion had materialized, the Indian taxpayer would have obtained a voice in determining the financial arrangements between the Government of India and the Provincial Governments. There were, however, certain legal difficulties in the way of giving effect to this suggestion. If the Budget was introduced in the Council and debate had followed upon it, such a proceeding would have offended against Section 38 of the Indian Councils Act (24 and 25 Vic. c. 67) and would have, therefore, been illegal unless the Budget involved some proposal for tax legislation. For, that Act had provided that the activity of the Legislative

Council should not be called into play except for strictly legislative purposes. If, on the other hand, there was to be no debate, there was no advantage in this mode of giving publicity to the Budget which was not equally secured by its publication in the official Gazette. As a solution of these difficulties, the Government of Madras proposed [1] to the Government of India

"that the Provincial Budget should form a schedule to an Appropriation Bill, the contents of which would, after all the necessary explanation and discussion, be voted section by section."

But the Government of India, which had first broached the subject, was shocked by this suggestion as being revolutionary. In reply [2] it observed :—

"2. His Excellency in Council does not . . . consider that the plan proposed . . . for bringing the annual financial statement within the terms of the Indian Council's Act, would be appropriate or possible. The passing of the Appropriation Bill in the House of Commons is a proceeding by which authority is given to carry into effect the Resolutions of the House in Committee of Supply which till the passing of the Appropriation Bill are not law. The Bill enumerates every grant that has been made during the whole session, and authorizes the several sums voted by the Committee of Supply to be issued and applied to each separate service. It also contains a provision that the various aids and supplies shall not be issued or applied to any other uses than those mentioned.

"3. Such a proceeding would, His Excellency in Council considers, be out of place in India, and might have the effect of transferring from the Executive to the Legislative Council, the power of disposing of all public moneys. His Excellency, therefore, does not consider that the introduction of an Appropriation Bill would be advisable."

Against this ruling the Government of Madras appealed

[1] Letter to the Government of India, Finance Department, No. 147 of April 18, 1871.

[2] Legislative Letter to Madras dated July 11, 1871, No. 765.

to the Secretary of State [1] and pleaded that either the proposal of an Annual Appropriation Act be approved or

> "such an alteration in the Council's Act be made as will allow the financial statement to be legally made and discussed in the Local Legislative Council."

But the Secretary of State upheld the decision of the Government of India [2] on the ground that

> "such mode of procedure is only applicable in a representative assembly, which has full powers of control over the Executive, and any such powers Parliament has advisedly withheld from the Legislative Council of India."

The suggestion was therefore dropped and was not given effect to till 1921. As the voice of the people did not prevail [3] in the framing of the financial contracts between the Imperial and Provincial Government, it is of no immediate advantage to seek for results that would have interested them to know, if they had been allowed their say in the matter. In so far then the results of the past influenced the policy of the future we have only to lay ourselves out to seek for results in which the two remaining parties to the contract were primarily interested, namely, gain to the Imperial treasury and adequacy to the Provincial Governments. Applying ourselves first to the test of adequacy to the provinces the results of the period may be gauged from the annual surpluses and deficits in the finances of each of the different provinces brought within the pale of the system of Provincial Budgets.

[1] Letter from the Government of Madras, Financial Department, dated September 19, 1871, to the Secretary of State and the whole of the correspondence accompanying it.

[2] Legislative Despatch No. 4 to the Government of India, dated January 18, 1872.

[3] In fact the point that decentralization should not be extended unless it was followed by devolution of political and financial power on the representatives of the people was not specifically raised till 1908, and that too only by the late Hon. Mr. Gokhale in his evidence before the Royal Commission on decentralization of India, *q.v.*

Provincial Surpluses and Deficits

Province.	1871–2.	1872–3.	1873–4.	1874–5.	1875–6.	1876–7.
	£	£	£	£	£	£
C.P. . . .	20,988	–8,423	2,268	13,108	8,307	16,800
Bt. Burma . .	27,634	33,832	–9,922	–21,889	–5,471	5,100
Assam . . .	—	—	—	5,159	590	9,833
Bengal . . .	180,622	74,622	393,955	271,044	27,397	46,978
N.W.P. and Oudh . .	31,595	64,036	36,358	11,693	20,945	128,501
Punjab . . .	109,828	28,008	–33,347	–117,644	–92,724	26,908
Madras . . .	40,787	–19,264	–56,381	4,303	–14,210	504
Bombay . .	65,553	128,805	–64,373	9,929	–18,354	–140,718

Compiled from the annual Finance and Revenue Accounts of the Government of India for the respective years.

It is evident from these figures that the surpluses outnumber the deficits in frequency and magnitude to such an extent that the deficit could have been easily met from the accumulated balances without seriously exhausting them. Care, however, must be taken in explaining the cause of this apparent prosperity of Provincial Governments. Did the province succeed in building up their balances from the savings from the assignments and receipts made over by the Imperial Government is what we have to find out. The answer to this question cannot be given in a categorical form, for the total resources and changes to which the above figures refer include more than the receipts and assignments set apart for provincial management. Besides Imperial assignments and receipts of incorporated services they include a part of what hitherto were known as Local Funds. It must be recalled that long before the separation of Provincial from Imperial Finance there was created since the year 1855 a separation between the Imperial and Local Finance in British India. The Local Funds when separated were under the immediate management of the several Provincial Governments and comprised of two different classes: (*a*) those which by law or custom were required to be spent within the districts in which they were collected and on the specific objects for which they were collected; and (*b*) those collected all throughout the province and over the disposal of which the Provincial Government possessed unrestricted discretion. When the scheme of Provincial Finance was inaugurated it was deemed natural to merge the second class of Local Funds into the Provincial Funds. The total addition made thereby to the Provincial resources it is difficult to ascertain. But it was the opinion of Sir John Strachey, the Finance Minister of the time,[1] that such addition was "inconsiderable" and could not therefore have affected materially the financial consequences of the new system.[2]

The question of estimating the gain to the Imperial treasury need not detain us very long. The indirect gain due to the economical management of the services by the Provincial Governments will come for discussion when we come to consider the influences that played a prominent part in bringing about the second state in the evolution of Provincial Finance. The direct gain made by the Imperial treasury was effected throughout the retrenchment in provincial assignments already referred to. It may be recalled that the Government of India had planned to obtain relief to the extent of one million sterling annually on the services transferred,[3] but the Government of India soon realized that all this retrenchment would necessitate some taxation by the provincial authorities. The burden had already grown since the Mutiny, and being anxious not to add to it directly by Imperial levy or indirectly through provincial levies, it decided to reduce the relief it sought by lowering the retrenchment on provincial assignments from £1,000,000 to £350,000, or more accurately to £350,801 if we deduct, as we must, the sum of £19,199 restored to Burma, being its quota of relief owing to the special circumstances of that province.

Summing up the results of the period, the Government of India, it must be said, realized full share of the benefits

[1] See his Minute, dated March 15, 1877, appended to the Financial Statement for 1877–8.

[2] This amalgamation was, however, abandoned with effect from 1876 to enable the Government of India to ascertain the financial consequences of the new system as compared with the old.

[3] Cf. Circular of August, 1870.

it had contrived to obtain by the annual relief of £330,801, though not without causing an insufficiency, however small, in the Provincial Finance. But notwithstanding the burden thrown on the Provinces their position as disclosed by the results cannot by any means be called unhappy.

One unwelcome feature marred the inauguration of Provincial Finance. That feature consisted in the large increase in the levy of rates and cesses for purposes of local improvement.

Receipts from New Resources of Income and Cesses enhanced since 1870

	1870–1	1871–2	1872–3	1873–4	1874–5	1875–6.
Oudh—						
Ord. cesses on :	£	£	£	£	£	£
Land Revenue .	38,813	29,018	34,354	34,259	33,208	33,146
Margin Fund .	7,363	3,461	—	—	—	—
Local rate . .	—	36,810	42,535	42,883	41,097	41,461
Total . .	46,176	69,289	76,889	77,142	74,305	74,607
Assam—						
Ord cess on land .						
Rev Old Fund .	6,506	4,333	711	1,916	*17,149	—
New Fund . .	—	—	—	—	15,267	16,300
Total . .	6,506	4,333	711	1,916	32,416	16,300
Bengal—						
Road Cess Fund .	—	—	22,917	59,039	120,128	158,516
N.W. Provinces . .	168,532	201,548	216,818	213,672	215,968	150,619
Punjab	58,330	214,441	216,194	208,063	211,862	193,573
Madras—Road Cess .	212,813	234,567	377,031	368,031	371,311	369,325
,, Tolls ,,	—	—	12,144	12,234	14,860	26,531
Grand Total .	492,357	724,178	922,704	940,333	1,040,850	980,545

* Balances recovered from Bengal on account of Road and Government Estates Improvement Fund.

For the new resources of income and cesses given above, refer to *Papers, etc., on the extension of the Financial Powers of the Local Governments*, p. 494.

This shows an increase in 1875–6 over 1870–1 of £488,188, chiefly by raising the cesses in the North-West Provinces, the Punjab and the Madras Presidency to 6¼ per cent. on Land Revenue in the two last mentioned, to about 5 per cent. in the North-Western Provinces (after deducting the rural police charge); by a road cess in Bengal and by granting an assignment to Assam, at the Imperial charge, of 6¼ per cent. instead of 3 per cent. on Land Revenue pending the levy of a cess of a corresponding amount on the ryots. In the Bombay Presidency the 6¼ per cent. was imposed some years before and hence is not included in the above table. The only province which did not levy any additional cess was the Central Province, though a cess of 6¼ per cent. on the Land Revenue was in 1870 considered practicable but not opportune.

Of what benefit, a cynic may say, was the institution of Provincial Finance if it did not obviate the necessity for further taxation? If further taxation was unavoidable, why did the Imperial Government throw the onus of facing it on the Provincial Government under the garb of Provincial Budgets when it would have done that itself? It must be said in reply that the merits of Provincial Finance are to be looked for in other directions, and it will be shown in its proper place that they justified its institution, even though a certain amount of enhanced taxation followed in its wake. It would indeed be unwise to decry against taxation in general, for no benefit can be obtained without a charge. But it would be equally unjust not to protest against the kind of taxation resorted to, for what really mattered was not the increase of taxation but the inequity of taxation. The method of taxation resorted to to make up the deficit in the Provincial Finance was an imposition of rates and cesses on the already over-burdened class of tax-payers, namely the landholders. Now the services incorporated into the Provincial Budgets, for whose support these rates and cesses were levied, though called local, were not more local in the sense of their being beneficial to the particular localities than those retained by the Imperial Government. On the other hand, the former were from the standpoint of the localities as onerous to them as the latter, and yet they were financed by rates and cesses levied from the localities as though they were directly beneficial to them, which as a matter of fact they were not. This is all the more lamentable when it is recalled that the necessity for retrenchment which caused the levy of these rates and cesses was occasioned by the abolition of the income tax. As a matter of justice we should have expected the continuance of the income tax to the relief of the State and the ratepayers. But justice was for a long time absent from the Financial Secretariat of the Government of India. A few cared for it in the abstract, but none looked upon it as an element worthy of consideration in providing for the exigencies of provincial or local finance; and as it was unrecognized, its violation by the Provincial Governments was no bar to the development of Provincial Finance.

CHAPTER V

BUDGET BY ASSIGNED REVENUES

1877–78 TO 1881–82

THE scheme of Provincial Budgets, the second stage of which we shall presently study, was launched not without mixed feelings. Boundless hopes were entertained, though not unmingled with a sense of misgiving. Just what was expected of the scheme may be correctly gauged from the remarks of Sir Richard Temple, who, when introducing the scheme in 1870, said :—

" We hope that this concession (of increased control over revenues and expenditure) will give the Local Governments an additional interest in the study and the enforcement of economy in expenditure ; will afford them a just inducement to supplement their local receipts from time to time by methods either most acceptable to the people or least fraught with popular objection ; will cause a more complete understanding to arise between the executive authorities and the tax-paying classes respecting the development of fiscal resources ; will teach the people to take a practical share in the Provincial Finance, and lead them up gradually towards a degree of local self-government ; and will thus conduce to administrative as well as financial improvement." [1]

While entertaining these hopes he also took the opportunity of asking the Council to be prepared for disappointment, for he went on to remark :

" the hopes which I am expressing, however sanguinely, or

[1] Annual financial statement for the official years 1860–1 to 1873–4, with Appendices : Calcutta, Office of the Superintendent of Government Printing, 1873, p. 348.

confidently entertained, are after all but hopes, and like all other hopes may or may not be fairly realized. But let all this eventuate as it may, sure I am with certainty free from shade of doubt, that the measure is advantageous to the Imperial Budget of British India. For it will have the direct effect of definitely limiting, for the present, the expenditure from the general Exchequer on certain important branches of civil expenditure, the very branches indeed, where, from the progressive state of the age, the demands for increased outlet have most arisen, and in which from the nature of the case the supreme Central Authority is least able to check the requirements of the local authorities."

The actual results, however, far surpassed these very moderate hopes and were more than necessary to dispel the misgivings that still lingered in the minds of those who looked upon the institution of Provincial Finance as a project of doubtful utility. Confining ourselves to the issues immediately affecting the Government of India or the Provincial Governments, it was abundantly proved that Provincial management was more economical than Imperial management. If we compare the expenditure incurred upon the services while they were an Imperial charge with the expenditure on them after they were provincialized, the superior economy of provincial management is overwhelmingly proved.

Year.	Total excess Expenditure on all Transferred Services except Registration over Total Receipts from them inclusive of all Contributions other than those for Bengal Famine under Imperial management.	Year.	Total excess Expenditure on all Transferred Services except Registration over Total Receipts from them inclusive of all Contributions other than those for Bengal Famine under Provincial management.
	£		£
1863–4	5,111,297	1871–2	4,835,238
1864–5	5,606,248	1872–3	4,964,407
1865–6	5,587,779	1873–4	5,329,180
1867–8	5,821,438	1874–5	5,379,509
1868–9	6,030,214	1875–6 Est.	5,135,677
1869–70	5,856,310		
1870–1	5,197,250		

Compiled from an official volume of Notes on Imperial, Provincial and Local Finance, 1876.

It was therefore with confirmed belief in its utility and

even with a sense of relief that the Government of India proceeded to incorporate into the Provincial Budgets additional services local in character or more amenable to local control. But these additions to the incorporated services made the problem of a supply of funds to Provincial Governments assume greater proportions. In the first period the gap between the receipts of incorporated services and the total charges for them was comparatively smaller than what it was found to be the case on the present occasion. The mode of bridging the gap entirely by assignments was deemed to be ill-fitted for the success of the scheme in its enlarged form. The most radical defect in the system of budget by assignment consisted in its rigidity. The provinces did not favour it as a mode of supply for the reason that while the outlay on the services under their management continued to expand the assignments made to them remained fixed in amount. Sir John Strachey, to whom belonged the credit of carrying the scheme a stage further, was particularly alive to this weakness of the system. In place of fixed assignments he desired to give the provinces certain sources of revenue, the yield of which largely depended upon good management. His primary object in doing this, no doubt, was to make better and more elastic provision for the growing needs of the provincialized services. But he had also another, and, as he conceived it, a far more important reason in the substitution for assignments of assigned revenues. That economy was the fruit of good management had by that time become a commonplace, but few were sure as to what good management consisted in. It was Sir John Strachey who, for the first time, defined in unmistakable language his notion of good management, which was since his time applied in an ever-increasing degree in the development of Provincial Finance. To him good management of finance was to be had

"not by any action which gentlemen of the Financial Department or by any other department of the supreme Government can take whilst sitting hundreds or thousands of miles away in their offices in Calcutta or Simla; not by examining figures or writing circulars, but by giving to the

RECEIPTS FROM INCORPORATED SERVICES

Allocated Services.	Under Imperial Management.					Under Provincial Management.				
	1865–6	1867–8	1868–9	1869–70.	1870–1	1871–2.	1872–3.	1873–4	1874–5.	1875–6.
	£	£	£	£	£	£	£	£	£	£
Jails	89,260	96,910	141,218	133,806	128,773	149,888	195,755	271,915	297,198	326,023
Police . . .	140,166	231,859	277,179	287,529	270,855	203,624	97,735	90,708	80,509	89,895
Education . .	53,256	66,869	67,207	72,848	60,740	76,789	80,869	101,306	99,537	101,909
Registration . .	86,997	127,070	153,488	165,048	147,152	155,262	171,735	121,470	172,111	184,461
Printing . . .	3,333	3,282	2,803	3,718	9,244	10,923	14,383	21,174	18,220	18,066
Medical . . .	—	—	—	—	3,273	20,594	30,649	36,370	43,097	26,583
Miscellaneous .	4,070	5,666	4,076	4,489	6,116	20,991	31,345	32,396	39,666	36,234

Compiled from the same source referred to above.

Local Governments . . . a direct and, so to speak, a personal interest in efficient management." [1]

And in this he had the strong support of recent experience; for, taking the results of the past stage the provinces not only managed the services at a lesser cost to the revenue than was the case under the Imperial regime, but the services yielded increased revenue under the more immediate and fostering care of the provinces than they did under the remote, uninformed, and therefore impotent vigilance of the Imperial Government.

Sir John Strachey had long held to the view that so long as the Provinces collected the revenues *for* the Government of India they did not care to check evasion, which they would have surely done if they had collected them for their immediate benefit, or, as he put it,

"when the Local Governments feel that good administration of branches of revenues will give *them*, and not to the Government of India alone, increased income and increased means of carrying out the improvements which they have at heart, then, and not till then, was to be had the good administration that every one desired."

This evidence of the expanding receipts of provincialized services were therefore a pleasant surprise which went a great way in confirming the view he had advocated. It was therefore for a double purpose, of augmenting the revenues and of introducing elasticity in Provincial Finance, that Sir John Strachey substituted assigned revenues for assignments as a mode of supply to the provinces.

The plan adopted by Sir John Strachey was not new, neither was it brought forward for the first time. It was present in the minds of the people who took part in the discussions of Provincial Finance in 1870, and was actually advocated by Sir John Strachey as early as 1872.[2] That the Government of India did not look upon the plan with favour in 1870 was due to the fact that it was afraid to permanently alienate the sources of revenue on the growth

[1] Financial Statement, 1877–8.
[2] See his Minute dated July 27, 1872.

of which its stability depended. By now, however, the financial position of the Government of India had a bit improved, and the six years' trial of provincial management had also engendered a greater confidence in the scheme in the minds of those who had never completely accepted the administrative utility of the project. To this was added the prospect of the plan being a means of increased productivity in their resources as it had been of increased economy in expenditure. The force of all these factors combined to bring a new stage in the evolution of Provincial Finance which, because of the distinct mode of supply adopted, may be well designated as a stage of Budget by Assigned Revenues.

To be sure, assignments still formed a part of the new system. But that was because of the difficulty of assigning such revenues the yield of which would have been precisely equal to the incorporated expenditure. Under any circumstances there was sure to be some difference. It happened that the normal estimated yield of the ceded revenues fell short of the requirements and the margin of difference had to be made up by some adjusting assignment in the case of each province.

The method of fixing the adjusting assignment for the different Provinces was on the whole a little too complicated, and may therefore be conveniently explained before proceeding to examine the constitution of the Provincial Budgets of the different Provinces as laid down under the second stage of their growth. It must be borne in mind that the total resources of the Provinces were made up under this system of (1) the receipts accruing from the incorporated services, (2) the yield of the revenues assigned, and (3) the adjusting assignment. How to fix upon an adjusting assignment for a particular Province was a question involving nice calculations. Before arriving at a definite figure for the adjusting assignments it was obviously necessary to have settled the normal yield of the receipts of incorporated services and of the revenues made over. The assessment of the normal yield was a contentious matter. As a rough and ready method the Government of India took the average yield of each over a series of years as the normal yield, and made it the basis from which to calculate the assignments. Similarly on the basis of the annual growth of the revenues in the past years it assumed a certain normal rate of increase for each of the sources, so that the normal for the succeeding years exceeded the normal for the preceding year at the normal rate of annual progression assumed. And as the normal yield of the assigned revenues increased at their assumed normal rate of growth the assignments fixed for the subsequent years diminished in like proportion. This normal rate of growth assumed for the assigned revenues was sometimes an assumption unjustified by their past productivity. At all events, as a higher rate of increase meant lessened assignments, the Provinces questioned its magnitude. To pacify the Provinces and to make due allowances for errors of estimating, the Government of India made a very ingenious concession. It agreed that if the actual results showed deviations from the estimated normal yield, either below or above, they should be equally divided between the Provincial and Imperial Governments. If the actual yield was greater than the normal the adjusting assignment from the Imperial Government fixed for the year would be reduced by half the excess, and if it were less than the normal the assignment would be increased by half the deficit.

All this very delicate mechanism was adopted primarily for the advantageous manner in which it enabled the Government of India to adjust the assignments without undue hardship being inflicted on either party. But there was also another advantage which, though unperceived at the time, was none the less effective. The consent secured from the Provinces to bear half the burden of a possible deficit in the normal estimate directly put a premium on economical and judicious administration of the ceded revenues. If the Government of India had agreed to bear the whole of the deficit below the estimated normal, it is doubtful whether the Provinces would have exerted themselves sufficiently to develop their resources to such a degree as to bring their yield to the level of the normal. But the fear that their obligation to bear half the deficit might assume a larger proportion, which would undoubtedly be the case if there was a great falling off in the revenue, compelled them to bestow greater vigilance than they would otherwise have done. Whilst an effectual check on relaxation was thus provided the scheme was not wanting in a stimulus to exertion. The prospect of gaining half the excess over the normal gave a more direct stimulus to the Provinces to develop their resources beyond the normal than would have been the case if the total excess had been entirely appropriated by the Imperial Government. In short, the deterrent effect of a deficit to bear and the stimulating effect of a gain to reap made the mechanism of Provincial Finance as perfect as it could be made from the standpoint of economy in expenditure and productiveness in resources.

Having noted the factors that led to the conception and execution of this new step in Provincial Finance and the features which marked its novelty, we may now proceed to the study of the constitution of Provincial Budgets and the revenue and charges that were incorporated into them. Unfortunately it is impossible to present a conspectus of Provincial Budgets as a whole, for the charges were not uniformly incorporated in all the Provincial Budgets. Each Province was treated individually. This compels us to enter upon the analysis of the Provincial Budgets as they were reconstituted in 1877–8 separately for each of the different provinces.

North-Western Provinces and Oudh [1]

The budget of the Province was recast rather than enlarged by additions to the already allocated items, as was the case with regard to some other Provinces. In its new form the budget of the Province incorporated the following heads of expenditure and revenue :—

[1] Financial Department Notification No. 1807, *Gazette of India*, Part I, March 31, 1877, p. 172.

Heads of Charges.		Heads of Revenue.
3. Refunds of all Assigned Revenues.		
4. Land Revenue (excepting settlements, allowances to district and village officers, and special temporary compensations to covenanted civil servants in N.W.P.)	I	Land Revenue—collections from the Terai and Bahbar estates and the Dudi estate in Mirzapore and from stone quarries.
6. Excise.	IV	Excise.
10. Stamps.	IX	Stamps.
14. Administration (excepting Account and Currency Officers).		
16. Law and Justice (excepting special temporary allowances to covenanted civil servants in N.W.P.)	XIII	Law and Justice.
17. Police.	XIV	Police.
19. Education.	XVI	Education.
21. Medical (excepting the pay of Medical Officers in charge of civil stations).		
22. Stationery and Printing.		
28. Miscellaneous (excepting remittance of treasure and any unenumerated item exceeding Rs. 10,000).	XX	Miscellaneous (excepting "Gain by Exchange," "Premium on Bills," unclaimed Bills and unenumerated items exceeding Rs. 10,000 each).
Public Works Ordinary; Roads and miscellaneous public improvements, civil buildings (except opium, post office and telegraph buildings) and tools and plants; also whole of the Public Works establishment of the P.W.D. excepting that in the Military works and irrigation branches; the imperial government paying towards their cost 20 per cent. on the outlay from the imperial funds and works and repairs executed by the establishment.		*Public Works Receipt* such as appertained to the Public Works charges incorporated into the Provincial Budget.

In assigning the heads of revenue the Government of India added the proviso that

"the Governments of North-Western Provinces and Oudh must surrender to the Imperial treasury half of any sum by which the net revenue from Excise, Stamps, and Law and Justice (omitting Jails and Registration), deducting Refunds under these heads and the charges under 6, Excise and 10, Stamps, exceeded Rs. 83,75,000"

and agreed to reimburse the province with a sum equal to

half the deficit if the yield fell below the above sum. This adjustment was effected by operating upon the balances of the Province so that if the expenditure of the North-Western Provinces and Oudh upon the incorporated services exceeded the enumerated revenues plus any Provincial contribution in support of them by less than Rs. 83,75,000, the difference was to be added to; and if such excess expenditure was more than Rs. 83,75,000 the difference was to be deducted from the balances of the Government of the North-Western Provinces and Oudh in the Imperial treasury.

Bengal

The budget of the Province of Bengal[1] was enlarged

Items of Expenditure incorporated in the Bengal Budget.	Grant as existing in 1877–8	Retrenchment.	Proposed Consolidated Grant.
3. Refunds of Revenue from Excise, Stamps, Law and Justice, and of Deposits	4,91,000	—	4,91,000
4. Land Revenue (Collectors', Deputy Commissioners', etc. Establishments and charges on account of Land Revenue Collections)	22,62,000	—	22,62,000
6. Excise on spirits and drugs	2,92,000	—	2,92,000
8. Customs	6,93,000	—	6,93,000
9. Salt	39,000	—	39,000
11. Stamps	2,38,000	—	2,38,000
15. Administration (excepting Account Office, Allowances to Presidency Banks, Stationery Office at Presidency and stationery purchased in the country)	12,61,000	—	12,61,000
16. Minor Departments (excepting meteorological and archæological departments, census and gazeteers)	1,68,000	—	1,68,000
17. Law and Justice (excepting Law Officers)	63,97,000	1,00,000	62,97,000
18. Marine	10,92,000	—	10,92,000
23. Political (Govt. House Police Guard)	7,000	—	7,000
26. Miscellaneous (excepting remittance of treasure)	25,000	—	25,000
Stationery and Stamps	4,98,000	50,000	4,48,000
27. Provincial allotment as now existing	1,10,59,000	4,40,000	1,06,19,000
Maintenance of Bishop's Palace, etc.	7,000	—	7,000
Total	2,45,29,000	5,90,000	2,39,39,000

[1] *Gazette of India*, Part I, March 31, 1877, p. 174.

rather than recast by additions to the already incorporated heads of revenue and expenditure. For the second stage of the scheme the Government of Bengal was made responsible for the charges shown in the table on preceding page.

To meet these charges the following revenues were handed over to Bengal for its use :—

ASSIGNED REVENUES (000 omitted)

Heads of Revenue.	Estimated Yield in 1876–7	Estimated Yield at the assumed Rate of Growth. 1877–8	1878–9	1879–80	1880–1	1881–2.
	Rs.	Rs	Rs	Rs	Rs	Rs
IV Excise in spirits and drugs	6,300	6,400	6,500	6,600	6,700	6,800
VI Customs (see, Customs Misc. and Warehouses and Wharf rents) . .	3,600	3,600	3,600	3,600	3,600	3,600
VII Salt (Rents of Warehouses, fines and forfeitures and misc.) . .	220	220	220	220	220	220
IX Stamps . . . . / XIII Law and Justice .	10,300	10,575	10,850	11,125	11,400	11,675
XIV Marine (pilotage receipts, registration and other fees and misc.)	1,091	1,084	1,084	1,084	1,084	1,084
XVI Misc. (all except premium on bills, unclaimed bills, and any unenumerated item exceeding Rs. 10,000)	771	792	792	792	792	792
Total .	—	22,671	23,076	23,421	23,596	24,171

Compiled from statements in the *Gazette of India* referred to above.

But as the revenues assigned were not sufficient for meeting the incorporated charges transferred, after taking account of the excesses over normal to be paid to the Government of India, the Government agreed to make the following assignments from the Imperial treasury to the Government of Bengal :—

Year.	*Assignments.*
1877–78	Rs. 48,32,000
1878–79	44,57,000
1879–80	40,82,000
1880–81	37,07,000
1881–82	33,32,000

Central Provinces [1]

In the case of the Central Provinces the following additional items were incorporated in its budget :—

Heads of Charge.	Grants as already fixed for 1877–78.	Re-trench-ment.	Proposed Net Consolidated Grants.
	Rs.	Rs	Rs.
Refunds of Excise, Stamp, Law and Justice and Miscellaneous	47,000	—	47,000
Excise	52,000	—	52,000
Stamps	14,000	—	14,000
Land Revenue exclusive of settlement charges	6,66,000	90,000	17,74,000
Administration (exclusive of Account and Currency Office)	3,39,000		
Minor Departments (exclusive of Meteorology and Archæology)	4,000		
Law and Justice	6,91,000		
Stationery and Stamps	69,000		
Miscellaneous (excepting Remittance of Treasure and Discount on Supply Bills)	5,000		
Add :— Existing allotment for provincial services	27,73,000	—	27,73,000
Total Grant for Services to be borne upon the Central Provinces Budget .	46,60,000	—	45,70,000

To meet these charges the Government of Central Provinces was authorized to appropriate the yield of the following sources of revenue :—

Heads of Revenue Assigned.	Estimated Yield in 1876–7.	Estimated Yield at the Assumed Rate of Growth in		
		1877–8.	1878–9.	1879–80.
	Rs.	Rs.	Rs.	Rs
Excise	13,90,000	14,50,000	15,10,000	15,70,000
Stamps	9,70,000	9,75,000	9,80,000	9,85,000
Law and Justice	1,67,000	1,75,000	1,83,000	1,91,000
Miscellaneous (excepting Premium on Bills, undrawn Bills of Exchange and any unenumerated items exceeding Rs. 10,000 each) . .	7,000	7,000	7,000	7,000
Total	—	26,07,000	26,80,000	27,53,000

Compiled from the *Gazette* referred to above.

[1] *Gazette of India*, Part I, dated June 2, 1877, p. 274.

As these revenues were insufficient the Government of India undertook to supplement them by the following assignments from the Imperial exchequer :—

Year.	*Assignments.*
1877–78	Rs. 19,63,000
1878–79	18,90,000
1879–80	18,17,000

These assignments were, however, subject to change because of the proviso applying to the assigned revenues. By virtue of that proviso the Government of India was to claim half the net increase of their combined annual yield over the estimated normal and was to bear half the deficit if their actual combined yield failed short of the normal. If there was an increase above the normal the assignments were to be reduced by a sum equal to half the increase, and if there was a decrease the assignments were to be increased by a sum equal to half the decrease.

Bombay

Coming to the Provincial Budget [1] of the Bombay Government we find the following charges were incorporated in it .—

Heads of Charge	Grant as already fixed for 1877–8	Retrenchment	Consolidated Grant
	Rs	Rs	Rs
3. Refunds . .	1,10,000		
4. Land Revenue . .	65,07,000		
6 Excise . .	80,000		
7. Customs .	8,09,000		
8. Salt . .	5,69,000		
14. Administration .	11,43,000		
15. Minor Departments . .	1,13,000		
16. Law and Justice . .	43,12,000	5,67,000	2,13,96,000
18. Marine	31,000		
20. Ecclesiastical	3,25,000		
21. Medical	2,68,000		
22. Stationery and Stamp . . .	2,29,000		
24. Allowances and Assignments .	64,81,000		
26. Superannuation allowances . .	8,00,000	—	
28. Miscellaneous	28,000		
Add :—			
Existing allotment for provincial services	1,04,54,000	—	1,04,54,000
	3,24,17,000	5,67,000	3,18,50,000

[1] *Gazette of India*, Part I, dated August 4, 1877, p. 468.

Besides the receipts accruing from the already incorporated services the Government of India assigned to the Government of Bombay the following sources of revenue :—

ASSIGNED REVENUES (000 omitted)

Heads of Revenue Assigned.	Estimated Yield in 1876–77.	Estimated Yield at the Assumed Rate of Growth in				
		1877–8.	1878–9.	1879–80.	1880–1	1881–2.
	Rs.	Rs.	Rs.	Rs.	Rs.	Rs.
I Land Revenue (receipts of Inamdari adjustments and service commutations) . .	5,199	6,624	6,624	6,624	6,624	6,624
IV Excise	3,946	4,000	4,100	4,200	4,300	4,400
Stamps	4,186	4,300	4,350	4,500	4,550	4,600
Law and Justice . .	277	270	270	270	270	270
Total	—	8,570	8,720	8,970	9,120	9,270
Miscellaneous (excepting gain by exchange, premium on Bills, and on Money Orders, lapsed Money Orders, Sales, Proceeds of Durbar Presents and unenumerated items — exceeding Rs. 10,000 each)	52	70	70	70	70	70
Total . . .	—	15,264	15,414	15,664	15,814	15,964

Compiled from the *Gazette of India.*

The adjusting assignments to cover the difference between the expenditure and revenue incorporated in the Bombay Budget were as follows :—

Year.	*Assignments.*
1877–78	Rs. 1,53,20,000
1878–79	1,51,70,000
1879–80	1,49,20,000
1880–81	1,47,70,000
1881–82	1,46,20,000

These assignments, it must be noted, were subject to the same proviso as obtained in the case of the Central Provinces.

Punjab

The only remaining Provincial Budget that was framed on the principle of assigned revenues was that of the Punjab.

The heads of charge incorporated in this budget were as hereinafter specified.

Heads of Incorporated Expenditure.	Grant as Settled for 1877–8.	Retrenchment.	Proposed Net Consolidated Grant.
	Rs.	Rs.	Rs.
Refunds	65,000		
Land Revenue, excluding settlement charges	16,21,000		
Excise	58,000		
Stamps	72,000		
Administration (excluding Account and Currency Offices and settlement Secretary)	9,74,000		
Minor Departments	16,00,000		
Law and Justice	20,94,000	2,24,000	51,38,000
Superannuation and Retired Allowances, Compassionate Allowances and Gratuities	3,38,000		
Miscellaneous, excluding Remittances of Treasure	41,000		
Stationery and Stamps	83,000		
Add :—			
Existing allotments for provincial services	54,22,000		54,22,000
Total	1,07,84,300	2,24,000	1,05,60,000

To defray these charges it was proposed to assign the following revenues to the Government of the Punjab :—

Heads of Revenues Assigned.	Net Revenue in 1876–7.	Estimated Net Yield in		
		1877–8.	1878–9.	1879–80.
	Rs	Rs.	Rs.	Rs.
Assessed Taxes	—	—	12,00,000	12,00,000
Stamps	—	24,85,000	25,05,000	25,25,000
Law and Justice	—	4,15,000	4,15,000	4,15,000
Excise	—	10,30,000	10,50,000	10,70,000
	—	39,30,000	39,70,000	40,10,000
Miscellaneous (excluding gain by Exchange, premium on Bills, and unclaimed Bills of Exchange)	—	60,000	60,000	60,000
Total	—	39,90,000	52,30,000	52,70,000

In making over these revenues the Government of India

had reserved to itself a share of the improvement in the net yield from Stamps, Law and Justice, and Excise. The estimated net yield having fallen short of the estimated expenditure the Government of India agreed to make the following assignments to the Government of the Punjab in order to restore balance in its budget :—

Year.	Assignment.	Less Share of Improvement in Net Revenue from Excise, Stamp, Law and Justice.	Net Assignment.
	Rs.	Rs	Rs.
1877–8	65,70,000	107,000	64,63,000
1878–9	53,40,000	85,000	52,55,000
1879–80	53,10,000	—	53,10,000

It should be noted that the Government of Madras refused to undertake the responsibility of a Provincial Budget based upon the new principle of assigned revenues. It preferred to remain on the old basis. Provincial Budgets of Assam and Burma are not included in this chapter. As the principle involved in their constitution appertains to the study undertaken in the following chapter it is deemed expedient not to include them in the present.

Before closing the study of the second stage in the development of Provincial Budgets it is advisable to take stock of the results achieved during its prevalence from the standpoint of sufficiency to the Provincial Governments and gain to the Imperial exchequer. The following is illustrative of the results of this stage from the standpoint of sufficiency to the provinces :—

Provinces.	Annual Surpluses or Deficits.				
	1877–8.	1878–9	1879–80.	1880–1.	1881–2.
	£	£	£	£	£
C.P.	5,992	7,049	–28,133	2,956	95,221
Bengal . .	173,380	158,932	82,523	–11,313	255,189
N.W.P. and Oudh . .	4,469	237,100	320,729	280,790	667,613
Punjab . .	18 ,578	48,195	7,017	59,497	135,979
Bombay . .	–609,672	61,249	–11,201	37,855	418,783

Compiled from the Finance and Revenue Accounts of the Government of India.

From this it is clear that except in Bombay the funds provided by the Imperial Government proved not only sufficient for the purpose of carrying on the services incorporated in the Provincial Budgets, but were such as to afford a safe margin of revenue over expenditure. That the provinces had enough and to spare is clearly proved by the assistance which they gave without much detriment to their finances to the Imperial Government in the years 1879-80 and 1880-1. In the year 1879 the financial position of the Imperial Government had become rather critical. The fall in the value of the rupee and the commencement of hostilities with the Afghans were expected to bring about a deficit estimated in 1879-80 at £1,395,000. As the first line of defence the Government of India urged on the several Local Governments and Administrations the necessity of reducing the ordinary expenditure of the country within the narrowest possible limits and directed that measures for suspending or postponing all optional expenditure, whether Imperial, Provincial, or Local, should be adopted forthwith and that no proposals for increase of salaries or establishments should be entertained without real necessity.[1] As a second line of defence the Government of India ordered that until further

> "arrangements could be settled with the Local Governments . . . no new work estimated to cost more than Rs. 2,500 shall be commenced at the cost of the Imperial or Provincial Funds, even though it may already have received the sanction of the Government "[2]

and decided to make large reductions in the expenditure on productive public works. When it was discovered that these restraints on expenditure were not enough to bring about an equilibrium in the Imperial Budget the Government of India adopted a plan of levying benevolences on the provincial balances as a better alternative to increased taxation. It was, of course, an abrogation of one of the most

[1] Resolution of the Financial Department, No. 4063, dated November 9, 1878.

[2] Finance Department Resolution of May 1, 1879, *Gazette of India*, Part I, May 3, 1879, p. 329.

fundamental conditions of Provincial Finance that the Provincial Balances, though in possession of the Imperial Government, were a sacred trust to be released only when required by the Provinces. But the solvency of India was deemed to be more sacred than the sanctity of the terms of Provincial Finance. Accordingly the following sums were appropriated by the Imperial Government from the balances of the Provincial Governments :—

Province.	Contributions to the Imperial Government.		
	1879–80.	1880–1.	Total in Lakhs.
	Rs	Rs.	Rs.
Bengal	10	10	20
N.W.P.	7½	7½	15
Bombay	4	4	8
Punjab	3	3	6
Burma	3	3	6
Central Provinces	2½	2½	5
Madras	2	2	4
Assam	1½	1½	3
Total	33½	33½	67

These contributions were repaid in 1882-3; but for the time being they were in effect a gain or at least a relief to the Imperial treasury. The real gain to the Imperial treasury consisted in the retrenchments made in assigning allotments for services transferred to provincial management. The amount of retrenchment secured in the case of each of the provinces may be summarized as follows :—

Province.	Rs.	Retrenchment.
N.W. Provinces	3,54,000	5 per cent. of the total allotment.
Oudh	73,000	,, ,, ,,
Bengal	5,90,000	,, ,, ,,
Central Provinces	90,000	,, ,, ,,
Bombay	73,000	,, ,, ,,
Punjab	2,41,000	,, ,, ,,

This does not exhaust the total gain reaped by the Imperial Government. Two other ways of gain must also be mentioned along with this. It should be borne in mind that by taking the standard yield of the assigned revenues at a level higher than what was justified by their history, the Government of India was able to assign reduced sums for the provincial services than what it would have been required to do if the standard yield had been fixed at a lower level. This reduction in assignments owing to abnormal estimates of the ceded revenues was a direct gain. The excesses above the standard also opened additional possibilities of gain owing to the clause governing the cessation of revenues, although it must be recognized that under the same clause the Government of India stood to lose in the eventuality of the actual revenue falling below the standard. How much it gained from these conditional channels of gain it is difficult to say. On the whole, it cannot be denied that the gain to the Imperial treasury was substantial.

Thus the results show that the scheme of Provincial Finance on the basis of assigned revenues was a success both from the standpoint of the Provincial and Imperial Governments, so that they agreed mutually to make a further move in the development of the scheme which constitutes its third stage.

CHAPTER VI

BUDGET BY SHARED REVENUES

1882–83 TO 1920–21

AT every step in the direction of enlarging the Provincial Budgets the crucial question, as has already been pointed out, was with regard to the difficulties of balancing the revenues and charges proposed to be incorporated therein. The two steps heretofore taken, one in 1871 and another in 1877, in the direction of the evolution of Provincial Finance, were marked by two distinct methods of balancing the Provincial Budgets. On the former occasion the Imperial Government supplied the Provincial Governments with fixed lump sum assignments from the Imperial treasury. On the latter occasion this mode of supply was partly replaced by assigning certain sources of revenue for the use of Provincial Governments. The plan of assigned revenues, though it went a great way to remove the most serious defect of the measures of 1871-2, which transferred to the Local Governments the responsibility of meeting charges which had an undoubted tendency to increase, with income which, although not quite fixed, had little room for development, fell short of the requirements of Provincial Finance from the standpoint of elasticity. Superior to those of 1871 though they were, the measures of 1877 were so short of the fullest requirements of elasticity in finance that the Government of Madras refused to accept the enlarged scheme and preferred to abide by the arrangements of 1871. The scheme of 1877 was not offered to Burma or Assam. But when the Government of India made such an offer in 1879 it was obliged to turn over a new leaf, for, though the difficulty of meeting expanding charges with fixed assignments was overcome in some of the provinces by economy and good management, it was considerably felt by the province of Burma. The expenditure of the province in the seven years preceding the scheme of Provincial Finance aggregated to Rs. 1,98,45,970, while the assignments for the following seven years, aggregated apart from special additions, Rs. 2,20,22,770, showing an excess of Rs. 21,76,800, in all or about 3 lakhs a year. But the expenditure during the same period amounted to Rs. 2,40,77,885, being an excess of Rs. 42,31,915 in all or about 6 lakhs a year. The difference therefore between the excess assignment of 3 lakhs, and the excess expenditure of 6 lakhs a year, had to be made good by the Imperial Government by special grants averaging 2¾ lakhs every year to maintain the solvency of the Province.[1] The Government of India while making the supplementary assignments was not unconscious of the demoralizing effect of such doles. In fact it was admitted that it would have been much better to have augmented the provincial assignments to Burma by 22½ lakhs at the start had it foreseen the necessity for it, than to have been obliged to grant an equal amount in the form of supplementary aids so detrimental to economy and good management. The experience of Burma had driven home the fatuity of assignments as a mode of supply and the Government of India had realized that elasticity in revenues was a vital condition for the success of Provincial Finance. To assign revenues to Burma was therefore inevitable. Being overborne by the needs of the Province and by the fact that the Province yielded a substantial surplus to the Imperial treasury, the Government of India conceded that the Province was "entitled to have its real wants supplied more liberally than heretofore."[2] It is in the method adopted for the purpose of giving a liberal treatment to the province of Burma that the new step in the method of supply to the Provinces was taken. In

[1] Finance Department Resolution No. 1488 dated March 26, 1879, para. 2.

[2] *Ibid.*, para. 22.

the settlements made in 1877-8 with the five Provinces—Central Provinces, N.W.P. and Oudh, the Punjab, Bombay and Bengal—the Heads of Account under Revenue and Expenditure comprising the Indian Budget were grouped under two distinct categories: (1) wholly Imperial and (2) wholly Provincial. But in the case of Burma the Heads of Account were grouped under three distinct categories: (1) wholly Imperial, (2) wholly Provincial, and (3) jointly Imperial and Provincial.[1] In so far as items of revenue and expenditure were in the exclusive keeping of the Imperial or the Provincial Government, the settlement did not differ in spirit from that obtaining in other provinces. The difference consisted in carving out a third category of Account to be made of *jointly Imperial and Provincial.* By it certain revenues and charges were marked off from the rest and were shared between the Imperial and the Provincial in some definitely fixed proportion. The object of the arrangement was to replace rigidity in the Provincial revenues by elasticity. In the finances of the other Provinces there was elasticity in so far as their assignments were replaced by assigned sources of revenue. But to the degree in which their revenues were made up of fixed assignments their finances inevitably suffered from rigidity. In the case of Burma, however, the substitution of shares of growing revenues for fixed assignments gave complete elasticity to the Provincial revenues without which it had become so difficult to shoulder the responsibility of meeting expanding charges.

In recasting the framework of the Provincial Budget of Burma on the principle of shared revenues, all the heads of receipts and charges were made wholly Provincial, with the exception of the following, which were treated as wholly Imperial :—

(1) The Army	Receipts and Charges.
(2) Post Office	" " "
(3) Telegraph	" " "
(4) Account Department . .	" " "
(5) Meteorological Department .	" " "

[1] Financial Statement, 1879–80, para. 24.

(6) Political . . . . . Receipts and Charges.
(7) Remittance of Treasure and Premium on Bills of Exchange and unclaimed Bills of Exchange . . . . " " "

The third category of revenues and charges, namely, jointly Imperial and Provincial, covered the following items :—

(1) Land Revenue, including capitation tax, but excluding Fisheries, with such Land Revenue Refunds, charges of collection and settlement as cannot be attributed to Fisheries only.
(2) Forest revenue. Expenditure and Refunds.
(3) Export Duty on rice, and Refunds.
(4) Salt Revenue, Expenditure and Refunds.

Items comprising the third category were divided between the Imperial and Provincial Governments in the proportion of five-sixths to the former and one-sixth to the latter. By adopting this method of supply Burma, unlike other provinces, secured funds of an elastic character, for, even though the shares remained fixed the amount they brought in in any one year varied with the variation in the total yield of the revenues assigned or shared. Of course everything depended upon how Burma nursed the revenues delegated to its control. But if it did its duty, unlike the other provinces, its labours were not to be unrequited.

The same principle of shared revenues was applied to the province of Assam, which had hitherto continued on the old basis of 1871. Although the settlement with that Province had been made after that with Burma had been carried out, the principle of shared revenues as a mode of balancing the Provincial Budget was not adopted on any appreciable scale. The reason for this break in the progressive realization of the principle is not to be attributed to any spirit of hesitation on the part of the Government of India, but is to be ascribed mainly to the necessity of the case. As it was contemplated to reincorporate the province into Bengal it was deemed expedient to frame the Provincial

Budget of Assam on the same plan as that of Bengal so that their financial fusion might be as easy as the administrative. Thus the heads of revenue and expenditure which were provincial in Bengal since 1877 were also made provincial in Assam in 1879, including "Law Officers," which for temporary reasons were reserved as Imperial in Bengal. The only point at which the new principle was applied consisted in making the Land Revenue head in Assam a joint head to be shared by the Imperial and the Provincial Governments in the proportion of four-fifths of its net yield to the former and one-fifth to the latter.[1]

The beneficial results of the new settlement with these two Provinces are easily to be seen from the following comparative table of the estimates of their budgets as prepared on the old basis and as recast on the new :—

000 omitted.

	Assam Budget Estimates				Bt Burma Budget Estimates.			
	Old Basis.		New Basis.		Old Basis.		New Basis.	
	1878–1879	1879–1880.	1878–1879.	1879–1880	1878–1879.	1879–1880.	1878–1879	1879–1880
	£	£	£	£	£	£	£	£
Revenue . . .	2115	2110	3657	3596	4013	4078	9459	9673
Expenditure . .	2253	2261	3480	3566	4169	5111	8926	10119
Surplus	—	—	177	30	—	—	533	—
Deficit	138	151	—	—	156	1033	—	526
Closing Balance .	206	55	521	555	873	161	1562	1436

From the Resolution of the Government of India in the Department of Finance and Commerce, No. 1249, dated March 13, 1879.

Once the new principle of shared revenues was established in the case of Burma and Assam it was not possible for the Government of India to withhold its application from the other Provinces. The settlements made in 1877 with the several Provinces were not only of short duration but were also of unequal durations. It was only in the case of Bengal and Bombay that the settlements were made for five years commencing from 1877–8. In the case of the Central Provinces and the Punjab the period fixed was three years,

[1] Finance Department Resolution No. 1598, dated April 17, 1879

while in the case of the North-Western Provinces it was as short as two years, from 1877–8. It is evident from this that the settlements with some other Provinces were to have expired soon after those with Burma and Assam had been completed, and would have required to be reconstituted on the basis of shared revenues. The Government of India, however, delayed the process, and in that it did wisely, for it was too soon to make the new principle of shared revenues and charges a basis for universal application. It was nothing but prudent to have regarded it as it were in its experimental stage. Secondly, the disadvantages of the *ex-parte* treatment of the Provincial Budget had come to be realized. It then dawned upon the Government of India that the several Provincial Budgets were only parts of an organic whole, viz., the Imperial Budget, and it was manifestly inadvisable to frame the Provincial Budgets each by itself without regard to the claims, needs and exigencies of all others. But in order that this comparative and compromising operation of judging the claims of one in the light of the needs of others be performed with the desired effect of treating the different provinces in an equitable manner, it was essential that all the Provincial Budgets be dealt with simultaneously. The importance of this consideration and the desire to gain time in order to profit by the experiences of Burma and Assam led the Government of India with the consent of the Provincial Governments to extend or shorten, as the case may be, the duration of their financial agreements with the Provinces so as to bring about a synchronous expiry of them all on March 31, 1882.

Financial Settlements of 1882–3

The new settlements made with all the provinces with effect from 1882–3 [1] were marked by an extension of the principle applied to Burma since 1878. Certain heads, as few in number as possible, of revenues and charges were

[1] Resolution of the Government of India in the Department of Finance and Commerce, No. 3353, dated September 13, 1881.

wholly, or with minute local exceptions only, grouped as Imperial. Others were classed as wholly Provincial. The remaining were placed in an intermediate category designated as joint and were in most part shared equally between the Imperial and the Provincial Governments. In those cases, however, where the provincialized expenditure exceeded the resources from the provincialized as well as the shared revenues, the balance instead of being provided as heretofore by fixed assignments from the Imperial exchequer was rectified for each Province by a fixed percentage on its land revenue—a wholly Imperial head of revenue except in the case of Burma, where the percentage was extended to the Imperial rice export duty and salt revenue as well.

Along with the enlargement of the scheme of Provincial Finance in 1882 the Government of India was also anxious to introduce simplicity and uniformity in the matter of grouping the different heads of revenue and expenditure under the three categories now established. It will be remembered that the agreements effected in 1877 were marked by diversity and intricacy. The same charges were not provincialized in all the Provinces. A charge which was Provincial in one was Imperial in another. Again, in transferring charges a grant was often broken up so that a part was made Provincial and a part reserved as Imperial. On the revenue side the arrangement was not a little intricate. The computations owing to the proviso in respect of the assigned revenues made the calculations far from simple. Both these defects were, however, removed when the settlements were framed in 1882, and it is to indicate what heads of revenue and expenditure were provincialized, what were imperialized, and what were divided and to what extent, that the following attempt is made.

Revenues

	Imperial.	Provincial.
I Land Revenue	The whole except as entered in the Provincial Column.	In *Burma*, Fisheries; in the *N.W.P. and Oudh* collections from the Terai, Bhabar and Dudhi Estates, Rents of Water-Mills and Stone Quarries; in *Bombay*, Rents of Resumed Service Lands and Service Commutations. In all Provinces, a fixed percentage on the Imperial land revenue to cover the difference between Provincial Revenue and Provincial Expenditure.
II Tributes .	The whole.	Nil.
III Forest . .	Half.	Half.
IV Excise . .	Do.	Do.
V Assessed Taxes	Do.	Do.
VI Provincial Rates	Nil.	The whole.
VII Customs .	All except as entered in the Provincial Column.	All items other than Customs Duties; and, in *Burma* only, the same percentage on Export Duties as on the Land Revenue.
VIII Salt. . .	All except as entered in the Provincial Column.	All items other than Duty on Salt and sale of Salt; and, in *Burma* only, the same percentage on the Salt Revenue as on the Land Revenue.
IX Opium . .	The whole.	Nil.
X Stamps .	Half.	Half.
XI Registration	Do.	Do.
XIII Post Office	Nil.	The whole.
XIV Minor Departments	Do.	Do.
XVI Law and Justice	Do.	Do.
XVII Police . .	Do.	Do.
XVIII Marine . .	As at present.	As at present.
XIX Education .	Nil.	The whole.
XX Medical .	Do.	Do.

Revenues

		Imperial.	Provincial.
XXI	Stationery and Printing	Nil.	The whole.
XXII	Interest .	All except as entered in the Provincial Column.	Interest on Government securities (Provincial).
XXIII	Pensions .	Book transfers from the Military and Medical Funds and subscriptions to these Funds.	The remainder.
XXIV	Miscellaneous	Gain by Exchange on Imperial transactions, Premia on Bills and unclaimed Bills of Exchange.	The remainder.
XXV	Railway .	As at present.	Whatever is now provincial in each Province.
XXVI	Irrigation and Navigation	Do.	Do.
XXVII	Other Public Works	Receipts from Military Works.	The remainder.
XXXI	Gain by Exchange on Transactions with London	The whole.	Nil.

Expenditure

	Imperial.	Provincial.
1. Interest	The whole except as entered in the Provincial Column.	Interest on local Debenture loans. 4½ per cent. on the capital cost to the commencement of the year, and 2¼ per cent. on the capital cost during the year, of all Public Works, whether classified as *Productive Public Works* or not, of which Capital and Revenue Accounts are kept: excepting, always, any portion of their cost supplied from the Provincial Revenues or by Local Debenture Loans. The rate of interest on the cost of *Protective Public Works* will be the subject of a special agreement.
2. Interest on Service Funds and other Accounts	Interest on Service Funds and deposits in Savings Banks.	The remainder.
3. Refunds and Drawbacks	Of the Imperial share of revenues.	Of the Provincial share of the revenues.
4. Land Revenue	The same percentage on charges for collection of Land Revenue and on the cost of Surveys (including expenditure hitherto charged in the Accounts of the Central Government) and Settlements elsewhere than in *Bombay* and *Madras*, as is retained of Land Revenue.	The remainder.
5. Forest . .	Half.	Half.
6. Excise . .	Do.	Do.
7. Assessed Taxes	Do.	Do.
8. Provincial Rates	Nil.	The whole.
9. Customs . .	Do.	Do.
10. Salt . . .	In *Madras* the whole. Elsewhere the purchase and manufacture of salt; and in *Bengal* the cost of preventive lines and operations; in *Bombay* charges connected with the administration of Salt Revenue in Portuguese India	The remainder.
11. Opium	The whole.	Nil.
12. Stamps . . .	Half.	Half.

Expenditure

	Imperial.	Provincial
13. Registration .	Half.	Half.
15. Post Office .	Nil.	The whole.
16. Telegraph .	Do.	Do.
17. Administration	Account and Currency Offices and allowances to Presidency Banks.	The remainder.
18. Minor Depts.	Archæological and Meteorological Depts., Census, Gazetteers and Statistical Memoirs.	The remainder.
19. Law and Justice	Nil.	The whole.
20. Police . .	Frontier Police and Police employed on Imperial State Railways on Salt preventive duties.	The remainder.
21. Marine . .	Whatever is now Imperial.	Whatever is now Provincial.
22. Education .	Do.	Do.
23. Ecclesiastical	The whole.	Nil.
24. Medical . .	Nil.	The whole.
25. Stationery and Printing	Stationery purchased for Central Stores.	The remainder, including cost of stationery obtained from Central Stores.
26. Political . .	The whole.	Nil.
27. Allowances and Assignments.	The whole except as in the Provincial Column.	In *Bombay*, items now Provincial.
28. Civil Furlough and Absentee Allowances	The whole.	Nil.
29. Superannuations	Items not provided for in the Provincial Column.	All pensions and gratuities, except pensions payable from the Military and Medical Funds brought to account in India; each Government being responsible for pensions and gratuities which it now pays, or hereafter grants or recommends, however earned and wherever paid.
30. Miscellaneous	Remittance of treasure, and discount on Supply Bills.	The remainder.
31. Famine Relief	Secondary liability.	Wholly Provincial.
32. Railways . .	As at present.	Whatever is now Provincial.
33. Irrigation . .	Do.	Do.
34. Other Public Works	Military Public Works, and, except in *British Burma*, Offices of the Supreme Government; Works in the Salt, Opium, Post Office, Imperial Telegraph and Ecclesiastical Depts. and Mint and Currency Offices; and Bengal Surveyor General's Offices.	The remainder.
38. Loss by Exchange	The whole.	Nil.

On the transactions of 1881–82 the Government expected to gain £470,000 a year. Of this sum, however, it returned to the Central Provinces £77,900, for improving the position of the subordinate civil services and other general purposes; to Madras, £20,000, for provincial public works; and to the N.W.P. and Oudh, £326,000, of which £10,000 was for additional kanungoes in Oudh, and the remainder, £316,000, for a remission of local taxation. Besides these benefactions the Government of India gave for a favourable start to Bengal, £285,000; Burma, £20,000; N.W.P., £55,000, to be added to their balances before the close of the year 1881–2. These benefactions, which amounted to £496,000 a year, were expected to turn the annual gain of £470,000 into an annual loss of £26,000 to the Imperial exchequer.[1]

In this connection it must also be recalled that the Government of India reimbursed the Provincial Governments of the amount of the benevolences it had levied on them in the years 1879–80 and 1880–1. But not long after the revision of 1882 the financial position of the Government of India, which had permitted of such a liberal treatment, suffered a reverse, and the necessity for levying benevolences on the balances of the Provincial Governments reappeared in 1886–7. In presenting the Financial Statement for that year the Finance Member of the Government of India argued :—

"22. Since the estimates for 1885–6 were presented . . . Indian administration and finance have entered on a new phase. The brief period of rest which the country had enjoyed since 1882 had drawn to a close. . . . By the events of the late years in Central Asia, India finds herself almost in contact with one of the great European Powers, and she cannot hope to escape the necessity which the position imposes on her of increasing her military strength. Events impending have occurred which have changed, as it was known they must change, the face of our estimates, and have thrust us violently out of the peaceful path of

[1] Financial Statement for 1882–83, p. 15.

internal progress in which we had hoped to have been left undisturbed."

Among the other means employed to weather the storm the Government of India resorted a second time to nibbling at the provincial resources, and gathered a sum of £400,000 in the year 1886–7 by appropriating from their balances the above amount.

The condition of Provincial Finance during this period may be summarized in the following table :—

Provinces.	Annual Surpluses and Deficits				
	1882–3	1883–4	1884–5	1885–6.	1886–7.
	£	£	£	£	£
C.P.	33,775	76,212	18,047	22,080	115,656
Burma. . . .	171,207	−90,030	−89,725*	†	71,743‡
Assam . . .	13,887	−5,216	−40,577	25,299	28,576
Bengal. . . .	539,611	146,027	48,910	26,777	52,911
N.W.P. & Oudh .	281,222	357,630	−69,276	−180,060	−12,408
Punjab . . .	−110,966	−15,765	−41,545	42,447	3,106
Madras . . .	108,421	10,820	−87,284	146,692	−78,689
Bombay . . .	−149,894	−2,585	6,006	291,976	−161,369

* No balance left at the close of the year.
† Equilibrium.
‡ Balance obtained by excess of current revenue over current expenditure of the year.
Compiled from the annual Finance and Revenue Accounts of the Government of India.

The settlements entered into with the Provincial Governments in the year 1882–3 not only differed from the preceding settlements in the replacement of fixed assignments by shares in the Imperial revenues, but they also differed in another important respect, namely, their duration. Though the results of the scheme of Provincial Finance have been presented in one Table covering the period 1871–7, it must not be supposed that the settlements with the various Provinces were made for the period of six years. On the other hand, the settlements were only annual and lasted up to 1877 by the process of constant renewals. The results have been presented together for a continuous period not because the settlements were made for that period, but because the principle on which they were based endured for that period. After 1877 the settlements no doubt were made for a longer period. In two cases they were for five years and for the rest the period ranged between two and three years. The short duration system, like the fixed assignment system, was of immense advantage to the Imperial treasury. The object of these settlements, it will be recalled, was firstly to put a definite limit on the demands of the Provincial Governments on the already too scanty resources of the Imperial Government. Evidently this object would have been better served had the duration of the settlements been longer than it was. But a longer duration would have deprived the Imperial treasury of its right to profit by an early revision of the revenue side of the contract. It was this consideration of not remaining too long out of pocket, that had hitherto prevailed upon the Government of India to shorten the duration of contracts as much as possible. But what was an advantage to the Imperial treasury was from the standpoint of the Provincial Government a serious drawback. Owing to the short durations of the settlements the Provincial Governments were not in a position to distribute the funds at their disposal on the incorporated services so as to open a new page in their financial history. They could not adopt a definite financial policy, for they feared that the new terms on renewal might compel them either to give up the policy or modify it so seriously as to prejudice its results. A single budget may seem nothing more than the conspectus of financial happenings of the year to which it pertains, yet to the financier who frames them year after year they embody a definite policy running towards its consummation. But a policy, however wisely adopted, may be thwarted by an unwise disturbance of the uniformity of conditions on which its fulfilment depends. This was just the flaw that deteriorated the sound working of Provincial Finance. Constant renewals had a general disturbing effect, and the duration between any two of them was indeed too short to give a stable state of conditions. Being impressed by the fact that the advantages of a short-duration-contract to the Imperial treasury were enormously counterbalanced by its disadvantages to Provincial Finance, the Government of India, on the occasion of revising the settlements in 1882–3, made it a definite rule that they shall be quinquennial in duration; that is, they shall not be subject to revision before the end of the fifth year from their commencement.

Revision of 1887-8

By virtue of this rule the settlements made in 1882–3 expired in 1887. The revision then undertaken, as well as the subsequent ones, left as a rule undisturbed the two categories of revenue and expenditure, namely, those wholly Provincial and wholly Imperial. It became almost a convention to leave them as they were since the separation in 1882, when the constitution of Provincial Budgets was thoroughly overhauled and consolidated. The only heads of revenue and expenditure that were revised, as revision fell due, were those that were grouped under the third category, namely, jointly Imperial and Provincial, otherwise known as "Divided Heads."

In the revision of 1887–8 the decisive factor was the unsatisfactory position of the Imperial Finances already referred to. To improve its financial position the shares in the joint heads were altered so that each Local Government was allowed to appropriate three-fourths of the stamps and one-fourth of the excise revenue, and required to bear the expenditure under those heads in like proportion. The proportions of land revenue were also altered so that three-fourths of it was made Imperial, and one-fourth Provincial. But the needs of the Imperial treasury were so great that the Government of India even revised some of the heads of the other two categories, namely, Salt, Customs, Interest, Irrigation and Railways, to its own advantage. The details of the gain to the Imperial treasury are as given on opposite page.

Revenue.	*Imperial Share* Increased. —Decreased.	Net Gain.
Land Revenue	437,500	
Stamps (share reduced from $\frac{1}{2}$ to $\frac{1}{4}$)	−810,000	
Excise (share increased from $\frac{1}{2}$ to $\frac{3}{4}$)	947,500	
Salt revenue of Burma imperialized	5,000	
Customs revenue of Burma imperialized	155,000	
Assessed taxes—divided in moieties	−290,000	215,000
State Railways gross earnings—		
Nagpur Chhattisgarh, Patna-Gaya, Cawnpore-Achneyra	−310,000	
Eastern Bengal, provincialized	−540,000	

Expenditure.	Increased —Decreased	Net Gain.
Land Revenue, entire provincialization of survey and settlement	145,000	
Salt in Bombay imperialized	−90,000	
Customs in Bombay imperialized	−50,000	
State Railways—		
Working expenses —		
Provincialized	305,000	395,000
Imperialized	−215,000	
Interest—Provincialized	−70,000	
Imperialized	−65,000	
Irrigation—Provincialized. Bengal	65,000	
" " Madras	230,000	
Add—Small items of accounts unenumerated		20,000

This gain to the Imperial treasury was distributed in the following proportion among the various Provinces :—

Provinces.	Increase of annual resources under the principal Provincial Heads of Revenue as estimated on comparison of 1882 and 1887			Amount by which Annual Provincial Resources were reduced by the Revision of 1887.
	Land Revenue	Stamps and Excise.	Total.	
	£	£	£	£
C.P.	2,200	45,500	47,700	15,600
Burma	4,700	9,200	13,000	—
Assam	22,300	21,300	43,600	24,600
Bengal	19,200	171,550	190,750	103,600
N.W.P.	8,000	130,150	138,150	100,000
Punjab	32,800	23,100	55,900	—
Madras	27,750	142,550	150,300	174,400
Bombay	99,000	198,550	297,550	221,900
Total	195,950	741,900	937,850	640,100

This would have been the net gain to the Imperial treasury had it not been for the fact that it conceded to Burma the sum of £10,000. The net gain was thus reduced to £530,100 per annum.

The condition of Provincial Finance during the period of 1887–92 may be judged from the following table presenting the annual surplus and deficit of each of the different Provinces :—

Province.	Annual Surpluses and Deficits.				
	1887–8.	1888–9.	1889–90.	1890–1.	1891–2.
	Rs.	Rs.	Rs	Rs	Rs
C.P.	13,148	22,583	−12,322	−31,573	17,540
Burma	77,028	11,560	64,072	106,216	50,598
Assam	7,751	26,343	20,090	−17,871	31,185
Bengal	131,007	−65,792	102,547	−120,377	−11,934
N.W.P. & Oudh	−53,900	45,949	102,710	−12,544	−4,399
Punjab	12,446	32,142	29,264	31,367	−1,719
Madras	105,371	113,932	144,571	−136,739	−241,770
Bombay	−24,574	18,322	41,361	−123,887	−53,189

Compiled from the annual Finance and Revenue Accounts of the Government of India.

Revision of 1892–3

The next revision of provincial settlements under the rule of quinquennial revisions occurred in 1892–3. The new settlements to commence from that year did not differ in principle from those of 1887–8. The shares in the Joint Revenue were so readjusted as to give to the Imperial treasury a larger gain from the growing yield of the provincialized sources. The amount resumed by the Imperial Government at this revision through readjustments of shares was estimated as follows :—

Province.	Increase of Revenue in 1891–2 (Revised Est) as compared with the Estimate for the Contract of 1887–8 to 1891–2.	Amount resumed by the Government of India.
	Rs.	Rs.
C.P.	119,200	22,700
Lower Burma .	334,900	58,900
Bengal. . . .	517,700	51,900
N.W P. & Oudh	53,300	56,900
Punjab . . .	195,400	41,000
Madras . .	313,200	103,800
Bombay . . .	399,200	131,100
Assam . . .	99,800	—
Total	2,042,700	466,300

But this gain to the Imperial treasury seriously disturbed the equilibrium between the expenditure of the Provinces estimated as normal for the ensuing period and the normal estimated yield of revenues left to them. To restore equilibrium between their normal expenditure and normal revenue the Government of India reverted to the discarded method of fixed adjusting assignments, so that while the actual revenues and charges deviated from what was estimated as normal for the period of the settlement, the adjusting entry allowed by the Imperial Government to each of the provinces remained fixed throughout the whole period. The following is a statement of estimated normal expenditure and revenues of the different Provinces with their respective adjusting assignments as fixed for the new period :—

Provinces.	Provincial Revenues.			Provincial Expenditure.
	Ordinary Revenue being a share of certain Receipts	Adjusting Assignments	Total	
	Rs	Rs	Rs	Rs
C.P.	567,600	220,500	788,100	788,100
Lower Burma . . .	1,427,500	414,300	1,841,800	1,841,800
Assam	657,700	−112,700	545,000	545,000
Bengal	4,249,300	−143,900	4,105,500	4,105,900
N.W.P. & Oudh . . .	3,403,500	−250,000	3,152,900	3,152,900
Punjab	1,370,400	348,500	1,718,900	1,718,900
Madras	2,479,300	325,400	2,804,700	2,804,700
Bombay	3,123,900	771,400	3,895,300	3,895,300

The evil effect of large resumptions and fixed assignments will be clearly seen in the condition of Provincial Finance as indicated by the annual surpluses and deficits over the period of the settlement :—

Province.	Annual Surpluses or Deficits.				
	1892–3.	1893–4.	1894–5.	1895–6	1896–7.
	Rs.	Rs.	Rs	Rs	Rs
C.P.	−21,798	−60,772	−105,108	19,653	−37,408*
Burma . . .	66,642	−90,653	−272,319	226,505	780
Assam . . .	9,336	28,532	−27,422	30,507	−25,421
N.W.P. & Oudh	−16,752	−25,155	−165,987	−139,798	−164,740
Bengal . . .	−9,826	36,887	169,796	149,808	−186,558
Punjab . . .	−106,050	−22,699	−24,811	−7,156	−64,073
Madras . . .	−159,081	33,636	92,328	44,118	−200,579
Bombay . . .	−23,888	19,443	−102,472	100,690	−221,119

* No closing balance left.

Compiled from the Annual Finance and Revenue Accounts of the Government of India.

It must, however, be admitted that the financial arrangements of the Provinces during this period were considerably disturbed by the outbreak of plague and famine towards the close of the settlements. The expenditure which the Provinces were obliged to incur to meet these two calamities depleted the resources of all and brought the Central Provinces and the North-West Provinces to the verge of bankruptcy, from which they were rescued by the following contributions made by the Government of India in aid of their balances in the year 1896–7 :—

To Central Provinces . . Rs. 526 lakhs.
To N.W.P. and Oudh . Rs. 1,609 „

Revision of 1896–97

This depression in Provincial Finance was alleviated to some extent at least in the revised settlements of 1896–7 by allowing a higher standard of expenditure and of revenue to the Provinces than was granted to them in 1892. The following table presents the old and the new standard of expenditure with the percentage difference between them :—

Provinces.	Standard Net Expenditure.		Increase per cent.
	1892	1897.	
	Rs.	Rs.	
Central Provinces	653,300	710,700	8·8
Lower Burma	1,064,600	1,206,100	13·3
Assam	467,600	564,900	20 8
Bengal.	2,816,700	3,125,500	10 9
N.W.P.	2,215,400	2,428,700	9·6
Punjab	1,384,600	1,537,300	11·0
Madras	2,054,800	2,238,600	8·9
Bombay	2,049,500	2,544,100	5 6
Total	13,066,500	14,355,900	9·9

This new and enhanced standard of expenditure called for a revision of the shares of the Imperial and Provincial Governments in the joint revenues. But the revision had to be so devised that while it gave larger resources to the Provinces it obviated the necessity of making fixed assignments as much as possible ; for the Government of India had learnt to its cost that fixed assignments on a large scale tended to make the resource side of the Provincial Finance rigid to such an uncomfortable degree that, if the variability of expenditure surpassed the expansibility of the revenue incorporated in the Provincial Budgets, it was perforce obliged to distribute benefactions to ease what would otherwise be a difficult situation. Secondly, these fixed assignments also created a certain degree of inequality as between the backward and the more advanced Provinces. In the advanced Provinces the fixed assignments formed a comparatively smaller part of their resources than they did in the case of the relatively backward Provinces, and, as larger expenditure could be undertaken by the Provinces only when their revenues expanded, the advanced Provinces, a larger part of whose resources were of an expanding nature, obtained a more favourable treatment than the relatively backward Provinces, a large part of whose resources were of a frozen character. This was rightly conceived by the Government of India as the reverse of what ought to have been, having regard to the fact that the needs of the backward Provinces were relatively more imperious than those of the advanced Provinces. To obviate this injustice the Government of India enhanced the shares of the backward provinces in the joint revenues by reducing *per contra* the fixed assignments made at the last revision. To the Punjab it gave ·4 and to the Central Provinces ·5 of the Land Revenue instead of ·25 only. The share of Burma in the Land Revenue was raised to ·66, and to make provision for the enhanced expenditure due to the addition of Upper Burma, and in lieu of the railway revenue withdrawn from it, Burma was allowed to appropriate ·5 of the Excise instead of ·25 only. The financial condition of the North-Western Provinces was not very happy. Its revenue had proved so very unprogressive that it advanced only 2 per cent. between 1892 and 1897. The treatment of the North-Western Provinces at the revision of 1892 was also a little unjust. The revision had left its revenues short by 5 lakhs of its standard expenditure, to be made up by reduction of its balances. To make amends for this the Government of India re-distributed the shares in the Land Revenue to the advantage of the North-Western Provinces. In addition to this the Government of India gave to that Province a grant of 4 lakhs for the year 1897–8, to enable it to establish district funds on a financially independent footing, a result accomplished long ago in every other Province in British India. To give an equitable treatment to the backward as well as to the advanced Provinces, it realized that an unequal treatment was the only proper way. It therefore adopted a less liberal attitude in revising the terms of the settlements with the more advanced Provinces of Bengal, Madras and Bombay. It allowed them a proportionately smaller increase of expenditure than the backward Provinces, as may be seen from the figures given above, and reduced slightly their shares in the revenues.

On the occasion of this revision the gain to the Imperial exchequer was practically negligible. In 1877 its total gain by retrenchment amounted to 40 lakhs a year; in 1882 the Imperial Government was so very prosperous that instead of contriving for a gain it surrendered to the

Provinces 26 lakhs of the annual imperial revenue. But in 1887 it resumed 63 lakhs and in 1892, 46 lakhs. On this occasion however its gain was nil, for what it got from the advanced Provinces it gave to the backward ones.

Just and liberal as the terms of the settlement were, the abnormal circumstances which disturbed the entire period of the settlement made such heavy demands on the Provincial resources that, ample though they were, they fell far short of the requirements of the Provinces. The famine of 1896 and 1897 affected all the Provinces, although in unequal degree. In the North-Western Provinces and Oudh, the Central Provinces, and Burma the effect was most severely felt. In Madras, Bengal and the Punjab it was serious, and in Burma it was slight. On the other hand, the famine of 1899 and 1900 affected Bombay and the Central Provinces most severely, the Punjab very seriously, and the rest of the Provinces slightly. And Assam, though unaffected by either of the two famines, suffered very severely from the great earthquake of June, 1897. Besides famine the plague was also making its ravages and taking its toll. As a result of these unforeseen calamities all the Provinces were forced to incur extraordinary expenditure on preventive measures, for which no provision was made in the standard of revenue fixed for the period of settlement. The expenditure on these unforeseen calamities being of an extraordinary nature was treated as imperial and defrayed from the Imperial exchequer, but even this much succour did not prove equal to the necessity and the Government of India was obliged to make special grants-in-aid of the Provincial Revenues as shown on page 118.

Thus the Government of India was not only obliged to pay for the cost of the famine, but to grant funds to restore equilibrium and to provide for useful public services held up or curtailed by the Provincial Governments owing to the extraordinary circumstances of the time. All this aid from the Imperial Government was made available because of the very prosperous condition of the Imperial Finances throughout this period. While it is better that governments in general should always be in penury, the surpluses in the

IMPERIAL SPECIAL GRANTS-IN-AID TO PROVINCES.*

Year.		India.	C P.	Assam.	Bengal.	N.W P and Oudh.	Punjab	Madras.	Bombay.	Burma
		Rs.	Rs.	Rs.	Rs	Rs.	Rs.	Rs.	Rs.	Rs.
1897–98 . . .		—	7,72,000	8,00,000	—	10,27,000	—	—	12,18,000	—
1898–99 . . .		—	5,00,000	18,00,000	17,00,000	10,00,000	5,00,000	16,96,000	48,75,000	—
1899–1900 . .		—	19,32,000	—	—	—	95,000	3,49,000	34,37,000	—
1900–01 . . .		—	34,15,000	—	—	—	5,98,000	—	64,79,000	—
1901–02 . .		—	26,89,000	2,00,000	—	—	12,40,000	32,14,000	91,00,000	—
			6,50,000	—	—	—	4,00,000	10,00,000	19,50,000	—
1902–03 .	1		2,00,000	1,00,000	10,00,000	5,00,000	4,00,000	8,00,000	6,00,000	4,00,000
	2	A 70,000	2,00,000	2,80,000	6,00,000	4,50,000	5,00,000	5,50,000	5,50,000	—
	3	B 1,00,000	2,00,000	1,50,000	—	3,50,000	3,00,000	3,50,000	3,50,000	—
1903–04 .	1	—	2,00,000	1,00,000	10,00,000	5,00,000	4,00,000	8,00,000	6,00,000	4,00,000
	2	—	5,00,000	5,00,000	2,00,000	3,00,000	10,00,000	5,00,000	10,00,000	—
	3	—	1,90,000	1,11,000	—	2,26,000	2,76,000	3,50,000	3,50,000	—

1. For education (recurring). 2. For use Public Works. 3. For improving district and other establishments.
A. Allotted for Public Works in Baluchistan, Rajputana and Central India.
B. Amount taken in the "India" estimates for subsequent distribution to the provinces.

* Compiled from the annual Financial Statements of the Government of India.

Imperial Finance proved a timely resource, the utility of which was doubled by the commendable way in which they were spent. Besides giving them grants for useful public works the superfluous funds of the Imperial Government were utilized in carrying out the following additional measures to the relief of the Provinces :

(1) Remission of Imperial Land Revenue Rs. 50,94,000 and reimbursement to the Provinces for their share remitted Rs. 59,81,000 ; in all Rs. 1,10,75,000.

(2) The abolition of the pandhri tax in the Central Provinces, costing Rs. 7,000 a year.

(3) The reduction of the patwari rate in Ajmere, from 10 per cent. on land revenue to 6¼ per cent. ; the amount of the local revenue remitted was—Rs. 13,000, but the contribution paid to the local fund was Rs. 23,000.[1]

Taking into account these various contributions in aid of Provincial Revenues, the following table is presented as indicative of the condition of the Provincial Finances during this period of settlement :—

Provinces.	Provincial Surpluses or Deficits.						
	1897-8	1898-9	1899-1900	1900-1	1901-2.	1902-3	1903-4.
	Rs	Rs	Rs	Rs.	Rs	Rs	Rs
C P . . .	(a)	12,288	−1,22,883	(a)	22,42,408	−705	−7,40,742
Burma .	1,69,435	4,11,494	26,14,312	15,16,220	7,55,285	—	—
Assam . .	−45,580	86,742	−8,15,488	−86,829	1,47,353	10,08,393	11,40,517
Bengal . .	−3,03,250	2,19,449	7,01,809	4,43,224	6,44,170	6,23,640	87,23,496
N W P . .	(a)	3,28,562	7,53,815	8,04,789	—	—	—
Punjab . .	−2,278	1,15,379	−16,53,794	(a)	14,96,350	10,28,770	6,74,880
Madras . .	−1,57,707	1,60,706	−17,58,029	−3,21,013	40,41,297	−15,810	52,40,809
Bombay	−1,29,663	1,00,427	−15,04,271	(a)	58,23,235	−24,23,235	−1,23,000
U.P of Agra & Oudh . .	—	—	—	—	−9,63,788	−64,372	37,11,281

(a) No closing balance left because of Budget equilibrium.

Compiled from the Annual Finance and Revenue Accounts of the Government of India.

Revision of 1902-3

Settlements made with the Provinces in 1897 should have ended in the ordinary course of time in 1902-3. The central

[1] Financial Statement of the Government of India, 1902-3, para. 146.

operation in the periodic revision of the settlements was to arrive at the standard provincial expenditure for the ensuing quinquennium and as a rough and ready method of decision the average expenditure during the expiring quinquennium was taken as a standard expenditure for the opening quinquennium. There is nothing grossly erroneous in such a procedure, provided the preceding and succeeding quinquenniums are equally normal with respect to the course of their events. But as we have seen, the events of the past quinquennium were entirely abnormal and could not have been made the basis of any calculations worthy of trust. To be on the safe side the Government of India thought it desirable to await the return of normal times before undertaking wholesale revisions of provincial settlements. The occasion of 1902–3 for revision was therefore postponed save in the case of Burma. For, the last settlement had become unduly favourable to that Province in comparison with the other Provinces, notwithstanding the very nice and equitable calculations on which the settlements of 1896–7 were based. The extent to which the revenues had exceeded its expenditure is indicated in the following table :—

Burma.	Estimated Standard for the Settlement of 1897–8 to 1901–2.	Estimates for 1902–3	Difference.
	Rs	Rs.	Rs
Revenues	2,93,81,000	3,73,86,000	80,05,000
Expenditure	2,93,81,000	3,31,86,000	38,05,000
Surplus	—	42,00,000	—

The continuance of such an outcome was deemed unfair to the Imperial and unjust to the other Provincial Governments. The financial settlement of the Province of Burma was accordingly revised notwithstanding the established canon of simultaneous revision, when the occasion presented itself in 1902–3. The revision resulted in the resumption by the Government of India of this surplus by readjusting the shares of the Province in the joint revenues. The share in the Land Revenue was reduced from two-thirds to one-half and that in the Excise from one-half to one-third, and a few minor heads were added to the already provincialized heads of expenditure. By these changes the standard revenue and expenditure of Burma for the new settlement of 1903 to 1906 assumed the following totals :—

Revenues Rs	Adjusting Assignment Rs.	Total Revenues. Rs.	Total Expenditure. Rs.
2,78,31,000	53,02,000	3,31,33,000	3,31,33,000

Another province whose settlement was revised was the Punjab ; but the reason of it was different. The territory covered by the North-Western Provinces was divided into the North-Western Frontier Provinces and the United Provinces of Agra and Oudh, usually styled U.P. Along with this some of the districts of the Punjab were separated from it and joined to the newly created North-Western Frontier Province. This caused a readjustment of the provincial revenues and expenditure, but not any wholesale revision of the settlement. The changes were confined to the necessary alterations in the adjusting assignment.

Quasi-Permanent Revision 1904–5

With the exceptions noted above the settlements of 1897 were extended up to the end of the year 1904. The primary cause of the postponement of the revision as explained above was the abnormality of the conditions prevailing in the year 1901–2. But there was also another reason why the Government of India was so very anxious for the return of normal conditions before taking any steps towards revision. It was about this time that the Government of India contemplated to introduce permanency in Provincial Finance. The five-year budget system which in 1881 replaced the annual budget system as the basis of Provincial Finance, though a marked improvement in the direction of continuity and stability, was not deemed to be quite sufficient. Under it the Provincial Governments were left free to enjoy the fruits of their economy in expenditure and of the successful nursing of their resources for the period of five years. Beneficial as far as it went, this time-bar was found to exercise a most pernicious influence on Provincial Finance. Under the quinquennial budget system it so happened that the Provincial Governments as the result of feeling their way under the new conditions were parsimonious in the first few years lest their expenditure should prove too much for their revenues, and extravagant in the last few years lest their expenditure should shrink below the standard and leave large margins to be cancelled by the Government of India on revision of their settlements. No Local Government could be expected to put into execution any carefully matured and well-thought-out scheme of improvement within the short span of a quinquennium. All that it could do was to spend the first two or three years in working out a scheme and utilize the last two or three years in rushing it through, as was done by most of the Provinces. This tendency to undertake such schemes, the only merit of which was that they could be carried through before the revision, and mainly in order to reach the standard expenditure, was a direct consequence of the quinquennial budget system. This is by no means an a priori conclusion. A glance at the annual surplus of the provinces will indicate how they tend to rise in the beginning of the quinquennium and fall at the end of it. To obviate these evils of parsimony and extravagance the only remedy was to do away with the principle of quinquennial revision, and this the Government of India courageously undertook to effect. The right to revise was a much cherished right, and the Government of India had not failed to exercise it in the teeth of all opposition from the Provinces. It was abandoned only because its exercise was deemed to be mischievous.

Taking the year 1903–4 as the normal one, the Government of India decided to revise the provincial settlements of all the different Provinces. The idea was to adjust the revenues between the Imperial and the Provincial Governments on the basis of the total expenditure they respectively controlled. It was found that the aggregate provincial expenditure represented less than one-fourth of the whole, while the Imperial expenditure, which included Army and Home Charges, aggregated in excess of three-fourths. These proportions of expenditure were taken as the basis of the division of revenue between the Imperial and the Provincial, and the following standard shares of revenue and expenditure under the joint heads were agreed upon :—

	Imperial.	Provincial.
Bengal, U.P., Bombay, Madras	$\frac{3}{4}$	$\frac{1}{4}$
Punjab, Burma . . .	$\frac{5}{8}$	$\frac{3}{8}$
C.P., Assam . . .	$\frac{1}{2}$	$\frac{1}{2}$

The reasons for adopting different standard rates of division in the case of the Punjab, Burma, C.P. and Assam was to give the backward provinces opportunities of development in the same proportion as lay within the reach of the advanced provinces.

Of the settlements made in 1904–5 the Government of India declared that those made with the Provinces of Bengal, Madras, Assam and U.P. were to be permanent and not subject to revision in future, except when it was found that the financial results were unfair to a Province or to others by comparison, or to the Government of India when it was confronted by an extraordinary calamity. Owing to this proviso their settlements were termed quasi-permanent. To obviate the recrudescence of unfairness during the currency of the settlements the Government of India felt it necessary to enter certain modifications in the standard ratio of division of the joint-heads of revenue and expenditure with regard to the Provinces brought under the quasi-permanent settlement. They were as follows :—

Provincial Share.				Provincial Share.			
Revenues	Bengal	Madras	U P	Expenditure	Bengal.	Madras	U P
Excise . . .	$\frac{7}{16}$	—	—	Excise . .	$\frac{7}{16}$	—	—
Stamps . . .	$\frac{1}{2}$	$\frac{1}{2}$	$\frac{1}{2}$	Stamps .	$\frac{1}{2}$	$\frac{1}{2}$	$\frac{1}{2}$
Registration .	Wholly	Wholly	—	Registration	Wholly	—	—
Irrigation . .	—	—	Wholly	Land Revenue	Wholly	Wholly	Wholly

Compiled from the Financial Statement of the Government of India for 1904–5, p. 67.

Besides these modifications the Government of India gave them the following grants :—

Bengal.	Madras.	United Provinces.
1. Addition of 4 lakhs to the assessment to improve the pay of Ministerial establishments.	1. Grant of 20 lakhs for Survey and Settlements.	1. Irrigation Revenue guaranteed up to 40 lakhs.
2. Further addition not exceeding 2½ lakhs for strengthening the staff of Deputy Collector.	2. Grant of Rs. 75,000 a year recurring for relief of certain local bodies.	2. Grant of 2½ lakhs a year in relief of local bodies.
	3. Rs. 50,000 a year for agricultural experiment.	3. Half a lakh a year to reform District Board Finance.
	4. Undertaking to bear charges for reorganizing district administration.	

Compiled from the same Financial Statement of the Government of India, p. 67.

The standard revenues and expenditure of the quasi-permanently settled provinces, after taking into consideration the alterations in their respective shares in the joint revenues, were as follows :—

STANDARD REVENUES AND EXPENDITURE

(in thousands of rupees).

Province	Expenditure.	Revenue		
		Revenues	Assignments	Total
Madras	3,50,48	2,90,82	5,966	3,50,48
Bengal	4,98,87	4,49,84	4,903	4,98,87
U.P.	3,66,64	3,62,64	400	3,66,64
Assam	72,07	60,07	1,200	72,07

The gain to the Imperial treasury on the revenue side brought about by the revision of the quasi-permanently settled Provinces was Rs. 2,06,000. But the revision also over-burdened the Imperial Government with a total charge of Rs. 36,000 hitherto borne by the Provincial Budget. Thus its net gain was only Rs. 1,70,000 a year on the normal.

As in the beginning of the scheme of Provincial Budgets, the Government of India thought it advisable to make to the quasi-permanently settled Provinces the following initial grants so as to give them a fair start:—

To Bengal,	Rs. 50 lakhs.	(Exclusive of 50 lakhs for Calcutta University.)
To Madras,	Rs. 50 ,,	(Inclusive of 20 lakhs for survey settlement.)
To U.P.,	Rs. 30 ,,	(Exclusive of $1\frac{1}{4}$ lakhs to compensate for expenditure on the purchase of encumbered estates.)
To Assam,	Rs. 20 ,,	

Of the remaining Provinces, Bombay and the Punjab were the next to obtain quasi-permanent settlements with effect from 1905–6.

In recasting their settlements the Government of India departed a little from the standard rate of division as applied to the Provinces quasi-permanently settled in 1904–5. With certain exceptions mentioned below the joint heads of revenue and expenditure were divided half and half, including Irrigation in Bombay, instead of three-fourths and one-fourth between the Imperial and the Provincial. The exceptions to this rule were the following :—

Revenue Heads of Account.	Provincial Share.		Expenditure Heads of Account	Provincial Share	
	Bombay.	Punjab		Bombay	Punjab
Land Revenue	Guaranteed up to $189\frac{1}{4}$ lakhs	$\frac{3}{8}$	Land Revenue	Wholly	Wholly
Registration	Wholly	Wholly	—	—	—
Irrigation	$\frac{1}{2}$	$\frac{3}{8}$ Guaranteed up to 28 lakhs			

Compiled from the Financial Statement of the Government of India.

The standard revenue and expenditure of these two provinces under the quasi-permanent settlement was as follows :—

Province.	Expenditure.	Revenue.		
		Revenues.	Fixed Assignments.	Total.
	Rs.	Rs	Rs	Rs
Bombay . .	4,91,75,000	4,48,98,000	42,77,000	4,91,75,000
Punjab . . .	2,49,50,000	2,46,50,000	3,00,000	2,49,50,000

The raising of the shares and the fixing of assignments on a liberal scale with respect to these famine and plague-stricken Provinces left the Imperial Government a loser on the transaction. On the basis of the new standard of revenues the Government of India lost Rs. 5,95,000 on the two Provinces together. The corresponding increase in the provincial shares of the joint heads of expenditure, however, lessened the Imperial expenditure by Rs. 2,21,000 a year. On the whole, therefore, the Imperial Government sacrificed a normal gain of Rs. 3,74,000 to give permanency and stability to the finances of these two Provinces. This was over and above the initial grant of Rs. 50,00,000 to each of them in order to enable them to set their sails in smooth waters.

A year after, the settlement of the Central Provinces was made quasi-permanent with effect from April 1, 1906. The shares in the joint heads of revenue and expenditure were raised, as they were in the case of Bombay and the Punjab, and particularly because of the addition of Berar, which was hitherto administered directly by the Imperial Government, from three-fourths and one-fourth to one-half between the Imperial and the Provincial, the share in the land revenue being guaranteed up to 82½ lakhs. The only exception to this rule of even division was the Registration revenue, which was made wholly provincial. To balance the revenue with the expenditure an assignment of Rs. 27,07,007 a year was fixed and an initial grant of Rs. 30,00,000 was given for a fair start.

Along with the settlement of the Central Provinces it

became necessary to reorganize the budgets of the quasi-permanently settled Provinces of Bengal and Assam owing to certain administrative changes. The two Provinces were reconstituted into (1) Bengal and (2) Eastern Bengal and Assam. In the revision of its financial settlement the new Province of Bengal was accorded the same proportionate share in the joint revenues as were granted to Bombay and the Punjab—namely, a share of a half in all the joint heads. Registration and that portion of the Land Revenue which was derived from Government Estates under the direct management of the Imperial Government were, however, made wholly provincial. In lieu of this favoured treatment the fixed assignment of the Province was reduced from 49·03 lakhs to 5·72 lakhs.

In the new Province of Eastern Bengal and Assam the principle of even distribution was applied to all joint heads of revenue and expenditure with the exception of Registration, which was made wholly provincial. This enhancement of shares so greatly augmented the resource side of the Provincial Budget that the balance had to be restored by a negative operation of a fixed adjusting assignment from the Provincial to the Imperial funds. The following figures show the standard expenditure and the standard revenue for the three provinces brought under the quasi-permanent settlements :—

Province	Expenditure.	Revenue.		
		Revenues	Assignments	Total.
	Rs	Rs	Rs	Rs
C.P.	1,76,43,000	1,49,36,000	27,07,000	1,76,43,000
Eastern Bengal and Assam .	2,12,19,000	2,18,42,000	6,23,000	2,12,19,000
Bengal . . .	4,72,73,000	4,67,01,000	5,72,000	4,72,73,000

Some modifications were later on introduced in the settlement of the Province, so that a positive adjustment had to be made by an assignment from the Imperial to the Provincial of Rs. 60,000 a year.

The only Province which was outside the pale of the quasi-permanent system was Burma. The last quinquennial settlement made with it in 1902-3 having expired, the Government of India decided to bring it in uniformity with the other Provinces by giving it a quasi-permanent settlement from April 1, 1907. In a spirit of perfect impartiality it was also given an even share in the principal joint heads of revenue and expenditure, salt being imperialized as in other provinces. It was given an adjusting assignment of Rs. 90,68,000 a year to cover the deficits in its standard expenditure and an initial grant of Rs. 50,00,000.

By the year 1907 all the Provinces were brought within the pale of the quasi-permanent settlement, and we would have expected the scheme of Provincial Finance to run its course undisturbed by any further changes. But it so turned out, as must have been noticed, that the quasi-permanent settlements made with Madras and U.P. in 1904 had become a little unfair to them in comparison with the terms offered to the Provinces subsequently dealt with. To remove this ground of injustice, which was one of those recognized for subjecting the quasi-permanent settlements to revision, the shares of the two Provinces in the joint heads were raised with effect from April 1, 1907, to one-half, with the following exceptions :—

Madras.	United Provinces.
Revenue.	*Revenue.*
1. Registration. Wholly Provincial.	1. Land Revenue. ⅝ Provincial. Minimum of 240 lakhs guaranteed.
2. Land Revenue. Minimum receipt of 308 lakhs guaranteed if the provincial share fell below that amount.	2. Irrigation. Minimum receipt of 60 lakhs from major irrigation works guaranteed, if the provincial share fell below that amount.
Expenditure.	
1. Registration. Wholly provincial.	
2. Land Revenue. Wholly provincial.	

The fixed assignments to cover the difference between the excess of standard expenditure over standard revenue were :—

To Madras	Rs. 22,57,000
To U.P.	Rs. 13,89,000

Thus the scheme of Provincial Finance in British India had advanced by gradual but distinct steps of assignment budgets, assigned revenue budgets and shared revenue budgets to a stage the terms of which were regarded by the parties concerned as sufficiently final. How far their expectations were fulfilled may be judged from the annual surpluses and deficits in Provincial Finance and from the range in their deviations as indicated in the following table :—

PROVINCIAL SURPLUSES AND DEFICITS

Province	1904–5.	1905–6	1906–7	1907–8.	1908–9.	1909–10.	1910–11	1911–12.
	Rs	Rs	Rs	Rs	Rs	Rs	Rs	Rs
C P *	−701000	3235000	1750607	−930617	—3097865	721755	280556	1214573
Burma	−1591796	−2613890	1890516	−3129590	−2060678	2515371	1900297	−1260040
Assam †	−269316	−3720027	−200140	−2596682	−2357687	549270	5539698	5218802
Bengal	−1252818	−1952312	−1877455	−2256994	−1330371	3274065	3960612	8296233
U P.	−869099	−2879192	795600	−3587066	1007260	2045221	3635904	144240
Punjab	4794387	−2796052	−661214	−2408818	−1576981	1300559	4199121	3398055
Madras	−1402344	220328	1217745	−44992	2025109	1266326	2316383	2938502
Bombay	4396000	−42892	1752202	−308925	−2618926	7137996	7585460	−541411

* Includes Berar since 1906
† Eastern Bengal and Assam since 1906

Compiled from the Annual Finance and Revenue Accounts of the Government of India

In judging of these results account must also be taken of the various benefactions made by the Government of India to the Provinces by way of grants-in-aid during the same period. These grants were as follows :—

IMPERIAL GRANTS-IN-AID TO THE PROVINCES

Province	1904–5	1905–6.	1906–7	1907–8	1908–9	1909–10	1910–11	1911–12
	Rs	Rs	Rs	Rs	Rs	Rs	Rs	Rs
C P *	2853710	6957793	110500	2752010	2903668	3588270	3465500	2080845
Burma	567500	1845000	7219000	682000	215253	1820952	4232742	3605164
Assam	—	3362916	827294	280030	2358947	4464435	4608965	6100732
Bengal	24794	4806984	475548	1362634	4157393	5753692	6137013	11131276
U P	136600	4036307	7641697	9879667	8770345	1624329	4513729	3136107
Punjab	7526436	2467579	4209531	5541529	6037990	5830014	9592844	3101681
Madras	700946	4430714	9980400	9473304	704885	613941	3691426	5008889
Bombay	10312928	3427325	4024512	4574284	5726162	5797603	12009360	4935159
Total	22122914	31334618	34982982	34543458	30874643	29502236	15475360	39099853

* Includes Berar since 1906

Compiled from the Annual Finance and Revenue Accounts of the Government of India.

But in taking account of these benefactions it must not be supposed that, barring a solitary case or two, they were necessary in order to preserve the solvency of Provincial Finance as it was defined by the terms of the settlement made with the different provinces. Far from being insufficient, the revenues settled upon the different Provinces proved quite ample for their needs if we take the last years, and they are the most typical years, into consideration.

Permanent Settlements of 1912

Soon after the series of quasi-permanent settlements were concluded with the different provinces, the subject of Provincial and Central Finance in British India among others of a like nature was investigated by the Royal Commission on Decentralization. In its Report issued in 1909 the existing method of allocating revenue and charges between the Imperial and Provincial Governments was upheld in principle. Of the many adverse criticisms passed by witnesses who appeared before the Commission only two were regarded by it as worthy of consideration: (1) The adjusting assignment and (2) Grants-in-aid, or doles as they were cynically termed. It was urged, and with some truth, that the adjusting assignments impaired the elasticity in provincial revenues by reason of the fact that while charges grew, that part of the provincial resource which was made up by assignments, and in some cases it formed quite an appreciable part, remained unaltered. Secondly, it was argued that doles were demoralizing and that it would be better to replace them by shares in growing revenue. The Commission seems to have been completely impressed by the disadvantages of large adjusting assignments, but it demurred, and rightly so, to the criticisms with regard to the doles. Every one extolled the benefits of decentralization to the Provinces, but few realized the anxieties that it involved to the Government of India. It must have been clear that by the process of decentralization the Government of India had given the Provinces more or less complete freedom in distributing their funds in any way they liked upon the services delegated to their management, while it had remained responsible for their efficient upkeep by the provisions of the law which governed its constitution. But the freedom which the provinces had obtained in carrying on the financial management of the services made over to their particular control, involved the possibility of their fostering certain services deemed to be of immediate utility to the people of the Provinces, and neglecting others the utility of which, though remote to the Provinces, was nevertheless real to the country as a whole. Neglect of nationally important services such as Education, Sanitation, Police, was especially to be avoided during periods of plague and famine. But the Government of India could not enforce distribution of provincial funds on such services; for one of the vital conditions of Provincial Finance was freedom of appropriation on provincialized services, which were not distinguished into obligatory and optional as is the case in the continental system of local finance. The Government of India was indeed not as powerless as the Central Government in England which, as is well known, cannot rectify cases of neglect by local authorities without resort to a writ of *mandamus*. But the way to bring a recalcitrant province to order, if easier, was not pleasant. For, the only way to mend such a situation was to end it by suspending the operation of Provincial Finance. Rather than resort to such a grave measure the Government of India happily hit upon grants-in-aid of particular services as a powerful and well-tried [1] corrective to the negligence of the Province, and require it to maintain a "national minimum" in those services which it regarded as onerous rather than beneficial.[2] Convinced of the virtue of grants-in-aid as a brake on decentralization degenerating into disintegration, the Commission only recommended that measures be taken to give Provincial Finance the greatest elasticity possible by diminishing the assignments to the smallest magnitude possible.

Following the recommendations of the Commission the Government of India decided to make certain modifications

[1] It is possible that the system was borrowed from England.
[2] S. Webb, *Grants-in-Aid*, 1911, p. 25.

in the existing allocation of revenue and charges and to make the quasi-permanent settlements permanent settlements from the year 1912. The permanent settlements did not differ from the quasi-permanent settlements which they superseded in any material point so far as the principle of allocation was concerned. The only point of difference between them in that respect was a partial replacement of the fixed adjusting assignments by increased shares in the following joint heads of revenue and expenditure :—

Modifications in Shares.

Revenues.		Expenditure.	
Heads of Account.	Provincial Share	Heads of Account	Provincial Share
1. Land Revenue including the portion credited to Irrigation	$\frac{5}{8}$ to Burma $\frac{1}{2}$ Punjab	1. Land Revenue	$\frac{5}{8}$ Burma $\frac{1}{2}$ Punjab
2. Excise . . .	Wholly in Eastern Bengal and Assam, Bombay. In C P., Bengal and U.P., $\frac{3}{4}$	2. Excise	Same as in revenue column
3. Assessed Taxes (P.W.D.) . .	$\frac{1}{2}$	—	—
4. Forest . . .	Wholly	4. Forest	Wholly
5. Major Irrigation works (excluding portion of Land Revenue credited to it)	$\frac{1}{2}$ in Punjab, minimum of 4 lakhs guaranteed	5. Major Irrigation	$\frac{1}{2}$
6. Major and Minor Irrigation	$\frac{1}{2}$ in Bengal	6. Major and Minor Irrigation	$\frac{1}{2}$ in Bengal

The effect of these modifications in the shares in the joint heads of revenue and expenditure was to reduce the adjusting assignments to the following figures :—

Province.	Assignments in Lakhs of Rupees from Imperial to Provincial.	From Provincial to Imperial.
Central Provinces	21·40	—
Burma	13·12	—
Eastern Bengal and Assam	13·55	—
Bengal	—	18·40
U.P.	—	19·26
Punjab	6·77	—
Madras	—	21·43
Bombay	—	9·38

During the permanent as during the quinquennial and quasi-permanent settlements the grants-in-aid of specific services, unobjected to as they were by the Decentralization Commission, were continued to be given to the different Provinces throughout the period although, as may be seen from the following figures, in a continually diminishing magnitude :—

SPECIAL GRANTS-IN-AID (in rupees)

Provinces	1912–13	1913–14	1914–15	1915–16	1916–17.	1917–18	1918–19.
C P.	4790480	2643264	5138256	4407802	3795784	3817540	2726008
Burma	8538948	2263939	3849763	3869472	216979	−2478482	2490
Assam	5530901	3283011	7533878	6577619	2497861	1922252	2444730
Bengal	15401885	6480800	7594894	7186436	6538732	7074773	9889717
Bihar and Orissa	6379420	4761028	3526567	4278854	3262214	4235205	4179425
U P	11470603	8542279	3842624	3229024	2453969	2706164	3590530
Punjab	6700924	2424404	3988117	5908023	4925830	4862616	5563665
Madras	12277591	5066343	1697803	1220785	1099165	1483708	1577446
Bombay	11192723	3996729	1468837	1200254	1065064	1154725	2479510
Total	82283565	39461797	38640739	37880069	25856498	24778501	35453521

Compiled from the Annual Finance and Revenue Accounts of the Government of India.

It was natural that the results of the permanent settlement should have been more anxiously awaited for with great interest by the Provinces, for the permanent settlement had the potentiality of a permanent gain or a permanent loss. That their anxiety on that score could not but have been completely allayed is amply supported by the repeated surpluses that meet the eye as it passes over the following figures of annual additions to and deductions from their balances during the period of its currency :—

PROVINCIAL SURPLUSES OR DEFICITS (in rupees)

Provinces.	1912–13.	1913–14.	1914–15.	1915–16.	1916–17.	1917–18.	1918–19
C.P.	5085246	1881245	−6544416	−13836	4235704	4870517	920121
Burma	8874174	914026	−3729808	1896621	9427702	12067708	4873587
Assam	3610494	−2217691	−4550789	658812	6044904	2800634	435872
Bengal	14705270	480842	−3967607	1028156	3708838	5280082	732237
Bihar and Orissa	7022199	−920062	−1870264	1133562	5919907	7176786	3643564
U.P.	9588749	50704	−4611080	−973090	3427808	−2268311	3686945
Punjab	7411069	−692512	−3730641	−1133541	500995	−695216	1185930
Madras	4330275	−5298411	−1207754	318508	2571241	1042303	−972354
Bombay	7083281	1558566	−2639924	−951099	122434	611321	1681066

Compiled from the Annual Finance and Revenue Account of the Government of India

While the condition of Provincial Finance was thus undoubtedly prosperous, the erratic movements in the provincial balances do not quite bear out the hope of orderly progress that was entertained of the permanent settlement. It should be noted, however, that the period during which the permanent settlement was current was not wholly a normal period. Part of the permanent settlement was no doubt a peace period, but it was not even as long as a quinquennium, and it should not on that account detract from the merits of a permanent settlement if it disclosed the faults of the quinquennial settlements. Most of the period covered by the permanent settlement was, however, a period of the Great War, the abnormal events of which could not have had any but disturbing effects on Provincial Finance.

Whether the permanent settlements would have been adequate for the purpose in view if sufficient length of time had been allowed for conditions to have become settled it is not given to us to say. For, from April 1, 1921, Provincial Finance in British India entered on an entirely new phase. That phase of it will be dealt with in another part. Here the study of the growth of Provincial Finance as it developed stage by stage under the old phase comes to an end. But this study will not be complete until we deal with the mechanism which inter-related the finances of the Central and Provincial Governments under the old phase. But before we proceed to do so it might be of interest as well as of value that the study of the final stage in the development of Provincial Finance were to close with the following retrospect of provincial revenue and expenditure which shows, as nothing else can, the small beginnings, the large strides and the vast proportions that Provincial Finance had reached during the half century over which it had been allowed to run its course.

GROWTH OF PROVINCIAL FINANCE

Provinces.	Provincial Revenues As a percentage of the total Revenues of India.						Provincial Expenditure. As a percentage of the total Expenditure of India.					
	1871–72	1882–83.	1892–93	1904–05	1912–13.	1918–19	1871–72.	1882–83.	1892–93.	1904–05.	1912–13.	1918–19.
C.P.	·655	1·055	·863	·905	2·52	1 715	·652	1·008	·87	·984	2·19	1·685
Burma	·572	1·66	2 256	3·023	4·73	3·57	·592	1·914	2·16	3 31	4·14	3·15
Bengal	2·8	5 9	4 72	4·12	5 56	4 00	2·7	6·68	4·52	4·26	4·56	3·84
N.W.P. and Oudh . .	1·99	4·16	3 6	—	—	—	2·04	4·4	3 32	—	—	—
Punjab	1·66	1 59	1 888	2 08	3 96	3 11	1·55	2 165	2·03	1 83	3·47	2 81
Madras	1·595	3 32	3 3	2 88	6·27	4·75	1·61	3·24	3·4	3·09	6·1	4·53
Bombay	1·8	4 9	4·49	4 05	6 17	5 45	1 836	5 08	4·4	3 77	5·7	5·00
Assam	—	·61	·738	597	1 38	1 00	—	·505	·617	·618	1·13	·857
U.P.	—	—	—	2 99	5 5	4 15	—	—	—	3 01	4·87	3 94
Bihar and Orissa . .	—	—	—	—	2·6	1 9	—	—	—	—	2·11	1·775
Total Provincial . .	11·11	22 8	21 75	20·4	38·6	29 2	10·8	25 00	21·3	20 8	34·3	27 6

Compiled from the Annual Finance and Revenue Accounts of the Government of India.

PART III

PROVINCIAL FINANCE: ITS MECHANISM

CHAPTER VII

THE LIMITATIONS OF PROVINCIAL FINANCE

To those who might be expected to have a knowledge of the anomaly—unparalleled in the annals of administration—involving the existence of Provincial Government without there being the necessary complement of Provincial Finance, the study could not but have been of profound interest as disclosing the manner in which the anomaly created in 1833 was rectified or seemed to be rectified in 1870.[1]

[1] There, however, prevails the idea that Provincial Finance existed long before 1870. But this is undoubtedly an error which may as well be corrected in this place by briefly recalling the history of financial decentralization prior to 1870. The year 1855 will always stand pre-eminent in the history of decentralization of Indian Finance. It is from that year that Local Finance dated its origin. It must not, however, be supposed that prior to 1855 there were no local revenues. On the contrary, there were very small funds such as Ferry Funds, Toll Funds, Cesses, etc., in existence and were spent on improvements of local utility, but the important point to note is that the balances from such funds were not carried to a separate account but as a rule merged in the general balances of the country, with the exception probably of Bengal and North-Western Provinces, where it seems that such balances were carried to separate Local Fund Accounts (cf. *Calcutta Review*, 1851, Vol. 16, pp. 464 and 466). It was by the Financial Resolution of May 11, 1855, that Local Funds were completely separated from Imperial Funds and were treated as "Deposits"—a sub-division of the Account Head "Debt" (cf. *Accountant's Manual*, by Y. Venkatramaiah, Part I, Madras,

On a purely a priori consideration of the matter, nothing could have been more natural than to suppose that the system of Provincial Finance thus established in British India was independent in its organization. Indeed it is difficult to imagine how one could emerge from the study of its origin and development without such a faith having silently grown upon him. But if Provincial Finance was independent in its organization, we should find the Provinces

1866, p. 79) and by the Resolution of September, 1863, Local Finance was established on a separate footing by the institution for each of the different provinces of a distinct Local Fund Budget as separate from the Imperial Budget. It so happened that in the absence of local authorities the Government of India entrusted the task of the preparation and execution of the Local Funds Budget to the respective Provincial Governments as being more in touch with local wants. It is this accident that has betrayed many into the supposition that this was essentially Provincial Finance. But nothing can be a greater blunder. What existed before 1870 was Local Finance, pure and simple, although under the supervision of the Provincial Government, in whose hands the Local Funds were essentially a kind of trust. The mere bringing together by the Provincial Governments of the receipts and charges pertaining to the Local Funds into a Local Fund Account for the whole Province can hardly be interpreted to mean the amount to be at their disposal—and that is the only sense in which Provincial Finance can be a reality—any more than the bringing together of the Local Rates levied in the United Kingdom in the budget of the Chancellor of the Exchequer can give an indication of its financial position. The Local Funds were not at the disposal of the Provincial Governments, for they could not be disposed of on purposes other than those which attached to them. In this sense they constituted Local Finance and not Provincial Finance. Some people mistake it for Provincial Finance probably because the term "Local Government" is used as a synonym for Provincial Government. But, while Local and Provincial Governments are often used as interchangeable terms, it must be remembered Local and Provincial Finance cannot be so used. As a matter of fact, there was a period in the history of Financial organization in India during which there was Local Finance without Local Government to be precise, and there was no Provincial Finance, even though there were Provincial Governments. It is probable that, as long as the habit of speaking of Provincial Government as Local Government continues, this confusion of ideas will not entirely vanish. While some have insisted that Provincial Finance had its being long before 1870, the Resolution of December 14, 1870, which instituted the scheme of Provincial Finance, is called "Resolution on Local Finance" as though it gave rise to Local and not Provincial Finance. Such absurdities can be avoided only by insisting upon precision of terminology.

in possession of financial powers which are commonly associated with the functioning of independent States. For the immediate purpose of finding out whether or not Provincial Finance was an independent system of finance, we may take the freedom of budgeting and everything that is involved in it as an evidence of the existence of these powers. Independent budget powers would involve the power to determine the services which, according to the needs of the country, a good government should undertake, and to decide upon the mode of raising either by taxation or loan sufficient money to meet the expenditure upon those services. Alongside these powers the budget system entails the obligation of keeping accounts and submitting them to independent audit.

Applying these tests to the Provincial Budget, the origin and growth of which have been treated in the foregoing parts of this study, we cannot predicate a tithe of the independence which characterizes the budgets of sovereign States. On the contrary, the budget system introduced into India with regard to the different Provinces was accompanied by the most stringent limitations. They were given a budget *without its powers,* and they bore the obligations of accounts and audit just because they were left free within the limits of their budgets. Why these limitations were imposed will be explained when we come to scrutinize the ways of enlarging the scope of Provincial Finance. It must, however, be emphasized that these limitations formed an integral part of the scheme, and the stringency of the former had grown *pari passu* with the scope and proportions of the latter. In fact they defined the law of the Constitution of Provincial Budgets. A complete comprehension of the operation of Provincial Finance in British India is therefore not possible without a thorough knowledge of its rules of government. Such being the importance of these rules it cannot but be to our advantage to analyse them at this stage.

These rules were laid down on various occasions during the interval between 1870, when the scheme of Provincial Finance came into being, and 1912, when the scheme reached through an evolutionary process its final and permanent stage, in the form of Resolutions of the Government of India in the Department of Finance. The rules framed in 1870 [1] were few and simple. Nor was there any necessity for a complex code to govern the operation of the very meagre budgets which were then constituted. Many supplementary rules were issued afterwards to dispose of unforeseen cases of order and procedure; but it was not till 1877 [2] that we come across a most elaborate set of rules and regulations governing the financial transactions of the Provincial Government. The Rules of 1877 were the basis of all those that were subsequently issued. With very small addenda or corrigenda they remained in force for a period of fifteen years, when they were superseded by a new series of Rules promulgated in 1892.[3] But only within a short span of a quinquennium this series was replaced by another issued in 1897,[4] and the latter formed the governing body of Rules till the year 1912, when a new series was brought out to regulate the working of the permanent settlement made in that year.[5] The same was reissued in the Financial Department Resolution No. 361-E.A. dated July 24, 1916. But as the alterations therein were not in any sense consequential, the series of 1912 may be taken as laying down the final regulations of Provincial Finance.

Recognize as we must the necessity for analysing the rules, we must determine beforehand the point or points of view from which to conduct the analysis. It must be premised at the outset that the object of entering upon the examination of the Rules is twofold: (1) to know what limitations there were and (2) why they were placed. Our immediate interest, it is true, is to state what limitations

[1] Financial Department Resolution No. 3334 dated December 14, 1870.

[2] Financial Department Resolution No. 1709 dated March 22, 1877.

[3] Financial Department Resolution No. 1142 of March 17, 1892.

[4] Financial Department Resolution No. 3551 dated August 11, 1897.

[5] Financial Department Resolution No. 249-E.A. dated July 15, 1912.

there were, but this is only a preliminary, if not a minor, object. The second is really the more important of the two. It is only as an aid to the proper understanding of the causes of the necessity for these limitations that a knowledge of them is to be sought. While keeping in our mind the immediate object of stating the limitations, it will be unimaginative not to foresee that in the following chapter, in which we shall be presently engaged, we will learn that the necessity for these limitations arose from the very peculiar nature of Provincial Finance itself. On the other hand, it is important to anticipate this conclusion, and instead of producing the Rules *seriatim* as they occur, arrange them in such a way that they shall be an external register of the internal conception of Provincial Finance which particularly pervaded the minds of its promotors. For the consummation of this end, the labours of the officials in charge of Provincial Finance who have laid down these rules are of no avail. To them these rules were only instruments of financial control, and it did not therefore matter in what order they were grouped. On the other hand, to get at the conception behind these rules it is necessary to classify and group them according to the purposes they were calculated to subserve. But the cardinal point in the matter of classification lies in defining the likely purposes which the originators of such an interrelated scheme of Provincial Finance as obtained in India must have had in view. Without being at all dogmatic, it may be said that for a successful working of such a scheme rules would have to be laid down for the purposes of defining (1) the Administrative and (2) Financial Powers of the Provincial Government. Each of the two categories may be further subdivided for a clearer understanding of the nature of Provincial Finance. Thus the Rules relating to Administrative Powers may be further subdivided into those pertaining to (i) Services and (ii) Staff. Similarly the Rules defining the Financial Powers may be conveniently grouped under the following subsidiary categories: Those (i) of a general nature and those pertaining to (ii) Provincial Revenues; (iii) Provincial Expenditure, (iv) Budget Sanction and (v) Audit and Account.

Taking purpose as the *fundamentum divisionis*, the above categories may be supposed to exhaust the possible purposes that the framers of the scheme may be said to have had in mind. On the basis of these categories we may therefore proceed to reduce the amorphous mass of Rules into a digest which, it may be hoped, will be convenient and instructive at the same time.

I. Limitations on Administrative Powers

(1) *Rules of Inter-Provincial Services*

For regulating the inter-provincial or inter-departmental relations affected by the creation of separate budgets for the different Provinces, it was ordained that—

(i) No inter-provincial adjustments were to be allowed.

(ii) No service previously rendered to other Departments at the charge of the Department made over to the control of the Provincial Governments was to be abolished, and no service previously rendered to these departments at the charge of other departments was to be increased.

(iii) No line of through communication was to be abandoned or allowed to fall out of repair.

(2) *Rules pertaining to Staff*

As to the staff engaged in the execution of the provincialized services the Provincial Governments were enjoined *not* to—

(i) Create a permanent appointment or augment the pay and allowance of any appointment.

Prior to 1912 this applied to appointments with a pay of Rs. 250 a month and above.[1] But after 1912 it applied only to appointments ordinarily held by a Gazetted Officer or by an Officer of the Imperial Service as defined in Article 29-B of the Civil Service Regulations.[2]

(ii) Create a temporary appointment or deputation for an Officer.

Prior to 1912 this applied to appointments with

[1] Rule 4 (3) (*a*) of 1897. [2] Rule 10 (1) of 1912.

a pay of Rs. 250 a month and above.[1] But after 1912 it applied to such of the appointments the remuneration of which exceeded Rs. 2,500 a month, or Rs. 800 a month, if the temporary appointment or deputation was expected to last for more than two years.[2]

(iii) Abolish a permanent appointment or reduce the pay and allowances of such an appointment.

This rule was in the beginning applied to such appointments the remuneration of which exceeded Rs. 250 a month.[3] After 1912 it was confined to such appointments as were held by Gazetted Civil Officers recruited in England or as were defined by Article 29-B of the Civil Service Regulations.[4]

(iv) Grant to a Civil officer in Government employ or in receipt of a service pension.

(*a*) *Land*, except where the grant was made under the ordinary revenue rules of the Province concerned without involving any special concession in money or its equivalent beyond the fact that the grantee received the grant in preference to others.[5]

or (*b*) An assignment of Land Revenue when the amount exceeded Rs. 600 a year, or the assignment though within that amount was not limited to three lives and reduced by one-half on each succession. All grants as assignments of Land Revenue made by Provincial Governments to civil officers were to be confined to cases in which the services were of a very distinguished and exceptional character.[6]

(v) *Revise* (*a*) permanent establishments which involved additional expenditure exceeding Rs. 50,000 a year; or (*b*) rates of substantive pay of any one branch of the service at a cost to that service alone of more than Rs. 25,000 a year, or (*c*) the average pay of

[1] Rule 4 (3) (*b*) of 1897.
[2] Rule 10 (4) (*a*) of 1912.
[3] Rule 4 (4) of 1897.
[4] Rule 10 (3) of 1912.
[5] Rule 10 (9) (*a*) of 1912.
[6] Rule 10 (9) (*b*) of 1912.

a service of which the maximum pay exceeded Rs. 500 a month and raise it above the average rate approved at the last revision of the service by the Secretary of State or the Government of India, or (*d*) the local allowances as compensation for dearness of living or for increase of rents in any localty.[1]

II. Limitations on Financial Powers

(1) *General*

Before actually detailing with the limitations on the financial powers of the Provincial Governments it is necessary to recall that the financial settlements made with the Provinces consisted in handing over to them certain *heads* of revenue and expenditure. From this accidental feature it is not to be supposed that the settlements were a collection of separate settlements for each head of revenue and expenditure incorporated into the Provincial Budget. To obviate such a construction by the Provincial Governments and the consequences thereof, it was ruled that—

(1) The Provincial Governments were to understand that the funds assigned to them formed a consolidated grant for all the services *en masse* entrusted to their respective administration and that no claim could therefore lie against the Imperial treasury on the ground that the actual cost of any service exceeded the amount at which it was estimated in the calculations of the consolidated grant.[2]

(2) And they were not to make any extra demands on the Imperial treasury, but were bound to maintain from the funds given to them all the services entrusted to their management in a state of administrative efficiency.[3]

With regard to the powers of the Provincial Governments concerning the custody of their funds it was ruled :—

(3) That the funds allotted for their use were to be lodged in the Imperial treasury, and were not to be removed for investment or deposit elsewhere ; nor were the Provincial Governments competent to withdraw such money except for expenditure upon the public services.[4]

[1] Rule 10 (6) of 1912. [2] Rule 7 of 1877 and 14 of 1897.
[3] *Ibid.* [4] Rule 1 (8) of 1877, 4 (11) of 1897, and 5 (6) of 1912.

(2) *Revenue Rules*

Turning from the general limitations to those pertaining to the revenues of the Provinces, it should be noted that they were required to maintain themselves within the funds allotted to them by the Central Government at each settlement.

The provinces could not *augment* their resources beyond the yield due to their natural growth by any possible means, for it was provided that Provincial Governments were—

(i) Not to impose any additional taxation or make any change in the existing system of revenue management.[1]

(ii) Not to alter or augment within its area the rates of discount upon the retail of Stamps, Court Fee labels, and duties on spirits and drugs.[2]

(iii) Not to raise *for its own* finances any loans in the open market.[3]

Powerless in the matter of augmenting their resources, the Provincial Governments were not free to will them away to any other authority subordinate to them. To guard against such eventualities it was ruled that Provincial Governments were—

(iv) Not to alienate any item credited to the general revenues, Imperial or Provincial, so as to form an asset of a Local or Special Fund.

This provision as regards the non-alienation of the resources of revenue made over to the Provinces was a little relaxed by the Rules of 1912 so that it was permissible for them to assign to a local body or special fund, as defined in Article

[1] Rule 1 (1) of 1877 and subsequent resolutions.

[2] Rule 1 (6) of 1877, also embodied in subsequent Resolutions.

[3] Rule 5 (13) of 1912. It is surprising that the various resolutions on the subject of Provincial Finance prior to 1912 do not contain this ruling, though it cannot be doubted that it has been in operation since the commencement of Provincial Finance. In the absence of a specific ruling prior to 1912, attention may be invited to the Resolution reviewing the Financial Statement for 1879–80, where it is said "so long, therefore, as a Local Government *does not incur debt* (*which is absolutely forbidden*), there is etc., etc." F. S., 1878, Calcutta, p. 5.

33 of Civil Service Regulations, constituted by law, petty items of Wholly Provincial Revenue of a recurring character, not derived from the proceeds of general taxation and not yielding on an average more than Rs. 25,000 a year.[1]

(v) Not to make grants, subventions or assignments from the funds at their disposal to Local or Municipal bodies so as to create a permanent charge on the revenues of India.

This by no means prevented grants, subventions or assignments from being made to local or municipal bodies by the Provincial Governments from their funds although the Government of India had sounded to them a note of warning by declining to bind itself to continue the grants after the expiration of the settlements or to provide for them in the succeeding settlements.[2] By the Rules of 1912, however, the power of making such grants was more clearly circumscribed so that a Provincial Government could not make (1) recurring grants to local bodies from provincial revenues exceeding Rs. 1,00,000 a year in any one case,[3] or (2) non-recurring grants to local bodies exceeding Rs. 10,00,000 in any one case,[4] or (3) a grant to a charitable or religious institution other than educational, not being outside India, in excess of Rs. 10,000 a year if recurring, and Rs. 50,000 if non-recurring.[5]

(vi) Not to make any grants to non-officials (1) on political considerations of (*a*) land, either free of revenue, or on favourable terms, or (*b*) of assignment of land revenue, if the value of the land or land revenue exceeded Rs. 1,000 a year[6]; (2) on the consideration of injury to himself or to his family in the event of his death during or in consequence of service rendered to Government, or (3) on the

[1] Rule 5 (5) of 1912.
[2] Rule 4 (10) of 1897.
[3] Rule 10 (12) (*a*) of 1912.
[4] Rule 10 (12) (*b*) of 1912.
[5] Rule 10 (10) of 1912.
[6] Rule 10 (7) of 1912.

consideration of exceptional services to the Government of a pension exceeding Rs. 1,000 a year or a gratuity exceeding Rs. 3,000 in any one case.[1]

(3) *Rules of Expenditure*

The powers of sanctioning expenditure granted to the Provincial Government were as limited as their revenue powers. While they were free to spend their funds on the services entrusted to them, certain limitations were laid down for the purposes of expressly ruling out certain objects and subjects of expenditure from the provincial domain.

With regard to the *objects* of their expenditure Provincial Governments were required—

(i) Not to sanction any expenditure from public money on anything outside the category of objects of expenditure recognized by the Government of India.[2]

(ii) To confine themselves to the carrying on of the services particularly entrusted to them by the terms of the settlement.

Prior to 1912 they could undertake a "new general service or duty" only if they satisfied the Government of India that they could provide the necessary funds temporarily if it was temporary, and permanently if it was permanent.[3] This provision was altered in 1912 so that a Provincial Government could undertake a new general service or duty provided it was not (*a*) of an unusual nature, or (*b*) devoted to objects outside the ordinary work of administration, or (*c*) likely to involve at a later date expenditure beyond its powers of sanction.[4]

(iii) Not to spend—

(*a*) On State ceremonies and assemblies, and on the entertainment at the public charge of distinguished visitors to India more than Rs. 1,00,000.[5]

[1] Rule 10 (8) of 1912.
[2] Rule 11 of 1897, also embodied in subsequent Resolutions.
[3] Rule 4 (2) of 1897. [4] Rule 5 (11) of 1912.
[5] Rule 10 (11) of 1912.

(*b*) On Railway Carriages especially reserved for the use of high officials otherwise than in connection with the maintenance of the carriage.[1]

(*c*) On the purchase of a Motor-car or Motor-cycle for the use of an official, or on the maintenance of it otherwise than from the "Contract Grant" with the Head of the province.[2]

(*d*) On the increase of the "Contract Grant" to the Head of the province.[3]

(*e*) On the construction or purchase of a vessel required for inland navigation and for use at ports, the cost of which exceeded Rs. 1,00,000.[4]

(*f*) On an Irrigation or other Public Works projects of which the estimated cost chargeable to the general revenues exceeded Rs. 20,00,000 inclusive of establishments, tools and plants. It was however competent for a Provincial Government to spend up to an amount 10 per cent. in excess of the original sanctioned estimate provided such excess was not more than Rs. 12½ lakhs inclusive of establishment, tools and plants.[5]

As to the limitations respecting the *subjects* of provincial expenditure, it was ruled that in virtue of the application of the general condition precedent to the delegation of all authority to disburse public money, that it shall be bona fide for a public purpose, Provincial Governments could not spend from their funds for benefiting—

(i) Any individual or body of private persons unless in accordance with some declared or established rule or principle recognized by the Government of India.[6]

(ii) Native States, directly beyond Rs. 10,000 a year on any one project or Rs. 50,000 if non-recurring.[7]

[1] Rule 10 (4) of 1912.
[2] Rule 10 (6) of 1912.
[3] Rule 10 (15) of 1912.
[4] Rule 10 (17) of 1912.
[5] Rule 10 (18) of 1912.
[6] Rule 10 of 1877, also embodied in subsequent Resolutions.
[7] Rule 10 (13) of 1912.

(4) *Budgetary Rules*

Besides being subject to the ordinary rules of the Budget System introduced into India for the first time by Mr. Wilson in 1860,[1] by which they were required to submit their budget estimates for sanction to the Government of India, and to observe the rules of appropriation in the execution of the grants, Provincial Governments were further given to understand that without the previous consent of the Government of India they—

(i) Could not exhaust their balances in the Imperial Treasury.

Prior to 1887 a Provincial Government could propose in its budget estimates to draw upon the whole of its balance. But by the Rules then framed the Provincial Government was required to maintain at all time a certain minimum balance in the Imperial treasury, the amount of which varied with each successive settlement.

(ii) Could not budget for a deficit, that is for provincial expenditure in excess of the provincial revenues of the year.

The stringency of this rule [2] was a little softened, so that a Province could after 1912 budget for a deficit, if it satisfied the Government of India that the cause was exceptional and non-recurring,[3] but it was at the same time provided that, if this drawing upon the balances to make up the deficits resulted in reducing the balance below the prescribed minimum, the budget for a deficit would be sanctioned only if the Government of India was able to allow the Provincial Government in question an overdraft to the extent necessary to restore the balance to the required minimum from the general balances to be repaid in such rates of interest and instalments as may be prescribed.[4]

[1] Rule 11 of 1892, 13 of 1897, and 19 of 1912.

[2] Rule 8 of 1892. [3] Rule 21 of 1912.

[4] Rule 21 and 22 of 1912.

(iii) Could not exceed during the currency of the year the expenditure on any head of account as finally sanctioned for it, for that year, by the Government of India.

It could increase the expenditure only if the increase was counterbalanced by re-appropriation, that is, reduction by the amount of the excess of the sanctioned grant under some other head of account under its control.[1] The powers of re-appropriation of Provincial Governments were very extensive, for it could sanction re-appropriation between the grants for provincial expenditure included in its budget, whether under a Wholly Provincial or a Divided Major or Minor Head provided that the aggregate grant of provincial expenditure was not exceeded.[2]

(5) *Rules of Audit and Account*

Though the Provinces were allowed considerable powers of re-appropriation within their budgets there was imposed upon them the obligation of audit and accounts of the money they spent. The important point to note in this connection is the fact that this obligation of the keeping of accounts and submitting them to audit was an obligation which the Provinces did not owe to their legislatures, but was an obligation which they owed to the Government of India, who had conferred upon them the financial power they exercised. Moreover, the Government of India did not leave the Provinces to discharge this obligation according to their own sweet will by employing their own audit and account staff. On the contrary the responsibility of realizing this obligation was entrusted to the imperial officers of audit and account stationed in the different Provinces, who acted as the critics and guides of Provincial Governments in the matter of administration and interpretation of the Rules discussed above. To facilitate their task Provincial Governments were instructed—

(i) Not to make any alterations in the form of procedure

[1] Rule 24 of 1912. [2] Rule 25 (1) of 1912.

of public accounts,[1] or direct the division of a charge between two or more heads of account. In all such matters they were to abide by the decision of the Comptroller General—an officer of the Imperial Government.[2]

(ii) To transmit the objection of the Imperial audit officer against its appropriation or sanction with regard to expenditure with the explanation of the Provincial Government concerned to the Government of India for final disposal.[3]

Such were the limitations on the Financial Powers of the Provincial Governments. Apart from these specific limitations the Provincial Governments were not altogether the free architects of their own destiny within the sphere allotted to them; for it was provided that the power of supervision and control in any Department still rested in the Governor-General in Council, and that the Provincial Governments should keep him fully informed of their executive and financial proceedings so as to enable the former to discharge its obligations for peace, order and good government.[4] Their general effect on the financial freedom of the Provinces could hardly have been concealed. It must therefore have been a most impervious mind which in face of these paralysing limitations had not lost its faith in the independence of the system of Provincial Finance and had not asked what was after all the nature and advantage of this illusive institution?

[1] Rule 1 (*a*) of 1897 also embodied in subsequent Resolutions.
[2] Rule 4 (2) of 1897. [3] Rule 30 and 31 of 1912.
[4] Rule 5 of 1877; Rule 15 of 1897; and Rule 6 and 7 of 1912.

CHAPTER VIII

THE NATURE OF PROVINCIAL FINANCE

The study of Provincial Finance cannot be said to be complete unless it furnishes a true answer to the question which is bound to be asked in the end, What was the resulting financial relationship under the old scheme between the Central and Provincial Governments in British India? The question is an important one, for the validity of the criticisms and proposals with regard to Provincial Finance, or any subject for that matter, depends entirely upon a correct understanding of its nature. Unfortunately it had not received the attention that its importance demanded, and consequently we find the rather distressing fact that no subject was so confidently discussed, and yet none was so grossly misunderstood, as that of the nature of the old system of Provincial Finance in British India. It therefore becomes necessary to explain what was the exact nature of the system of Provincial Finance established in British India.

In an inter-related system of polities, such as is composed of Central and Provincial Governments in British India, it is always difficult to grasp the exact nature of their financial relationship; for, what may appear on the surface may be very different from what it may really be. None the less, the view was commonly held that the Indian system was based on a separation of sources between the Provincial and the Central Governments, and contributions from the yield by the former to the latter, much the same as was found in the federal system of finance which obtained in the German Empire. Whether such a view was wrong or right there were various incidents of the relationship between the Central and Provincial Governments in India, which, there can be no doubt, went a long way to strengthen that view. Among such incidents must be mentioned the division of functions between the Central and Provincial Governments. An onlooker could not fail to observe that in this distribution of functions the former controlled matters pertaining to Military Affairs, Foreign Affairs, General Taxation, Currency, Debt, Tariffs, Posts and Telegraph, Railways and Audit and Accounts; while the latter administered matters of ordinary internal administration, such as Police, Education, Sanitation, Irrigation, Roads and Buildings, Forests, and the control over Local Bodies. If this incident encouraged the view that there was a separation of services, there was another incident of the relationship which encouraged the view there was also a separation of revenues between the Central and Provincial Governments in British India. That incident was the collection of most of the taxes in India by the agency of Provincial Governments. As observed by the Royal Commission on Indian Expenditure [1]

"in the United Kingdom the Revenue Administration is centralized . . . under the Chancellor of the Exchequer in London. In India the administration of some branches of revenue is centralized, though not always under the Finance Minister (of the Government of India). That of other branches is decentralized. The Land Revenue is under the control of the Central Department at Calcutta, but that department is subject not to the Finance Minister but to the Minister in charge of the Home and Revenue Departments. The Telegraph Department is under the Minister of Public Works. The Central Government controls the collection of part of the Salt duty and of part of the opium revenue, of Post Office revenue and of other revenues. . . . The remainder of the revenue is collected by the Provincial Governments. . . . As regards . . . a large portion of the revenue, the Provincial Governments are units of administration and are efficiently equipped for their duties."

[1] Para. 25 of the Final Report.

As a third incident supporting the same view, reference must be made to the peculiar mode of presenting Indian Accounts adopted in official Blue Books. As might have been noticed, to the General Accounts of the Government of India is attached a supplementary account professing to show the distribution of the different heads of receipts and expenditure among the various Provinces into which British India has been divided. This mode of showing the accounts is beyond doubt misleading. It appears as if the aim was to show the financial position of the Provinces. But as a matter of fact the figures given in the columns in which the revenues and charges are shown in their provincial distribution do not represent the respective claims and responsibilities of the different Provinces. Far from showing the financial position of the Provinces, the figures in the columns merely represent the geographical distribution of the different agencies through which the financial business of the Government of India is conducted, and through which the revenues are collected and the expenditure is defrayed. The revenue and expenditure, for instance, shown under "Bombay" represent the income and outgo which pass through the books of the Accountant General of the Government of India stationed at Bombay, and the same is true of entries under the heads of other Provincial Governments. The figures really represent the transactions of the Government of India distributed geographically, and there is nothing provincial about them in the least. However, such a system of account bears the impression that the system of finance in India is primarily Federal.

With these three incidents before one's mind it was easy to fall into a federal line of thinking in reasoning about the financial relationship between the Central and Provincial Governments in British India. So deep seated was the view that the Indian system was one of separation of sources and contributions from the yield, that many witnesses giving evidence before the Royal Commissions on Indian Expenditure (1892) and on Decentralization in British India (1909) sallied forth to assail the Commissioners with the criticisms on the inequity of the system and proposals for amending it according to what they considered to be the requirements of justice. Nowhere have they stated the reasons for their assumptions in explicit terms.[1] Yet their proposals are an unmistakable proof that they held that view. Unless they had taken for granted that the Provinces had separate revenues and separate services, they could not be expected to have wasted their energies in directing as they did their efforts to getting redressed what appeared to them as a piece of injustice embodied in the unequal contributions made by the different Provinces from their revenues to the support of the Central Government.

If their view of the financial relationship between the Central and Provincial Governments was acceptable, then a good deal could not but have been conceded in favour of their criticisms and their proposals. Contributions, if the Imperial share could have been conceived of in such a light, as between the different Provinces whether in ratio to their revenues or population, were certainly unequal if calculated on the somewhat questionable but generally accepted hypothesis that all the revenues collected within a Province belonged to the Province.

PROVINCIAL CONTRIBUTIONS TO THE IMPERIAL GOVERNMENT

Province	Ratio of Amount Surrendered to the Government of India to the Total Revenues raised in the Province.					Ratio of Amount Surrendered to the Government of India per Head to the Population of the Province				
	1871–2	1882–3	1892–3.	1904–5	1912–13.	1871–2	1882–3.	1892–3	1904–5	1912–13.
C P	655	464]	615	297	·204	·9	·69	1 3	55	59
Burma	728	575	598	497	38	3 4	39	7	4 37	3 08
Assam	—	438	390	376	—	—	75	75	87	—
Bengal	903	746	761	·742	596	2 4	1 99	2 9	2 29	2 39
N W P and Oudh	785	617	435	—	—	1 5	1 24	1 4	—	—
Punjab	768	648	726	·512	391	1 7	1 5	2 4	1 57	1 64
Madras	828	664	·667	638	479	2 3	2 0	2 3	2 34	1 79
Bombay	·845	·648	·66	614	58	5 0	4 1	5 4	4 75	5 6
U P	—	—	—	·567	381	—	—	—	1 48	93
Bihar and Orissa	—	—	—	—	220	—	—	—	—	17

Compiled from the Finance and Revenue Accounts of the Government of India and the Decennial Census Reports.

[1] Cf., however, Indian Expenditure Commission Minutes of Evidence, Vol. 3, Q. 18094, and Decentralization Commission Evidence, Vol. 2, Q. 9497.

Similarly, whatever may be said of the relative merits of the proposals[1] of changing the system of divided heads of revenue into one of complete separation supplemented in favour of the Central Government by contributions from the Provinces in the form of (1) a fixed sum revisable every few years, or (2) a lump percentage on provincial revenues, or (3) a fluctuating contribution from the provinces on their population, revenues or wealth, there can be no doubt that they were all aimed at reaching some such intelligible basis of distributing the burden of the Imperial exchequer as equality of payment or ability to pay. No one who had cared to scrutinize the true nature of Provincial Finance could have been expected to take these proposals with the same seriousness with which they were offered by their authors. However, strange as it may seem, none of the two Commissions questioned their propriety. The Royal Commission on Decentralization did make it clear, though not quite forcibly, that equal contributions were not necessarily equitable contributions, but neither it nor the Royal Commission on Indian Expenditure challenged the language which spoke of the Provinces as surrendering *their* revenues to make contributions to the imperial treasury after paying for *their* services. It therefore becomes all the more necessary to examine at some length the grounds which supported that view which argued that the system was based on the principle of separation of sources and contributions from the yield. Indeed the question of equity of contributions would hardly be worth discussion until it is settled that the Provinces had revenues which they could call their own and services for the efficient discharge of which they were primarily liable.

What is the criterion by which to judge whether the provinces had revenues and services which they could call their own ? There is, of course, the administrative criterion by which it would be possible to say that anything which a Province administered was provincial. But that criterion cannot be a final criterion. For, whatever may be the

[1] See *Report of the Royal Commission on Decentralization* (hereafter abbreviated into R.C.D.)

view regarding the origin of administrative polities or regarding what their position should be in an ideal organization, yet all regional rights of an administrative polity are in modern times exercised in the main, not in virtue of any social compact or the mere discharge of certain functions, but in virtue of a general law. The question must therefore be decided with reference to the law which defined the status of the Provincial Governments in British India.

Did the Provinces have a legal title to the revenues? Although it is uncertain whether or not those who spoke of Provincial revenues invested the term provincial with a legal status there is no doubt that it had acquired such a connotation in ordinary parlance. Even the Provincial Governments, who ought to have known better, thought and argued that by the provincialization of revenue what the Government of India passed on to them was not the mere usufruct but a title to the revenue. But the Government of India had always been prompt in suppressing such pretences. The facts are patent that provincial settlements were revisable every five years, that the usufruct was not perpetual and that the Government of India could resume it at the end of five years if it wanted. This is made quite clear in answer to the pretensions advanced by the Government of Bengal in a letter No. 284 of January 14, 1882, from which the following is extracted:—

"For the sake of diminution of friction and other well-known objects which need not be specified, the Imperial Government delegated a share in its administration to Local Governments. It makes a rough calculation that a certain portion of the general income, together with the increment thereon, will suffice to meet the expenditure which it retains under its own control, and it hands the rest over to Local Governments, with the obligation to meet out of it certain necessary expenditure. . . . But it cannot bind itself to this proportion for ever, because the calculation must necessarily be a rough one, and is liable to be vitiated by unforeseen failure of resources, or growths of charges, whether in the share of financial administration which it retains or in that which it delegates. An examination of the appropriation and a readjustment of it in any particular found necessary are indispensable. A surrender of the right to this would be analogous in its nature and effects to the Permanent Settlement of Bengal."

Although anxiety was expressed for the provinces the revisions were primarily conducted in the interests of the Imperial Government as the resumptions incontrovertibly proved, and the Permanent Settlement was delayed because the Government of India did not desire to relinquish its control over its revenues. Under the quinquennial settlement the usufruct was permitted to be undisturbed for five years only. But how tentative was this surrender, which, even for five years, was looked upon as highly impolitic by the Secretary of State,[1] was proved by the Government of India, which did not take back to exercise its inherent right to resume the usufruct of its revenues at any time it liked as is indicated by the not too uncommon levies or benevolences, as they were called, which it forced upon the provincial balances. Not even the Permanent Settlement can be interpreted to mean that the revenues settled upon the different Provinces became their revenue in anything like a legal sense, for in the eye of the law all revenues including those provincialized still remained the constitutional possession of the Government of India. Whether the Government could have effected a legal separation by divesting itself of the revenues of India in favour of the Provinces is doubtful. The Parliamentary enactment which vests the revenues of India in the Government of India had limited the legislative powers of the Government of India by a clause which prevented it from

"making any laws or Regulations which shall in any way repeal, vary, suspend or affect any of the provisions of this Act (of 1833) . . . or the Prerogative of the Crown, or the Authority of Parliament."

At least it is significant that it has required an Act of Parliament to do so. But the Government of India had

[1] Cf. Despatches to the Government of India No. 51 dated February 16, 1882, and No. 208 dated July 6, 1882.

not made any legal separation of the title to the revenues, and if it could have done that by its own law it could have undone it as well. Nor can it be said that the separation of Provincial revenues involved separate possession. If the Provincial Governments had been allowed to establish their own treasuries to receive the collections from Provincialized revenues, then Provincial revenues in the sense of separate possession could have had a meaning. But by the rules, Provincial Governments were not to deposit their funds elsewhere than in the treasury of the Imperial Government. Consequently the possession of the revenues remained in the hands of the Government of India and the disbursement from the provincial revenues was carried out from the Imperial Treasury by the officers of the Imperial Government. None the less, the view was hard to die. But such an erroneous view was never more confidently stated than by The Honourable Mr. Sayani, and never more forcibly controverted than by Sir James Westland in a passage-at-arms between the two on the occasion of a Budget debate in the Council Hall of the Government of India from which the following is reproduced :—

The Honourable Mr. Sayani said :—

"The whole theory underlying the system (of Provincial Finance) is that the revenues of the country, far from belonging to the Provinces which raise them or being available for their own requirements . . . constitute a common fund to be absolutely at the disposal of the Central Government, out of which it is to dole out what amount it pleases for provincial services."

Catching the condemnatory tone of these comments, the Finance Minister, Sir James Westland, rose to say :—

"The Honourable Mr. Sayani, if I correctly followed him, stated that the arrangements of the Government of India were made upon the theory that the revenues were not the revenues of the separate Provinces and were not applicable to the expenditure of the several Provinces, but were the revenues of a common fund, the Local Governments being merely the agents of the Government of India for their realization. I think he mentioned the theory in some words like these, only for the purpose of condemning it. Well, I wish to assert that theory in the most positive manner I can. The revenues are the revenues of the Government of India—its Constitutional Possession. The Government of India is a body created by Act of Parliament, and if reference be made to that Act of Parliament it will be seen that the revenues of India are the revenues of the Government of India and of that Government alone. Every action that the Local Government takes in respect of them must be justified by a specific order of the Government of India; the Local Government derive their powers entirely from the Government of India, and apart from that Government they exercise no financial powers whatsoever." [1]

Again, if the financial relationship between the Central and Provincial Governments in India were based upon the principle of separation of sources and contributions from the yield, what ought to have been shown was the existence of legal responsibility of the Provinces for the services they administered. It is true there was a certain division of functions between the Central and Provincial Governments in India analogous to what existed between the Central and State Governments in most of the federal countries. But it must, however, be remembered that this division of functions had no sanction in law and no legal responsibility attached to the provinces for any of the services, not even for those provincialized. The entire responsibility by law rested on the shoulders of the Imperial Government and it could not absolve itself of that responsibility by transferring it on to any of the Provinces. That the Provinces accepted the financial responsibility for some of the Imperial services was their choice. That they could not be compelled to undertake them was proved in a singular manner by Madras refusing to accept such responsibility in 1877. By law it was thus the Government of India which was responsible for peace, order and good government in the country. All services were therefore necessarily Imperial in status under-

[1] Financial Statement, 1897-8, p. 110, etc.

taken by the Government of India in discharge of its constitutional obligations.

It is therefore obvious that the view which posited that the relationship between the Central and Provincial Governments in British India was one of separation of sources and contributions from the yield was an untenable view. The Government of almost every country in these days is carried on by an inter-related group of polities operating in specific areas and discharging specific public functions; and it may well be that in any two given countries the number of polities engaged in carrying on the work of government is the same. But it is quite erroneous to argue from that fact that the nature of their inter-relationship must have been alike. It is therefore as well to invite attention to the point that the ordered relationship between such inter-related polities depends upon which of them is the law-giving polity. It will be granted that in such group of polities there is one that is supreme in the sense that from a variety of reasons mostly historical it is competent to give law to the other polities. In federal countries it is the State Governments which are the law-giving polities. They occupy a pivotal position. They are the depositories of sovereign powers original as well as residuary. They can claim independent existence, have their own resources and discharge their own functions. The Federal Government, on the other hand, is the creature of the State Governments. It can have no powers and no functions other than those which the States have been pleased to transfer to it by an act of self-abnegation. It is therefore truthful as well as becoming to speak of the financial relationship between the State and Federal governments as one of separation of sources and contributions from the yield.[1] For there the States have their separate resources which they lawfully own and can therefore be spoken of as surrendering their revenues to make contributions to the

[1] Of course, it is not necessary that there should be a federal system. A legalized system of decentralization will be equally compatible with separation of sources and contributions from the yield.

Central Government after paying for their own services. But the same was inconsistent with the position of the Provincial Governments. Far from pivotal, the Provincial Governments formed the weakest entities in the group of administrative polities functioning in India. Up to 1833 the Provinces had separate rights to surrender in a *foedus* and had the government of India been then organized on a federal basis the position of the Provinces would have been very much the same as those of the States in federal countries. But with the establishment of the Imperial system by the Act of 1833 the last chance of creating a federation in India vanished. By that Act the sovereignty of the Provinces was so entirely crushed that no trace was left of it to permit of a truly federal element ever to enter into their relationship with the Central Government. Since that Act the government of the country has been entrusted to a single authority charged with the sole responsibility for the good government of the country. As no single administration could support the Atlantean load of governing such a vast country with the help of central bureaux, great powers were delegated to the Provincial Governments. But this must not obscure the fact that they were literally the "agents of the Government of India." Common usage had elevated the term "Provincial" to a proud position. Along with Provincial Revenues it had been usual to speak of Provincial Services, Provincial Civil Servants, Provincial Courts, etc., as if all these and other things constitutionally belonged to the Provincial Governments. But the usage was full of irony. For, when one recalls the provisions of the constitutional law of the land, so far from thinking of them as Sovereign authorities one felt inclined to say that notwithstanding their high-sounding apparatus of Governors and Councils it was not appropriate to call them Governments. In any case the Provincial Governments had no legal powers or functions which polities designated as Governments have been known to possess. The fact is the Indian system of polity was diametrically opposed to the federal system of polity. It was a centralized system in which there was nothing Provincial; what appeared to be Provincial was but the regional aspect of the Imperial. It was therefore untruthful and over-becoming to speak of the financial relationship between the Provincial and Central Governments in India as being one of separation of sources and contributions from the yield. For here the Provinces had no separate resources which they lawfully owned, and could not therefore be spoken of as surrendering their revenues to make contributions to the Central Government after paying for what may be supposed to have been their own services—a supposition rigorously excluded by the law of the constitution.

If the complex code of limitations discussed in the last chapter had had the effect, which it was not unreasonable to expect, of revealing the true nature of Provincial Finance, such a view as the one herein criticized could never have prevailed. That notwithstanding the existence of these limitations there should have been men who instead of wondering as to what remained of Provincial Finance when it was regulated by such limitations, argued with the confidence of the ignorant that the system was independent in its organization, is itself a proof that in their study of Provincial Finance the study of its limitations formed no part. Otherwise a reference to that code would have shown that if the Provinces had separate revenues and separate services they would have had powers of alienating whatever revenues they liked, of spending on any service they desired, of framing their Budget Estimates with a view to any particular policy they decided to adopt, and of arranging for supplementary grants in any manner they chose. But such powers they never had. Indeed no greater proof could be furnished in support of the view that everything had remained imperial in status after 1870, as it was before 1870, than is afforded by these limitations on the working of Provincial Finance.

If separation of sources and contributions from the yield as a theory of the financial relationship between the Central and Provincial Government in India was incompatible with the facts of the case, what theory was there which could be said to have been compatible with the position as defined by law? We may at once proceed to state that the only theory of financial relationship between the two governments which accorded with facts and agreed with law was that of *aggregation of the sources and distribution of the yield.*

It may seem fallacious to speak of aggregation of sources when what the Government of India gave to the Provinces was assignment of revenues and shares of revenues. To this the reply is not difficult. It has already been made clear that Provincial Finance did not involve a *de jure* separation of sources. Nor was there a *de facto* separation either. For as has been remarked before, all revenues whether assigned or reserved were collected into the Imperial treasury and were thence paid out on all approved Government transactions. Obviously, when all the revenues are thrown into a common pool, it cannot be said without unduly straining the imagination that what the Provinces were given were revenues.[1] The collections from all sources of revenue being inextricably mixed up, the only proper view is to say that what was given to the Provinces were funds. The expressions Budget by Assignments, Budget by Assigned or Shared Revenues are in a certain sense all fictitious phrases. In all the stages of Provincial Finance what the Provinces were supplied with were funds. Under the assignment stage the supply granted was a definitely fixed sum and the only difference made as a consequence of the replacement of Assignments by Assigned or Shared

[1] The remarks made by Captain Pretyman, M.P., in his evidence before the Royal Commission on local taxation in England with regard to the revenues assigned to Local Governments may be cited in this connection. He said: "I absolutely hold that it is impossible to say that you give a contribution from Imperial Taxation from a particular source. A man might just as well pour a bucket of water into a pond and then go and hook it out again and say that he had hooked out the same bucket of water. The taxes are paid into the Imperial Exchequer and the contribution is made from the Imperial Exchequer, and to say that you select a particular sum of money as the produce of a particular tax and that you hand that over is, I think, a fallacious statement altogether." Vol. 1 of Min. of Evid. C. 8763 of 1898, Q. 9873.

Revenues was that the supply, instead of being a fixed sum, was a sum which varied in amount with variations in the yield of the Assigned or Shared Revenues. But all the same it was a supply of funds and nothing more. It is even incorrect to say that the Government of India *gave* funds to the Provincial Governments for meeting the expenditure on the services the responsibility for which was undertaken by them. As a matter of fact, the receiving as well as the disbursing of all public money, including the provincial portion of it, remained in the hands of the Government of India. The only proper expression, if it is to be true to facts, would be to say that Provincial Finance simply meant that the Government of India opened a Provincial Services Account in its Treasury books which varied with the yield of the Assigned or Shared Revenues and on which and to its extent only the Provincial Governments were permitted to draw.

Thus there was a complete aggregation of the sources of revenue in the hands of the Government of India. From this fact it follows that instead of the Provinces contributing from their funds it was the Government of India which distributed the yield of its taxes among the Provinces. The situation could not be otherwise. For it should be recalled that in virtue of the Act of 1833 the financial responsibility for the services undertaken to subserve the ends of peace, order and good government rested upon the Government of India. While some of the services were administered directly by the Government of India, owing to the well-nigh impossibility of managing directly from a central bureau the affairs of a country as vast as the continent of Europe minus Russia, many of the services attaching to the Imperial Government were left to be administered under its supervision by the Provincial Government. The weak point of the situation, as has been remarked, consisted in the fact that the administrative and financial responsibility did not rest on one and the same authority as should have been the case. On the other hand, at the end of every financial year all Provincial Governments sent in their estimates of the charges for the services they administered to the Government of India in the Financial Department, leaving the obligation of refusing, curtailing or granting the supply asked for to the Government of India to discharge as best it could. Not having the obligation to find the money, the Provinces tended to make extravagant demands. And the Government of India, not being in possession of the details, was unable to judge of the true requirements of each service. Being afraid of failure of its responsibility as much by too little trust as by too much trust in the estimates sent to it, it was often obliged to submit to extravagance of the Provinces, which as we saw brought on the crisis of 1859. To avoid this fatality there was instituted the system of Provincial Finance under which the Government of India distributed its funds among the Provinces, and the Provinces in their turn undertook to manage *some* of the services which they administered for the Government of India *within* the sum which came to them severally out of this distribution.

This being the nature of the financial relationship, the criticisms of the system of Provincial Finance on the ground of inequity were quite inapplicable. Contributions must be according to ability, but distribution must be according to needs in order to make it equitable. If the system of Provincial Finance was to be impeached on the ground of inequity, then it was necessary to have shown that the distribution was unfair. Even here it may perhaps be shown that the different Provinces got different amounts if measured by their population or their area. But it must be remembered that the distribution was not primarily among the Provinces, but among the various departments, whether controlled by the Government of India or by the Provincial Governments. This could make a considerable difference in the equity of the distribution; for, the needs of the areas within the jurisdiction of the different administrative polities must be very different and cannot certainly be held to be coterminous with the needs of the departments maintained under them. The distribution of funds by the Government of India was not based upon the principle of each Province according to its needs but upon the principle of each department according to its needs. It was therefore futile to criticize the equity of the system on any other principle.

Thus interpreted, the system of Provincial Finance must strike as of the nature of what may be called Departmental Finance, something quite different from Decentralized Finance or Federal Finance. This view cannot be far wrong from the true view as supported by the facts of the case. As in the case of Departmental Finance every Department of the State has a certain grant fixed for it in the Budget and it then draws upon the Treasury to the extent of the grant. In the same manner Provincial Governments were given a certain consolidated grant for the departments they managed and for the expense of which they were to draw upon the Imperial Treasury to the extent of the grant. Notwithstanding Provincial Finance, nothing was provincial in its status. The revenues, the services, the Civil Service, were as strictly Imperial in status after 1870, when Provincial Finance came into being, as they were before 1870, when there was no such thing as Provincial Finance in existence. It is therefore no exaggeration to say that Provincial Finance, instead of being an independent system of Finance involving freedom to tax and freedom to spend, was only a matter of accounts, the operations on the debit and credit side of which were subject to stringent control on the part of the Government of India.

This means that there was no change in the nature of the financial relationship between the Central and Provincial Governments as a result of the introduction of the scheme of Provincial Finance. The relationship of aggregation of sources and distribution of the yield was not a new one but was as old as 1833. It was a financial counterpart of the Imperial system then established. It was because there was no alteration in the relationship that Provincial Governments, even with Provincial Finance, far from becoming separate clocks, each with its own mainsprings in itself, remained as before the departments of the Government of India. Such a conclusion is bound to be regarded as somewhat of a startling character. There can, however, be no doubt that it is true and that no other conclusion is possible, given the legal relationship of the Provincial and Central Governments in British India. But if Provincial Finance is only a matter of accounts then, were there no changes that followed in its wake, in the financial organization of the Imperial system? It would be idle to deny that any change took place in the financial organization of Imperial system owing to the introduction of the scheme of Provincial Finance, and equally idle to assert that some fundamental change had taken place in consequence thereof. To be just, only two changes worth speaking of may be said to have resulted from the introduction of Provincial Finance:—

(1) Before 1870 balances on *all* services lapsed to the Government of India at the close of the financial year. After 1870 all unspent balances on the services delegated to the management of Provincial Governments remained at their disposal and formed a part of their resources for the ensuing year.

(2) Before 1870 Budget estimates on all services had to be sanctioned by the Government of India and the Provinces could not undertake any reappropriations between the different grants for the year, even if it was found necessary, without the previous sanction of the Government of India. After 1870 the Provinces were left to a greater extent free to distribute their expenditure in any way they thought proper among the various services delegated to their management, provided their total expenditure did not exceed the funds lying in the Imperial treasury to their credit respectively.[1] But by the rules they were required to maintain

[1] Whether they could materially alter the distribution of the grants on the different services delegated to them is doubtful. In his despatch No. 30, dated December 10, 1874, in the Revenue Department, on a proposal by the late Lord Hobart, Governor of Madras, to discontinue the grant made from provincial funds for Roads and to devote the money to education, the Secretary of State wrote: "I am unable to reconcile it with the principles which govern the so-called provincial administration of the revenue. I am not, indeed, of opinion that the same relative proportion which existed, on the introduction of the system, between the services made over and the expenditure upon them, should always be main-

all the services under their management in a state of administrative efficiency. Similarly after 1870 the Provincial Government had complete freedom which they never enjoyed before to carry on reappropriations between the grants under their management without the sanction of the Government of India, provided their total expenditure did not exceed the amount budgeted for the year.

For the purposes of visualization the financial relationship between the Provinces and the Government of India may be likened to the Hindu Joint Family System with the Patria Potestas vested in the latter. Before 1870 the similarity between the two was more or less exact. Like the family property of the Hindus the revenues of India were jointly enjoyed by all the departments whether under Central or Provincial management without metes and bounds being fixed to the shares of any one of them. After 1870 the only change that took place consisted in the cesser of commensality and the fixing of metes and bounds to the shares of each in the common property according to their respective needs. The system remained a joint family system, although separate accounts were opened by the head of the family, namely the Government of India, to guard against any member overdrawing the amount placed to his credit.

Were these results worth striving for? On the results achieved in consequence of Provincial Finance a variety of opinion has been expressed. But if we judge of the results as we ought to in the light of the antecedents that gave rise to the system in 1870, it cannot be said that the hopes entertained were in any way belied. It is only when critics,

tained. But I agree with Mr. Sim, that there was an implied engagement to maintain all these departments in full efficiency and integrity and an implied understanding that no one of them should be wholly sacrificed to the others, or to any other. The new financial arrangements in question were most fully discussed, both by the various Indian Governments as constituted at the time, and by the Home Government. During this discussion it was certainly never suggested that an effect of the change might be to put a stop to the construction of new roads in some parts of India; if such an eventuality had been considered probable, I doubt whether the change would have been made."

solely because of their misunderstanding of the nature of Provincial Finance, sought for results which were never intended by its promotors that an adverse pronouncement came to be made. But if we keep clear of these misunderstandings and never lose sight of the fact that in 1870 what the Provinces wanted was freedom and the Government of India stability, none can assert that this compromise between Imperialism and Federalism was tried in vain. How great was the freedom gained by the provinces can be appreciated only when it is realized that before 1870 the Governor of Bengal could make

> "no alteration in the allowances of the public servants . . . establish a new school or augment the pay of a daroga (watchman) to the extent of a Rupee," [1]

nor could the Governor of Bombay have a lock made [2] without a vote of the Council of India. Nor can the importance of the large measure of stability derived from it be fully realized unless it is borne in mind how before 1870 the Government of India was left between the devil and the deep sea by having to refuse or to accept the bewildering demands ranging from dustbins for a Department to education for the people made by the Provinces on its not too large resources. The Provincial Governments had been saved the delay and the indignity in having to depend upon the Government of India for sanction of the meanest of their wants. The Imperial Government on the other hand was saved the fumbling task of scrutinizing the most trivial of demands and grant or reject it, but always under the apprehension of having done wrong by acting either way. The system not only gave freedom to the Provinces and stability to the Government of India, but had replaced the irresponsibility and extravagance which had proved the bane of the Imperial System by economy and responsibility, for by setting bounds to the funds of the Provincial Governments the Government of India had ended in setting bounds

[1] *Calcutta Review*, Vol. 3, p. 169.

[2] Report of the Committee on the Affairs of the East India Co., 1852, Vol. 10.

to itself. These results, it is true, did not satisfy the critics of Provincial Finance. More in other directions was expected of it, but that could have been possible only if Provincial Finance was a system independent in its organization. So long as Provincial Finance was a part of Imperial Finance, inseparably linked to it, it could have yielded no greater results than have followed from it, and those that have followed are by no means slight.

There, however, remains the question that, although it was not possible to alter the nature of Provincial Finance, whether it would not have been feasible to enlarge its scope by relaxing the limitations imposed upon it by the Government of India without in any way interfering with the due discharge by it of its own responsibilities. That aspect of the question will be examined in the next chapter.

CHAPTER IX

THE ENLARGEMENT OF THE SCOPE OF PROVINCIAL FINANCE

It used to be made a matter of complaint that the system of Provincial Finance was unjust in that under it the Government of India conscripted, at every revision of the financial settlement, the increases in the revenues given over to the management of the Provinces, either for its own benefit on the pretext of meeting the requirements of the Central Exchequer or for the benefit of such of the Provinces as had by inertia not cared to improve their resources on the pretext of tempering the wind to the shorn lamb. There was a good deal of truth in this complaint in the early period of Provincial Finance. Being the custodian of the funds, the Government of India did often put the consideration of Imperial Services above that for the Provincialized Services. In the early period of Provincial Finance the prevailing idea [1] in the distribution of funds was not how much of the revenues assigned under the expiring settlement could be continued to be usefully spent on heads of expenditure controlled by Provincial Governments, but how much of the general revenues consistently with its obligations, and having regard to the growth of demands upon its resources during the currency of the settlement, could the Government of India surrender for a further period to the Provincial Governments in order to enable them to meet whatever expenditure was essential to the conduct of their administration. This attitude of the Government of India, justifiable as it was by the financial

[1] Finance Department Resolution No. 458 of January 28, 1881.

stringency of the period, changed as the financial condition became easy, so that in the latter period

> "the distribution of revenues between the Provincial and Central Governments was made, except on occasions of grave emergency, with direct reference not to the needs of the Central Government, but to the outlay which each Province might reasonably claim to incur upon the services which it administered. The first step taken in concluding a settlement was to ascertain the needs of the Province and assign revenue to meet them; the residue only of the income of the Province coming into the Imperial Exchequer." [1]

With the shifting of emphasis on the competing needs of the Central and Provincial Governments the complaints on the score of unfair distribution of funds ceased, and no fear of an adverse revision remained when the settlements were declared permanent. There, however, remained the other main objection to the system of Provincial Finance, namely, that the limitations imposed upon it tended to reduce the Provincial Government to a nonentity by restricting the scope of their activity within the field allotted to it.

It was said that if the system of Provincial Finance was inaugurated on the understanding by which the Government of India said to the Provinces

> "Take what we are able to give you, and for the residue take certain powers of taxation and raise it yourself . . . for there are subjects which can be dealt with far better by local than by imperial taxation,"

there was no reason why the Provinces should not have been allowed the freedom to tax. Again, if certain resources had been made over to the Provinces, what justification was there in not allowing them to raise loans for promoting purposes of local utility? This restriction was particularly resented; for, it was pointed out that even the humblest Local Authority in India enjoyed the power to raise loans to effect improvements in its respective

[1] Finance Department Resolution No. 27 dated May 18, 1912.

jurisdiction, while such an important polity as a Provincial Government was deemed unworthy of shouldering such a responsibility. Indeed it was felt as a most galling restriction, for under it it happened that a Provincial Government which was deemed to have enough credit to be accepted as security by the Government of India against loans to other local bodies subordinate to it, was ruled to have no credit to pledge in its own behalf!

What, again, was the justification for limitations on the spending powers of the Provincial Governments in the matter of staff and establishments? If the administration of certain services had been entrusted to the Provincial Governments, why should they have been circumscribed in the matter of creating new or abolishing old appointments or revising the establishments of their departments? If under the system of Provincial Finance the Provinces were responsible for the services they managed, why should they not have been trusted with powers to make needful changes in the agencies which carried out those services?

Further, it was asked, what justification was there for the limitations on the preparation and execution of the Provincial Budgets? If separate Budgets had been carved for each of the Provinces out of what once formed an Imperial Budget for the whole of India, why should the Provinces have been required to submit their Budgets to the Government of India? Merely as a matter of conveying information the requirement was comparatively of a trifling character. But why should the Government of India have claimed to alter their estimates and compel them to abide by the grants as fixed by it? Was such a scrutiny of Provincial Budgets a cover for dictating a policy to the Provincial Governments? If this was so, what was the scope for initiative and freedom left to the Provinces which it was the primary object of Provincial Finance to promote and of the permanent settlements to ensure? Again, why should a Provincial Government have been required to come to the Government of India for a supplementary grant as it had to do where the excess over estimates could not be met by reappropriations, even when it had balances to its credit so sufficient as not to be reduced below the required minimum by a draft to meet the excess?

For each of these limitations which fettered the Provincial Governments and contracted the scope of Provincial Finance, the Government of India was of course ready with abundant excuses.[1] In the matter of revenue restrictions it urged that the revenues of India were its constitutional possession for the proper disposal of which it was responsible to the Secretary of State and Parliament. That being the case it was fair that the Government of India should require that the sources assigned to the Provinces should not be alienated nor spent on unauthorized grants or unapproved services. Again, being responsible for all services it followed that the Government of India could not have afforded to weaken its position as to managing the resources of the country by partitioning the taxing or borrowing powers. The field for taxation in India being considerably limited, an indiscriminate levy of taxes by a competing authority, it was feared, would have led either to discontent by additions [2] to the Imperial imposts or to a retrenchment of the field for imperial taxation. The concentration of borrowing powers in its hands, the Government of India urged, was a natural corollary of the statutory hypothecation of all-India revenues to all-India needs. The Government of India could not allow its revenues to be mortgaged by a Provincial Government for its own needs. Besides it was afraid [3] that if this freedom to borrow were granted

"the temptation to hypothecate revenues in advance might become inconveniently strong, and the future administration of a Province might be starved because a former Government had been in a hurry to proceed with some costly ambitions and non-productive project."

[1] In this connection, cf. Evidence of Mr. J. S. Meston before the Royal Commission on Decentralization. Mit. of Evid., Vol. X, Q. 44807–45336.

[2] Between 1870 and 1879, when the Provinces had a freer hand in the matter of local taxation, all of them selected the already overburdened basis of taxation, viz. land for their levy.

[3] *R.C.D.*, Mit. of Evid., Vol. X, Q. 45310.

Moreover, the loan market in India, it was said, was as limited as the taxable capacity of the country. Therefore

"if many buckets are dipping into one well and drought cuts short the supply of water, obviously the chief proprietor of the well must take it upon himself to regulate the drawings." [1]

In the matter of specific restrictions on spending powers with respect to staff and establishments, the defence of the Government of India was that such restrictions were necessary in the interest of uniformity and economy. It was urged that if each Province was allowed the freedom to regulate the remuneration of the Public Service which carried on the actual work of administration the result would probably have been unequal pay for equal work. Such a consequence would have engendered discontent in the servants of the State which it was desirable to prevent in the interest of good administration. Again, if the Provinces had been given full freedom to revise establishments it might have resulted in considerable additions to the recurring expenditure of the Provinces, thereby jeopardizing the stability of the Provincial as well as of the Imperial finance, for in the last resort the Government of India was responsible for maintaining the Provincial Governments.

In the matter of control over the preparation and execution of Provincial Budgets the Government of India urged that the scrutiny was not motivated by a desire to control an unwelcome policy,[2] but was inevitable because of the three important ties by which the Provincial Budgets were bound up with the Budget of the Government of India. These were (1) the incorporation of the income and expenditure of the Provincial Governments into the Budget and the Annual Accounts of the Government of India as an integral part thereof; (2) the system of divided heads of revenue and expenditure, and (3) a common treasury involving

[1] Report on Indian Constitutional Reforms, Cd. 9109 of 1918, p. 94, herafter called Joint Report.

[2] *R.C.D.*, Mit. of Evid., Vol. X, Q. 44981.

a combined "ways and means" for the transaction of the Central and Provincial Governments. The first two points of inter-relation required that the Government of India should examine the Budget Estimates of the Provincial Governments. It was urged [1] that the power to make such alterations was rendered specially necessary by the inveterate tendency of Local Governments to over-estimate their expenditure and under-estimate their revenue. Estimates which departed widely from actuals meant bad finance and also a provision of larger ways and means for the working of the Treasury. But even if this tendency was absent it was incumbent on the Government of India to scrutinize the Provincial Estimates in order to preserve accuracy in the combined accounts. Besides the interests of accuracy, the Government of India had to ascertain by a scrutiny of their estimates that a Province did not impair the stability of its finances by (1) including in its budget expenditure on schemes which had not received due administrative sanction, or was not likely to receive such sanction in time to be incurred during the year; or (2) by entering on an enhanced scale of expenditure a Province was not unduly depleting its balances. But by far the strongest reason why the Government of India needed to scrutinize the Provincial Estimates consisted in the fact that in so far as some of the Heads of Accounts were shared, the ultimate result of the Central Budget, whether there was to be a surplus or deficit, depended upon the accuracy of the estimates. The Government of India, it was urged, was thus directly interested in the Provincial Budgets, and could not have abandoned its right to scrutinize them without exposing its budgetary system to serious derangement. The third point of inter-relationship necessitated that the Provincial Governments should work within the grants as fixed finally by the Government of India. To have allowed the Provincial Governments the liberty to exceed the grants because they had ample balances to their credit would have been incompatible [2] with the responsibility of the Imperial Government to provide the ways and means

[1] *R.C.D.*, Mit. of Evid., Vol. X, Q. 44863. [2] *Ibid.*, Q. 44865.

for the whole administration of the country. A provincial balance, it was pointed out, was not a separate balance locked up in a separate provincial chest. It was a part of the general balances on which the Government of India operated daily. If a sudden demand uncontemplated in the Budget were to be made upon these balances, as would have been the case if the Provincial Governments had exceeded their budget grants, it would have disturbed the ways and means transaction and would have involved the Government into insolvency by causing insufficiency of cash.

All these defences of the restrictions on Provincial Governments were plausible defences and could have been decisive if the centralized system of administration in favour of which they were urged could be deemed to have satisfied the ends of good government. But it was not unreasonable to argue as was done by the Provincial Governments [1] that modern tendencies were all moving in the direction of forms of government which placed fullest powers as low down in the administrative scale (i.e. as near the section of population immediately affected) as could be safely arranged. It is reasonable to centralize such powers as could not be efficiently exercised otherwise. But it is equally unreasonable to centralize powers where central control or uniformity is not clearly essential or is impracticable. By centralization all progress tends to be retarded, all initiative liable to be checked and the sense of responsibility of Local Authorities greatly impaired. Besides, centralization involves and must involve a serious sacrifice of elasticity, for it is naturally disagreeable to a central department to have to deal with half a dozen different ways of managing the same branch of administration, and which therefore aims at reducing all types to one. Further centralization conflicts with what may be regarded as a cardinal principle of good government, namely, that when administrative business reached an authority fully compe-

[1] In this connection see the very trenchant memorandum by the Government of Bombay on Decentralization, *R.C.D.*, Mit. of Evid., Vol. VIII, Appendix II.

tent to deal with it, that authority should deal with it finally. Even when there is a higher authority equally competent, to pass the business on to it would at best help to transfer power to the hands of the lower ranks of the official hierarchy, by causing congestion of business in the Central Department. Thus centralization, unless greatly circumscribed, must lead to inefficiency. This was sure to occur even in homogeneous states, and above all in a country like India where there are to be found more diversities of race, language, religion, customs and economic conditions than in the whole continent of Europe. In such circumstances there must come a point at which the higher authority must be less competent than the lower, because it cannot by any possibility possess the requisite knowledge of all local conditions. It was therefore obvious that a Central Government for the whole of India could not be said to possess knowledge and experience of all various conditions prevailing in the different Provinces under it. It, therefore, necessarily became an authority less competent [1] to deal with matters of provincial administration than the Provincial Governments, the members of which could not be said to be markedly inferior, and must generally be equal in ability to those of the Central Government, while necessarily superior as a body in point of knowledge.

To these arguments the only reply the Government of India could make was that it concentrated all power in its hands, not from principle but from necessity. That necessarily arose out of its constitutional obligations. The law had invested it with the superintendence, direction, and

[1] In this connection if may be of interest to draw attention to the semi-serious suggestion made by Mr. A. C. Logan, in which he argued that if decentralization "cannot be effected, then there is an alternative method of so remodelling the constitution of the Government of India as to replace the present departments by departments of various local areas each with its own Secretary and Member; thus there should be a department of Bombay with Secretary and Member appointed from that Province dealing with all Bombay questions and the like for other (six) provinces. Thus each Province could govern itself from Calcutta under the supervision of the Governor General,"—*Vide R.C.D.*, Mit. of Evid., Vol. VIII, Q. 35531.

control of the civil and military government and the ordering and management of the revenues of the country. It could not therefore relax its control over the powers it had delegated to the Provincial Governments. It was, of course, impossible to deny the force of this argument. So long as the Government of India remained the authority solely responsible to Parliament it was reasonable to hold that it should be the controlling authority in all matters pertaining to the administration of the country. But it was equally reasonable to ask whether it would not have been possible in the interests of cordiality between the Central and Provincial Governments to have relaxed such of the restrictions on the financial powers of the Provinces as would not have been incompatible with the due discharge by the former of its own responsibilities. That it was possible so to enlarge the scope of Provincial Finance by a relaxation of the limitations without injury to the position of the Government of India must be said to be evident from the following analysis of the suggestions made by the Provincial Governments. These suggestions were:

(i) Power of taxation and borrowing on the security of Provincial Revenues.

(ii) Power of sanctioning expenditure on Staff and Establishments up to a limit higher than that allowed by the Government of India.

(iii) Separation of Provincial Estimates from the Imperial Budget and Accounts.

(iv) Abolition of the system of divided heads of revenue and expenditure and the replacement of it by a system of separation of sources and contributions from the yield.

(v) Power to spend part of their balances up to a defined amount, without the previous sanction of the Government of India in meeting an excess of expenditure over Budget Estimates.

What objections were there, from the standpoint of the constitutional responsibilities of the Government of India, to the grant of these demands? Clearly it was possible for the Government of India to have marked off certain sources of taxation best suited for provincial levy and unconnected with the imperial imposts. Similarly it was possible to have permitted the Provincial Governments to borrow to a limited extent on the security of the revenues assigned to them. To suggest, as did the Government of India, that the Provincial Governments would abuse these powers to the extent of causing discontent or jeopardizing the stability of their financial system, was to believe that such legally recognized polities as the Provincial Governments were run by incompetent administrators unmindful of their obligations. The second demand could have been granted with greater ease. It is to be noted that the Civil Service of the country which deals with revenue and general administration has been divided into

(i) The "Indian Civil Service" recruited in England by competitive examination, at which natives of India, like other subjects of His Majesty, can compete; and

(ii) The "Provincial" and "Subordinate" Civil Services, recruited in India, and, as a rule, only open to persons who are natives of the country or domiciled therein.

Each Province has had its own separate "Provincial" and "Subordinate" Services, but while it has a free hand in recruiting for the latter, appointments to the former have been regulated by rules laid down by the Government of India. That being the case it would have been only logical that the Government which had the power of recruiting for an appointment should also have the power of regulating the salary. There can be no reason why the salaries of posts of similar grades should be equal in all Provinces; nor can they be equal having regard to the differences in the economic conditions of the Provinces. A Local Government knows better the economic value of a local man, and should therefore have been trusted with powers up to a limit covered by the Provincial and Subordinate Services. The suggestion of the Government of India that the grant of such powers would have resulted in heavy additions to the recurring expenditure of a Province must be said to be too ungracious to be taken seriously.

The acceptance of the third recommendation could not have in any conceivable way affected the responsibility of the Government of India. The only objection which the Government of India urged was that such a separation would have been unwise. To have published accounts or estimates of the Imperial Government which excluded the accounts of the Provincial Governments, when the items excluded covered such a large magnitude, would have misled the public and rendered a wholly incomplete idea of the financial position of the Government of India.[1] Now it must be granted that if such a separation of accounts could have avoided the scrutiny and the consequent restraint on budget-making by the Provinces, not to have done so was to have put the supposed convenience of the student of Accounts above the administrative convenience of the Provincial Governments. Besides, it is to be pointed out that the suggestion was not a novel one. It was only a revival of the old practice which obtained between 1871 and 1877. During that period of financial decentralization Provincial figures did not appear in the Imperial Budget. The Provincial Budget as framed by the Accountant General was passed by the Provincial Government and no more reference was required to the Government of India except to inform it that the estimate was a probable one and that it was within the limits of the revenues assigned to the Province. It is therefore obvious that there could not have been any constitutional objection to the granting of the demand for a separation of accounts.

The fourth recommendation was of the same class as the third, in that it too could not be said to have involved any infringement of the constitutional responsibilities of the Government of India. The abolition of the divided heads of revenue would have clearly eliminated the interference of the Government of India in the preparation of the Budget Estimates by the Provinces. Similarly the abolition of the divided heads of expenditure would have

[1] *R.C.D.*, Mit. of Evid., Vol. X, Q. 44866, 45179–180.

given the Provinces greater [1] freedom in the matter of spending the revenues assigned to them. Under that system a Provincial Government could not spend more on a particular service if it was a divided head unless the Government of India consented to increase its figure for expenditure under that service. If the Government of India reduced its figure the Provincial Government was perforce obliged to reduce its own. The substitution of a system of separation of sources and contributions from the yield for the system of divided heads would have clearly resulted in a greater freedom to the Provincial Governments, without any evil consequence to the Government of India. The objections which the Government of India was able to oppose to this demand was far from convincing. It was urged [2] that the Provincial Governments under complete separation may cease to take such interest as it took in respect of revenues which were divided. But it is evidently a mistaken view that a Provincial Government could not have been trusted to administer a tax efficiently unless it had a financial interest in the result. This view supposed that the people engaged in the collection of revenue really knew whether it went to the Imperial or the Provincial credit. As a matter of fact the ultimate credit could in no way have affected the collection of the revenue. And even if that view were true the difficulty could easily have been met by each government having its own staff to collect its own revenues. The employing by one Government to execute its functions the agencies of another, as has been the case in India, is obviously a complicated and awkward system. If separation of agencies had resulted from the separation of sources it would have been a reform all to the good. Besides it was overlooked that the fact that the divided heads gave a personal interest to the Provincial Governments was indeed a point against the system rather than in favour of it. A system which created a vested interest in a revenue apart from the interest of the public was a bad system, for such an interest was sure to lead to

[1] *R.C.D.*, Mit. of Evid., Vol. VIII, Q. 35225-28.
[2] *Ibid.*, Vol. IV, Q. 15100, 16791.

harshness and rigidity in collection.[1] As an instance of this may be cited the notorious unwillingness of Provincial Governments in the matter of remitting taxation.[2] If humanizing the Provincial Governments was a desirable end, then the abolition of divided heads was a good means. The other objection which the Government of India was able to oppose was that such a change would have given the share of the Government of India from the revenues raised in the Provinces the character of a tribute, and the Government of India would have appeared to be the pensioner of the Provincial Governments, depending upon them rather than controlling them. This objection must be ruled out as being sentimental.

The fifth and the last suggestion for the enlargement of the scope of Provincial Finance was least obnoxious to the responsibility of the Government of India. There is no reason why there should have been a single-treasury system for both the Governments, Provincial and Central. It is true that a common treasury permits a high state of economy in the cash balances of the country, which it is the duty of every Government to effect, just as any business firm looks upon it as its duty to economize its till money or floating cash. But if a common treasury hindered the use of the balances the gain in freedom would have more than compensated the loss involved by the increase in the cash balances that would have followed the institution of separate treasuries and separate ways and means. But the demand of the Provincial Governments did not ask for a complete separation of Provincial balances from the balances of the Central Government involving separate treasury system and separate ways and means, probably because they anticipated that as such a proposal meant separate possession of provincial revenues the Government of India would raise a constitutional objection to such a demand. All they asked for was a power to spend part of their balances up to a defined amount without reference to the Government of

[1] Cf. in this connection *The Fee System*, by Prof. Urdhal.

[2] *R.C.D.*, Mit of Evid., Vol. X, Q. 44866.

India. The suggestion was accepted [1] as "reasonable," for its consequences, provided it was not a big amount, would have been not a deprivation of the Government of India's power of control over nor a disturbance in the ways and means, but only a slight increase in the cash balances of the country.

Thus it is clear that the scope of Provincial Finance was unduly restricted by a too narrow and too legalistic an interpretation of the constitutional obligations of the Government of India. From the above analysis of the suggestions made by the Provincial Governments it is clear that without making any breach in the constitutional position of the Government of India it would have been possible, with a more charitable view of their sense of responsibility, to effect the changes they desired. Such concessions would have made Provincial Finance as self-sufficient and as autonomous as it was capable of being made. The system would no doubt have rested on pure convention: none the less its benefits would have been as real as though it was based on law.

But the time had arrived when the financial arrangements could no longer be looked upon as a matter which concerned the Central and Provincial Governments. There arose a third party whose counsels were rejected in 1870, but which now insisted on having a voice in the disposition of the financial resources of the country. It was the Indian taxpayer, and his clamour had grown so strong that it compelled the powers that be to alter the system so as to permit him to take the part he claimed to play.

The changes that followed upon this event will form the subject-matter of Part IV.

[1] *R.C.D.*, Mit. of Evid., Vol. X, Q. 44900.

PART IV

PROVINCIAL FINANCE UNDER THE GOVERNMENT OF INDIA ACT OF 1919

CHAPTER X

THE NECESSITY FOR A CHANGE

As two types of governmental systems, the Presidential and Parliamentary are often contrasted [1] to the advantage of the latter. For the Parliamentary type of government it has been claimed [2] that no other arrangement seems able quite so effectively to place the centre of authority under the control of those who are supposed to represent the popular will: that it means government by consent: that it ensures the exercise of the functions of government by a body of persons who are amenable to and whose views are in accord with those of the majority of the Legislature: that it is the only form of government which provides for a powerful Executive so very necessary for a stable government without rendering it so irresponsible as to endanger the essentials of a good government: that it throws upon the holders of high office the onus of vindicating their acts or, failing, suffer dismissal: it renders the Legislature supreme both in legislation and administration so that it forms a government not only to make life possible but also to make life good. No other form of government, it is urged, can so effectively prevent order degenerating into tyranny or progress blocked in the name of peace. So eminently has

[1] Cf. James Bryce, *The American Commonwealth*, 1910, Vol. I, Chap. XX.

[2] Cf. Sir Sidney Low, *The Governance of England*, 1914, Ch. III, *passim*.

Parliamentary Government demonstrated its supreme virtue in securing orderly progress that, though originally developed as an accident in the evolution of the British Constitution, it has been most eagerly adopted as the most fundamental institution by many countries whose political convulsions have required them to prepare anew or alter the existing framework of their governmental systems.

If the fact of the Executive being a part of the Legislature be a sufficient indication of the Parliamentary type of government, then the system of government in India since 1853 may be said to be analogous to the Parliamentary system. Indeed it would hardly be possible to deny this characteristic to the Indian constitution, for the provision of the constitutional law has since then been that the additional (i.e. the Legislative) members *and* the ordinary (i.e. the Executive) members shall *together* form the Legislature for the making of the laws and regulation for the peace, order and good government of British India.[1] But judged in the light of its *de facto* consequences the Indian system falls lamentably below the *de jure* connotation of the class of governmental systems to which it belonged. If in other countries the record of Parliamentary government is one of submission of the Executive to the Legislature, in India it had been one of the Executive thwarting, often of flouting, the Legislature. In vain may one search the proceedings of the Legislature to find the Executive ever paying deference to the wishes of the people.[2] Reforms have been inces-

[1] Cf. the important note by that eminent lawyer Sir Bhashyam Iyengar on the Reform proposals of Lord Minto in 1908.

[2] The following table from N. C. Kelkar's *The Case for Indian Home Rule*, p. 81, is illustrative of the fact :—

Legislative Council.	No of Resolutions moved	No of Resolutions withdrawn	No of Resolutions rejected.	No of Resolutions accepted
Supreme . .	3	2	1	0
Madras .	32	26	6	0
Bengal . .	38	26	12	0
U.P.	22	10	12	0
Bihar and Orissa	5	5	0	0
C.P. . . .	4	2	2	0

santly, asked for by the Legislature only to be denied with equal tenacity by the Executive.

The reason why the Indian Parliamentary system was but an empty form is to be found in the fact that it was a Parliamentary system without a Parliamentary Executive. In other words, the Executive under the system was not responsible to the Legislature and was not removable by it. The Indian Legislature could neither make nor unmake the Indian Executive. The Indian Executive made peace or war as it liked without being afraid of dismissal by the Legislature. It taxed as it pleased and spent as it liked, without the slightest compunction as to the wishes of the Legislature. It undertook acts or refused to undertake them according to its own sweet will, but had no fear of a vote of censure from the Legislature. The nearest approach to the Indian system of Parliamentary Government is to be found in the position of the Irish Parliament which existed from 1782 to 1800. The peculiarity of the case lay mainly in the fact that while this Irish Parliament, commonly known as Grattan's Parliament, was during the period it lasted admittedly a sovereign Legislature, the Irish Executive of the time was as regards the Irish Parliament in no sense a Parliamentary Executive. The Irish Executive, instead of being appointed and dismissed by the Irish Legislature, was in reality appointed and dismissed by the Crown on the advice of the English Ministry. In the same manner the Indian Executive was appointed and dismissed by the Crown on the advice of the Secretary of State for India who is a member of the English Ministry and was in no way responsible to the Indian Legislature.

It is true that the Executive in India was ultimately responsible to the Secretary of State for India and through him to the British Parliament. But it must not be forgotten, said Mr. Fisher,[1] that

"the affairs of India are in the hands of the Government of India . . . Proposals may come from the Indian Govern-

[1] Fisher, H. A. L., on Imperial Administration in his *The Empire and the Future*, 1916, p. 58.

ment to London and be vetoed by the Imperial Government. The large lines of Indian policy may be shaped by a Secretary of State in the India Office, and a powerful Secretary of State may make his influence felt strongly on the direction of Indian affairs if he encounters no serious opposition from the Government of India. But in reality the last word lies with the Indian official opinion (i.e. the Executive in India), that a measure would not be forced upon India against the united opposition of the Indian bureaucracy."

As a matter of fact neither was the Secretary, though all-powerful in Indian affairs, inclined to restrain the Executive in India from doing what the people regarded as evil nor to constrain it to do what he thought to be for the good of the people.[1] Hardly can it be said that the British Parliament, wherein every member has been supposed to be a member for India, has made the acts of the Indian Executive a matter of anxious scrutiny.[2] On the other hand, its inter-

[1] The only two cases in which the Secretary of State is known to have run counter to the wishes of the Executive in India were those concerning the Punjab Drainage and Canal Act and the Indian Tariff Act of 1875. The latter was obviously detrimental to the interests of India.

[2] The salary of the Secretary of State for India being paid out of the revenues of India, Parliament had no occasion, as it had in the case of the Colonial Secretary, to annually review his actions in the full activity of the Parliamentary Session. At the end, generally after the Appropriation Bill had been read a second time, the Indian Budget used to be submitted to Parliament which, after a somewhat desultory discussion, used to pass a Resolution proclaiming in solemn terms that the Indian Accounts show certain totals of income and expenditure! Many attempts were made to improve the control of Parliament on Indian affairs. But Parliament never cared to increase its control. In 1873 Mr. R. N. Fowler moved "that in the opinion of this House it is desirable that the Statement of the financial affairs of India should be made at a period of the Sessions when it can be fully discussed." Again in 1883 the same motion was brought forward by Mr. Fowler. Both of those attempts to furnish the House with a better opportunity to review Indian affairs fell to the ground. In 1899 the same Resolution was moved by Mr. Cladwell, M.P., with the addition that the Salary of the Secretary of State for India be placed on the British Estimates. It was opposed by Mr. Fowler, who was then the Secretary of State for India, and was in consequence lost. By the provision of the Government of India Act of 1919 the House has a better opportunity to criticize Indian affairs owing to the salary of the Secretary of State having been placed on the British Estimates.

ference in Indian affairs has on some occasion been positively harmful to the interests of the Indian people.[1] Indeed, there can be no doubt that the interest of Parliament in Indian affairs since the assumption of the Government of the country by the Crown instead of increasing has considerably diminished as compared with the interest it took when the affairs of the country were in charge of the Company.[2] Nay, the influence of the British Parliament over Indian affairs, it may be said, has undergone a decided change for the worse,[3] inasmuch as all its influence is exerted to strengthen the Executive in India against popular clamour rather than restraining it from flying in the face of public opinion.

It is therefore evident that the control of the Secretary of State and of Parliament over the Executive in India was only a nominal control, and the Indian Executive was in reality an uncontrolled body of bureaucrats in the exclusive charge of Indian affairs. How was this trust discharged by this irresponsible Executive ?

The answer to this question may be summed up in the statement that the Indian Executive has sacrificed progress to order. Whether we examine its actions in the field of legislation or finance, the truth of this statement becomes painfully evident.

There are very few countries in the world where there may be said to prevail so many social evils as has been the case in India. Law is a means by which society from time to time repairs its ills in order to effect its conservation.

[1] Cf. the Resolutions of the House of Commons in 1877 and 1879 condemning the Indian Tariff policy in the interest of Lancashire.

[2] In support of this may be cited the fact that Parliament never granted a lease of power without making harassing inquiries into the affairs of the East India Company.

[3] Compare the Parliament which subjected the Indian Executive to the Judicature with the Parliament that has freed that Executive from Judicial and Legislative control. Compare the Parliament which laid stringent regulations on the Europeans in India with the Parliament which not only allowed them free ingress but kept them above the control of the Magistracy. Compare the Parliament which impeached Hastings with the Parliament which supported General Dyer.

But with very few exceptions[1] the rule of *personal* law of a most pernicious character has been allowed to govern the social relations of the citizens, notwithstanding the fact that enlightened public opinion has long since raised its voice of protest against its perpetuation.[2] So religious has been the regard of the Executive for the preservation of the personal law, notwithstanding the fact that it has disabled millions of its subjects from enjoying the most elementary rights of citizenship, that it has been careful not to allow in cases of conflict the rational provisions of the civil law to override or chasten the irrational rulings of that archaic code.[3] Judged by the modern standard of legislation the Executive must be pronounced to be extremely conservative. In the matter of securing economic rights its response was of a very halting character, and the legislation it has been persuaded to undertake for giving security or fixity of tenure to the agricultural[4] or ease and comfort to the industrial[5] population sank in comparison to what it refused to undertake for liberating the rest from a species of industrial slavery notwithstanding incessant demands for its abolition.[6]

[1] Bengal Regulation of 1829 prohibiting *Sati*; Act V of 1843 (prohibiting slavery); XXI of 1850 (*re* enacting Sec. of Reg. VII of 1832) prohibiting forfeiture of rights or property as a result of loss of caste or religion, XV of 1856 authorizing the remarriage of Hindu widows; XXI of 1866 enabling native Converts to Christianity to obtain divorce; XXVII of 1871 restricting unnatural practices; III of 1872 providing a form of marriage for all persons who are neither Christians, Jews, Hindus, Mahomedans, Jains, nor Sikhs.

[2] It was first accepted by Warren Hastings in 1772 and was embodied in the East India Company's Act of 1780 (21 Geo. III, c. 70, ss. 17 and 18); the provisions have been incorporated in later Statutes.

[3] Cf. the provisions in favour of the personal law in the Indian Succession Act X of 1865; the Transfer of Property Act IV of 1882, and the Indian Trust Act II of 1882.

[4] Cf. the Tenancy Acts of 1859, 1868, 1881 and 1885 in Bengal; Oudh Rent Act of 1868 in U.P.; the Deccan Agriculturists Relief Act of 1879 in Bombay, and the Central Provinces Tenancy Act of 1883.

[5] The Factory Acts did not begin in India till 1881. The Act of 1881 was amended in 1891 and replaced by another in 1911 which lays down the conditions governing factory labour in India.

[6] Students of Indian economic problems will perceive that the reference is to the scandalous system of indentured labour.

Its financial system was similarly characterized by the desire to preserve peace and order by taxing the masses and exempting the classes. It has been urged that the revenue system be so altered as to give relief to the poorer classes. Indirect taxes are justified as a method of making the poorer classes pay their share of the burden of the State without their being sensible of the fact. But there is a limiting principle which forbids the imposition of certain kinds of indirect taxes. It may be said to be agreed by students of public finance that indirect taxes be such that the poor on whom they impinge rather heavily relatively speaking, must be able to adjust the burden of such taxes to their means. When such indirect taxes fall on luxuries it is possible for them to apportion for themselves the burden they need must bear by regulating their purchases. But in those cases where they fall on necessaries of life this elasticity is not possible. The pernicious character of the salt tax in India was urged as a sufficient ground for its elimination from the revenue system of India. But not only did the Executive refuse to accept the demand, it actually increased the salt tax whenever a deficit has occurred instead of tapping some other source of revenue, which it could have done with equal ease and greater justice. In 1886, to cite one example, it was admitted [1] that

"There can, after all is said and done, be no manner of doubt, but that one great fact remains established, one great blot not only unremoved but aggravated by the course of events in recent years. . . . It is that . . . the classes in (India) which derive the greatest security and benefit from the British Government are those who contribute the least towards it."

But in the Budget of 1887–8 the Executive eschewed its own conviction and increased the salt duty to make up for the deficit caused not by any extraordinary measure of internal improvement but by an enormous act of external

[1] Cf. the speech by Sir A. Colvin on the License Tax Amendment Bill in the Supreme Legislative Council on January 4, 1886.

aggression, namely the conquest of Burma, as though the income tax of 1886 which left untouched the incomes of the Bengal zamindars, the Assam Tea planters and the Talukdars of Oudh, in making the richer classes pay, made them pay, at the very moderate rates it levied, all they could be made to pay.

But the salt tax is not the only instance of inequity under which the masses paid for the classes. The land revenue as it has been levied in India may be cited as another example of inequity in the Indian Tax System. The sources of inequity are various. There is first of all the glaring fact that in some cases the amount of the tax is permanently fixed, while in other cases the amount of the tax payable in respect of land revenue is periodically revised. Now there is no justifying circumstance why some citizens should be exempted from contributing their quota to the growing needs of the State when the same is rigorously exacted from their fellows. This is, however, only one point of injustice to those whose taxable capacity in respect of land revenue is subject to periodical revisions. There is another which consists in the adoption of a wrong measure of capacity to pay. The cardinal feature of this revisable part of the land tax in India is to be found in the basis of the tax which, as is well known to every student of Indian Finance, is a certain unit of land. Now nobody has ever suspected the pernicious effect of the system which bases the tax on a unit of land held ; but surely there can hardly be a system more mistaken in thought or more mischievous in practice. It ignores the commonplace of economists which asserts that taxes are paid not by things but by persons,[1] and if it is persons who ultimately pay the taxes then it is manifest that they must be required to contribute not according to the land they hold but in proportion to the total income derived. On the contrary the system, in undertaking to tax per unit of land, taxes the poor peasant with only one

[1] Cf. the criticism by Prof. Cannan on the Terms of Reference to the Royal Commission on Local Taxation in the Memoranda chiefly relating to the classification and incidence of Imperial and Local Taxation, C. 9528 of 1899, p. 160.

PERCENTAGE OF EXPENDITURE

(Excluding expenditure on commercial services, i.e., Post Office and Telegraph Dept., Railways and Irrigation).

In thousands of rupees.

Periods.	District Administration.	Forest.	Other Heads, including Opium.	Debt Sources.	Civil Depts	Civil Changes.	Civil Works.	Army (including Military Works and Special Defence Works).	Famine Relief and Insurance	Total
1877–78 to 1881–82	5 2	8	5 6	8 9	18·7	6 8	5 8	39 2	2 6	93 6
1882–83 to 1886–87	6 0	1·2	6 6	8·2	21·4	7·5	7 6	35 6	2·3	96 4
1887–88 to 1891–92	6 0	1 3	5 4	7 6	22 1	7·5	7·3	37·7	2 8	95 7
1892–93 to 1896–97	6·1	1 3	4 9	6 4	22 5	8 4	6·9	38 5	1·6	96 6
1897–98 to 1901–02	5·8	1 4	5 5	4·3	22 6	7 8	6 8	35·2	4·8	94 2
1902–03 to 1906–07	5 9	1 6	8·2	3 1	23 2	7·3	9	37·1	1·8	97 2
1907–08 to 1911–12	6·3	1·8	7·1	3·5	25·7	7·7	8 5	35 6	2·1	98 3
1912–13 to 1916–17	6 0	1 9	6 2	2 1	28 2	7·3	9 3	35·1	1·5	97 6

From the statistics of British India, Vol. II, Financial Statistics, 1920, p. 7.

acre to cultivate and the landlord owning hundreds of acres at a *uniform* rate without realizing that as the total incomes of the two must be vastly different this uniformity of taxation must produce a glaring inequity of treatment as between the rich and the poor.

If the revenue thus raised by sacrificing equity to the dictates of order had been spent on services promoting progress there would have been some compensation. But such was not the case.

All the revenue that was collected was spent on Services such as Police, Military and Administration which are calculated to maintain order. Such services as Education, State aid to industries, hardly found any place in the scheme of public expenditure as managed by this irresponsible Executive. But it may be asked as to why the Executive, sovereign as it was, should have stood for order and against progress? The answer is that an irresponsible government, however sovereign, is incapable of progress, for in the exercise of its sovereign powers it is hampered by two very serious limitations.[1] There is first of all the internal limitation which arises from the character, motives and interests of those who are in power. If the Sultan does not abolish Mahomedanism, Pope ban Catholicism, the Brahmin condemn caste, or the British Parliament declare the preservation of blue-eyed babies illegal, it is not because they *cannot* do things, but it is because they *will* not do these things. In the same way if the Executive in India did not do certain things most conducive to progress it was because by reason of its being impersonal[2] and also by reason

[1] For an illuminating discussion of this, cf. A. V. Dicey, *Law of the Constitution*, 1915, pp. 74–82.

[2] Impersonal because the higher and controlling grades of public services are devoid of Indian element. Although the eligibility of the natives of India for employment in public services was proclaimed as far back as 1833, the regulations made by the Secretary of State for admission to the Public Services in India has had the tendency to exclude them from the employment of the right granted to them by statute. Under the regulations made by the Secretary of State for War, candidates for Commission in the Army were to be of pure European descent and a similar regulation was adopted by the Admiralty for cadetship in the Navy, thereby excluding

of its character, motives and interests it could not sympathize with the living forces operating in the Indian Society, was not charged with its wants, its pains, its cravings and its desires, was inimical to its aspirations, did not advance Education, disfavoured Swadeshi or snapped at anything that smacked of nationalism, it was because all these things went against its grain. But an irresponsible government is powerless to do even such things as it may like to do. For its authority is limited by the possibility of external resistance. There are things which it would do but dare not do for the fear of provoking thereby resistance to its authority. Cæsar dare not subvert the worship of the Roman people, a modern parliament dare not tax the Colonies, however much they would. For the same reason the Government of India dared not abolish the caste system, prescribe monogamy, alter the laws of succession, legalize intermarriage or venture to tax the tea planters. Progress involves interference with the existing code of social life and interference is likely to cause resistance. None the less a government which is of the people and is not detached from them can venture on the path of progress, because it is in a position to know where obedience will end and resistance will begin. But the Indian Executive not being of the people could not feel the pulse of the people. The gist of the matter is that the irresponsible Executive which had been in power in India was paralysed between these two limitations on its authority and much of what went to make life good was held up. Part of the programme it would

Indians. As to the Civil Service the Statute (Government of India Act, 1858, s. 32) laid down that all "natural-born subjects" of the Crown be admitted for examination, thereby including the natives of India. But the ruling of the Secretary of State that that examination should be held only in London had indirectly debarred many natives of the country from benefiting themselves under the statute. Regulations for admission to other public services varied. For the Indian Medical Service, candidates were to be natural-born subjects of European or East Indian descent; for the Indian Police Service they were to be British subjects of European descent; for the Forest Service they were to be natural-born British subjects; for Public Works Department one-tenth might be natives of India who are British subjects.—Cf. in this connection Halsbury, *Laws of England*, Vol. X, pp. 588–9.

not undertake and the other part it could not undertake. As a result of this, so far as the moral and social life of the people was concerned, the change of government by the Moghuls to a government by the British was only a change of rulers rather than a change of system. Owing to the adoption of the principle of non-interference partly by preference and partly by necessity by the British

> " the natives of India found themselves under a government distinguished in no vital respect from those under which they had toiled and worshipped, lived and died through all their weary and forgotten history. From a political standpoint, the change was but the replacement of one despotism by another. It accepted the arrangements as it found them [1] and preserved them faithfully in the manner of the Chinese tailor who, when given an old coat as a pattern, produced with pride an exact replica, rents, patches and all." [2]

That there was some advancement in material progress is not to be denied. But no people in the world can long remain contented with the benefits of peace and order, for they are not dumb brutes. It is foolish to suppose that a people will indefinitely favour a bureaucracy because it has improved their roads, constructed canals on more scientific principles, effected their transportation by rail, carried their letters by penny post, flashed their messages by lightning, improved their currency, regulated their weights and measures, corrected their notions of geography, astronomy and medicine and stopped their internal quarrels. Any people, however patient, will sooner or later demand a government that will be more than a mere engine of efficiency. Under the influence of Western ideas of representative government the Indian people had for some time been demanding a change in the form of the government. A Parliamentary form of government with a Parliamentary Executive was the goal they had laid before themselves.

The popular agitation for achieving this end assumed such proportions that, in the course of time, there was

[1] The poll tax has been continued in Burma simply because it was found to exist there on the day of conquest.

[2] Bernard Houghton, *Bureaucratic Government*.

presented a serious issue for the consideration of the Executive in India. How was the government of the country to be carried on? By force or by consent. Power seldom commits suicide of its own accord. Rather, when it fails to secure the willing compliance of the people, it resorts to force. That was the resource adopted by the Executive in India. Not satisfied with the aid of the power with which the Executive was endowed by the provisions of the Criminal and Penal Codes to anticipate offences by preventive acts, it besmeared the Indian Statute Book with a set of repressive laws hardly paralleled in any other part of the world. The Criminal Law Amendment Act XIV of 1908 empowered a magistrate with special sanction of the Government to hold an *ex-parte* inquiry without the presence of the accused or of his legal representative and commit him for trial to be conducted without a jury. Under another provision of the same Act the Executive could declare unlawful any association which in its view interfered with the maintenance of law and order. The State Prisoners Regulations [1] and Acts [2] authorizing the Executive to place under restraint any person whom it suspected but against whom it had no proof, constituted by themselves a perpetual suspension of the Habeas Corpus Act: [3] while under another Act [4] the Executive was empowered to proclaim "a State of Siege" or martial law in any area and suspend therein the jurisdiction of the Civil Courts in favour of the military courts. The Indian Press Act of 1910 put a complete muzzle on the Press. So wide were its provisions that in the opinion of a learned judge [5] of one of the Indian High Courts it was "difficult to see to what length its operation might not be plausibly extended by an ingenious mind" and "that they would certainly apply to writings that might even command

[1] Bengal Regulation III of 1818; Bombay Regulation XXV of 1827; Madras Regulation II of 1819.

[2] Act XXIV of 1850 and Act III of 1858.

[3] N. Ghose, *Comparative Administrative Law*, 1918, p. 480.

[4] Act IX of 1857.

[5] Sir Lawrence Jenkins, C.J., *in re* Mahomedali, I.L.R. 40, Cal. 466 (1913), quoted by N. Ghose, *op. cit.*, p. 567.

approval" and "much that is regarded as standard literature might undoubtedly be caught." The right of public meeting was suppressed in the same manner and with the same sternness as was the right to personal freedom and the right to freedom of discussion; for, over and above the restrictive provisions contained in the ordinary law of the land,[1] the Executive armed itself with discretionary powers under a special enactment to prohibit any public meeting on the excuse of what it regarded as the interest of the public.

The rigour of this regime of *lettre de cachet* and the *Bastille* was quite untempered by any fear of responsibility on the part of the Executive for any excesses committed in putting these repressive laws into operation. For it is to be noted that the Executive had, coupled with the large grants of these discretionary powers to suppress the liberties of the people in order to preserve law and order, the gift of an equally generous measure of immunity to its agents in carrying out those powers.[2] The Police Acts and the Press Act *all* contained provisions which barred all action in a civil court against these agents for damages to be done in pursuance of these Acts. Officers and soldiers taking part in the suppression of riots were not criminally responsible for acts done in good faith and were not to be prosecuted for other acts without the sanction of the government.[3] In like manner superior Executive officers could not be prosecuted for crimes committed in discharge of public functions except with the permission of the government, and then only in the manner prescribed by government.[4] There is no wonder then if such discretionary powers, exercised extra-judicially, substituted a reign of terror in place of a regime of peace.

But it was soon found out that force was not a sure means of carrying on the government of a country. The

[1] Sections 108 and 144 of the Criminal Procedure Code and Sections 120 A and B, 124 A and 153 A of the Indian Penal Code.

[2] N. Ghose, *op. cit.*, p. 601.

[3] Code of Criminal Procedure Act V of 1898, Ch. IX, Sections 128, 130 and 132.

[4] *Ibid.*, sect. 197.

verdict of history was well summed up by Burke[1] when he said:

"The use of force alone is but temporary. It may subdue for a moment, but it does not remove the necessity of subduing again: a nation is not governed which is perpetually to be conquered. (The) next objection to force is its uncertainty. Terror is not always the effect of force, and an armament is not a victory. If you do not succeed, you are without resource; for conciliation failing, force remains, but force failing, no further hope of reconciliation is left. Power and authority are sometimes bought by kindness, but they can never be begged as alms by an impoverished and defeated violence. A further objection to force is, that you impair the object by your very endeavours to preserve it. The thing you fought for (to wit the loyalty of the people) is not the thing which you recover, but depreciated, sunk, wasted and consumed in the contest . . ."

Government by consent was indeed long ago accepted by the Indian Executive as a principle of political wisdom, and the changes introduced from time to time in the constitution of the Indian Legislature were avowedly for the purpose of making it reflect the popular will. The result for a time was an astonishing degree of accord between the Indian Executive and the Indian Legislature; so much so that the regime of *lettre de cachet* and the *Bastille* had the sanction of the majority of the *Indian Legislature.* But all this government by consent or conciliation was a camouflage. On the other hand, an analysis of the changes introduced from time to time into the constitution of the Indian Legislature clearly shows that the motive behind these changes was to make it an impotent body or a willing tool in the hands of the Executive. A Legislature as distinct from the Executive was first[2] inaugurated in 1853.[3] But

[1] Speech on conciliation with America.

[2] Up to 1833 the Executive was also the Legislature. In 1833 a law member was added to the Executive Council, whose duties were confined to merely giving assistance to the Executive Council in the matter of making laws. By the Act of 1853 he was merged into the Executive Council.

[3] 16 and 17 Victoria, c. 95.

in 1861 [1] the constitution of the Legislature then established was altered. The ground urged was that that Legislature was not a body representative of the Indian people.[2] Its members were drawn from the official class representing the several Provincial Governments. In order to make the Legislature representative of the people, the Act of 1861 directed that it should be composed of *nominated* members chosen by the Governor-General from among the public, of course on the advice of the Executive. Again, by the Act of 1892 the Governor-General was directed to nominate such persons to the Legislature as were selected by public, bodies in the country. These changes in the constitution of the Legislature appear to be aimed at liberalizing it. But was this tendency towards making the Legislature representative accompanied with a tendency to make it more powerful as regards the Executive ? Quite the reverse. As the Legislature gained in its representative character it lost in its controlling power. The powers exercised by the Legislature under the Act of 1853 were far vaster than anything possessed by the Legislature under the Act of 1861. Under the former the Indian Legislature modelled itself on the procedure of the House of Commons in England, and not only dealt with matters of legislation, pure and simple, but also with matters of administration. In the words of Sir C. Ilbert, it showed an inconvenient degree of independence by asking questions as to and discussing the propriety of the measures of the Executive Government —deeming itself competent to inquire into abuses and grievances, calling for reports and returns from local administrations, debating long on questions of public interest and introducing motions and resolutions independent of the Executive Government. In a despatch of Lord Canning at the time, he pointed out that the Legislature had become invested with forms and modes of procedure closely imitat-

[1] 24 and 25 Victoria, c. 67.

[2] By the Act of 1853 the Supreme Legislature was composed of nominated members comprising two Judges of the High Court of Bengal and four nominated officials representative of the Bengal, Madras, Bombay and N.W.P. Governments in addition to the members of the Executive Council of the Government of India.

ing those of the House of Commons, that there were 136 standing orders to regulate the procedure of a dozen gentlemen assembled in council, that in short, in the words of Sir Lawrence Peel, they had assumed jurisdiction in the nature of that of a grand inquest of the nation. This was deemed to be a very grave defect (! !) in the Legislature as constituted by the Act of 1853. Its reform was therefore looked upon as very necessary for maintaining the supremacy of the Executive, and its non-popular character was made the ostensible excuse for its reconstruction. Under the pseudo-representative system introduced in 1861 the Legislature was a meek body entirely in the hands of the Executive. Being composed of *nominated* members, division in the Legislature was directly influenced by that fact. In every legislative body a man must sit, unless he has a hereditary right, by what in modern parlance is called a mandate. That mandate usually proceeds from the authority to whom he owes his seat. The nominated members, official as well as non-official, owed their elevation to the Legislature to the pleasure of the Executive, and as such were bound to support the Executive on any measure on which a division was taken. The Executive had always at its command the official block of nominated members, who gave implicit obedience to its mandates either because of its convictions or by reason of its being a part of the same. The nominated non-officials, who may be said to be opposed by conviction to the Executive, were not men of independent character and were largely concerned to make themselves agreeable to the Executive rather than make themselves reckoned with. But had they been men of independent character they could not have made themselves masters of the Executive, for by the provisions of the Constitutional law and the rules of procedure made under it, the Legislature was rendered entirely powerless to compel the Executive to do anything against its wishes. From 1853 to 1861 the Legislature dealt with both legislative and administrative questions. From 1861 the Legislature met only for legislative purposes. As a consequence of this limitation the Legislature was debarred from asking a question, moving a resolution or dividing on the Budget. During the first thirty years of its existence the Legislature did not even discuss the annual budget on more than sixteen occasions, and that too because some new tax legislation had been called for, and which the Executive could always carry through with the help of the nominated official block as it did every other kind of legislation it deemed necessary. The right of discussing the annual financial statement and the right of asking questions in regard to matters were first conceded to the Legislature by the Rules of Procedure framed under the Indian Councils Act of 1892. But it may be doubted whether these concessions of powers to the Legislature amount to a restoration of the position which it occupied and dominance it exercised under the Act of 1853.

Even the reforms of Lord Morley fell short in the matter of according a real measure of independence and power to the Legislature over the Executive. In the reforms which he introduced in 1909 nomination, directly or after selection, was in principle replaced by election as a basis for the constitution of the Legislature. At the same time the procedure of the Legislature was liberalized so as to give power to the members to put supplementary questions along with interpellations, to move resolutions on the Financial Statement and on matters of general public interest. But a little analysis is enough to show that even this attempt was of a piece with the old endeavour of liberalizing the Legislature without impairing the supremacy of the Executive.[1] This supremacy of the Executive was maintained (1) by means of a permanent majority of officials of the government nominated to the Legislature, and (2) by controlling the rules of procedure. Although election[2] was admitted

[1] It was Lord Morley, of world-wide fame as a champion of Liberalism by supporting the cause of Irish Home Rule, who said in introducing the political reforms in India: "If I knew that my days, either official or corporeal, were twenty times longer than they are likely to be, I should be sorry to set out for the goal of a Parliamentary system in India. The Parliamentary system in India is not the goal to which I for one moment aspire."

[2] It was, however, a system of selection. The only difference between the Act of 1861 and the Act of 1892 was that under the

by the Act of 1892 as a basis of the composition of the Legislature, the elected members were in a minority, so that they could not give effect to the wishes of the people whom they represented. They were entitled to move resolutions if permitted by the Executive [1] but the Executive was not bound to carry them out. They served only as recommendations, and were not binding upon the Executive. This direct thwarting produced irritation between the Executive and the elected members of the Legislature. In a certain sense the reforms of 1909 were a bad piece of engineering. Before 1909 whatever conflict there was was manifested outside the Legislature. For by the rules of election and procedure the Legislature was entirely muzzled: it could do no mischief. By the reforms of 1909, however, an attempt was made to make the Legislature independent and at the same time to muzzle it. This attempt, ingenious as it was, only served to bring to the surface the deep-seated conflict between the Executive and the forces agitating the minds of the people. Election procedure or business procedure governing a Legislature is, in the words of Prof. Redlich, as it were a political pressure gauge, indicating the tension in the parliamentary machine and thence in the whole organism of the State.[2] It is possible that this pressure gauge in the first instance may either be badly constructed or may become worn out so as to give a false reading of the actual tension. But there can be no doubt that in the case of India the Executive, in the alterations which it introduced from time to time and particularly in 1909 in the election and business procedure of the Legislature, had all along

former Act the Executive Government was to nominate anyone it liked to the Legislature. Under the latter the Executive Government was to nominate "upon the advice of such sections of the community as are likely to be capable of assisting in that matter." But as the Government was not bound to appoint the person selected, the second, howsoever concealed, must really be regarded a case of nomination by the Executive as much as the first.

[1] Legally the President of the Council, i.e. the Viceroy; but he is supposed to be invariably acting on the advice of the Executive Council.

[2] Cf. J. Redlich, *Parliamentary Procedure*, Vol. III, p. 198.

constructed it badly of purpose and had attempted to conceal thereby dangerous pressure of the steam in the political machine, so as to cause it to give a false reading of the situation. So long as the members of the Legislature derived their mandates from the Executive, owing to the fact that all of them were nominated members, such an artifice worked well, with the entry of the elected members holding their mandates from the people, the weakness of the artifice became evident. The mortification of the elected members led them to obstruct and challenge the great fundamental principles recognized as the theoretical basis of procedure. Now if a party complained of inequality among members, of the rules of conducting proceedings, of freedom of speech or of the majority principle, it is a danger signal indicative of the existence of some serious defects in the life of the State. When such a conflict arises it is for a political statesman to judge whether he has to face a reform of the procedure of the representative assembly or a reform in the constitution of the State.

While inside the Legislative Assembly there were signs of hardening opposition and weariness which comes from sterile efforts, outside the Legislature the tide of feeling was rising more quickly, for, all the time the sense of national consciousness and the desire for political power were growing rapidly in the minds of educated Indians, no doubt, because the Legislature with its limited powers was found to be an insufficient safety valve. As a result of the realization of this fact those who had given their thoughts to the political reconstruction of the country agreed that a mere reform of the procedure will not do. Only a reform of the constitution will save the state from anarchy.

There was, however, a considerable diversity in the reforms suggested for effecting an alteration in the constitution of India. One scheme may here be noted in passing and that was the scheme propounded by the Indian National Congress and the Moslem League, shortly known as the Congress-League-Scheme.[1] The scheme demanded a four-

[1] This will be found in East India Constitutional Reforms, pp. Cd. 9178 of 1918, p. 98.

fifths majority of elected members in the Central Legislature. As to the Executive, it demanded that one-half of the total number of the Executive members should be Indians and that they should be elected by the elected members of the Legislature. The Legislature was to have complete financial and legislative powers. Nay, its recommendations, passed in the form of resolutions, were to be binding on the Executive. Such " was the latest, most complete and most authoritative presentation of the claims of the leading Indian political organizations " on behalf of the Indian people. But when we come to analyse the scheme it speaks poorly of the political genius of the Indian politicians. The scheme was formulated as a fulfilment of *responsible* government in British India. But in practice it was not only not a measure of responsible government, but it was deficient even to subserve the ends of good government. The scheme did not ask that the legislature should have the power to make or unmake an Executive as it pleased. If it had asked that, then the scheme would have been a scheme for responsible government. But what it asked for was to compel an Executive, which was irremovable, to conduct the administration of the country according to the orders of the Legislature. The scheme was of a piece with that of Lord Morley in an enlarged form. He had introduced an Indian element into the Government so that Indian opinion and Indian advice might have some weight with the Executive in addition to what it exercised through the legislative organ of the Government. Those who framed the Congress-League-Scheme merely increased the Indian element in the Executive and the Legislature, and added provisions aimed at converting advice into control without realizing what was to happen if the Executive refused to be bound by the wishes of the Legislature. The essence of the project was an Executive with a divided mandate legally responsible to Parliament, and practically to an elected Legislature. Such a separation of mandates, it was obvious, would have enabled the Legislature to paralyse the Executive without having power to remove it. Being without any constitutional means to change the Legislature in cases of conflict by an appeal to the Electorate it would have been obliged to carry on the Government even where it did not respect the wishes of the Legislature. The scheme was unsound, like all previous attempts at the reform of the Indian Constitution, because in it the Executive and the Legislature derived their mandates from and were responsible to different powers. It was unsound because it overlooked the possibility that two mandates may not agree, in which case there would be a conflict. That conflict is inherent in a non-parliamentary executive. Some form of a Parliamentary government with a Parliamentary executive was the only way of avoiding it.

It is from this standpoint that the announcement of August 20, 1917, forms a landmark in the annals of the development of the Indian Constitution. On that date the Secretary of State for India announced in the House of Commons that—

"The policy of His Majesty's Government, with which the Government of India are in complete accord, is that of the increasing association of Indians in every branch of the administration and the gradual development of self-governing institutions, with a view to the progressive realization of responsible government in India as an integral part of the British Empire. They have decided that substantial steps in this direction should be taken as soon as possible . . ."

"I would add that progress in this policy can only be achieved by successive stages. The British Government and the Government of India, on whom the responsibility lies for the welfare and advancement of the Indian peoples, must be judges of the time and measure of each advance, and they must be guided by the co-operation received from those upon whom new opportunities of service will thus be conferred and by the extent to which it is found that confidence can be reposed in their sense of responsibility."

This momentous announcement marks the end of one epoch and the beginning of a new one. It definitely abandoned the old conception under which the Executive might, as it saw fit, consult the wishes of the Legislature, which were only given an increasing share in the administration of the country and increasing opportunities for influencing and criticizing, but never for controlling, the Government. Under the new conception the aim was to endow the Legislature with the power to make or unmake the government, so that it would be not only a government of the people and for the people, but by the people. The adoption of such a change of policy in the basis of the political institutions of the country involved far-reaching changes in their relations with one another, administrative, legislative and financial. The changes in the system of Provincial Finance introduced in consequence of the Reforms Act of 1919 were not caused by any inherent defects in the system as it stood at that date. On the other hand, the system was eminently workable. They were effected because the system as a whole was inconsistent with the great revolution which that Act had sought to effect in the governmental system of that country.

The nature of the changes, their extent and their adequacy will form the subject-matter of the two following chapters.

CHAPTER XI

THE NATURE OF THE CHANGE

THE announcement of August 20, 1917, spoke of progressive realization of responsible government as the goal of the future British policy in India, and the Montague-Chelmsford Report on Constitutional Reforms surveyed the ways of giving effect to that announcement. One of the merits of that Report consisted in showing that the Congress-League-Scheme of political reforms did not embody the principle for the recognition of which they were agitating so long. Instead of inaugurating a responsible government in India, the scheme would have saddled the country with a non-parliamentary executive under a parliamentary system of government. Being convinced of their error the Congress-League politicians, be it said to their credit, abandoned their scheme in favour of the proposals contained in the Joint Report. But in their turn they demanded the introduction of a more or less complete responsible government in most of the political institutions at one stroke. But the framers of the new constitution pointed out that the emphasis on the word progressive in the announcement was as great if not greater than the emphasis laid on the word responsible.[1]

In consonance with this view it was decided to introduce, as a substantial step in the progress towards the realization of the goal laid down in the announcement, a responsible government of a limited character in the Provincial Governments. The Provincial Governments in India, like the Central Government, were irresponsible governments. The changes made in the constitution of Provincial Legislatures

[1] Report of the Joint Select Committee on the Government of India Bill, pp. 203 of 1919, p.s. para. 7.

were of the same nature as the changes in the Central Legislature, in that both were calculated to enable the Executive to consult the Legislature without being amenable to its control. Only on one occasion were the frame-works of the two machines of governments, the Provincial and the Central, constructed on a slightly different basis, and that was in the Morley-Minto Reforms of 1909. Under those reforms the Central Legislature was dominated by *official* members who with the members of the Executive formed a standing majority in the chamber. In the Provincial Legislatures this principle of a standing majority of official members was dispensed with. The second point of departure in the constitution of the Provincial Legislatures as compared with that of the Central Legislature consisted in the Budget procedures in the two governments. In the Central Legislature the Finance Member early in each calendar year presented to the Legislature his preliminary estimates accompanied by an explanatory memorandum. On a subsequent day he made such further explanations as he thought necessary. Members of the Legislature could thereupon move resolutions regarding (*a*) any proposed alteration in taxation, (*b*) any proposed loan, or (*c*) any additional grant to a Local Government. The first stage in the discussion of the Budget of the Government of India was over when once these resolutions were voted upon. The second stage commenced when the estimates were taken into consideration by groups. At this stage also it was open for members to move resolutions on any heads of revenue and expenditure, except those that were declared by rules of procedure to be not open for discussion to the Legislature. After the resolutions had been moved and voted upon the Finance Member took the whole discussion into consideration and made such changes as were agreeable to him and then presented his final Budget. At this, the third stage, the Finance Member explained his reasons for the acceptance of some and the non-acceptance of other suggestions made during the course of the Budget debate. A general discussion of the Budget then followed, but no resolution was allowed to be moved upon the final Budget or a vote taken.

The Budget procedure in the Provincial Legislatures was a little different. There the first stage commenced with the preparation of a rough draft of the provincial estimates, accompanied by a schedule including in it all projects involving an expenditure of over 5,000 rupees, divided into two parts, the first containing all allotted, i.e. obligatory, items of expenditure and the second containing unallotted, i.e. non-obligatory, items of expenditure. The Government of India to whom this draft Budget was submitted corrected the estimate of the revenue and determined in consultation with the Provincial Government the aggregate expenditure for which the latter should provide, and if need be, altered or added to the items in the first part of the schedule. When the figures of the altered revenue and the aggregate expenditure as fixed by the Government of India were communicated to the Provincial Government it marked the close of the first stage of a Provincial Budget. The second stage commenced when this draft Budget was submitted by the Provincial Government to a committee of the Provincial Legislature. The Committee was composed of officials and non-officials in equal number, the former nominated by Government and the latter elected by their fellows. It was presided over by the member of the Executive in charge of Provincial Finance; the proceedings of the committee were informal and private and decisions were by majority votes. The Committee concerned itself only with the second part of the Schedule containing non-obligatory items of expenditure and, provided it did not exceed the aggregate expenditure fixed by the Government of India, it was free to make variations and even to insert new items occasionally. On the conclusion of its labours the Committee reported the changes it made to its Government. With this ended the second stage in the Provincial Budget. The third stage began when the Provincial estimates as a whole were presented to the Provincial Legislature by the member in charge of finance. The Budget was then considered in a committee of the whole House and resolutions moved on each group of estimates discussed. When all resolutions were debated and voted upon the result of the discussions was communicated to the Provincial Government. But the resolutions were not binding. The fourth stage commenced when the Provincial Government introduced the final budget and explained its reasons for the acceptance of some and the non-acceptance of the rest of the suggestions made by the Legislature. A debate followed, but no resolutions were in order at this stage ; nor did the Legislature divide upon the Budget. It was adopted as passed by the Executive.

From these differences in the constitution and procedure of the Central and Provincial Governments, it must not be supposed that the Provincial Governments were less irresponsible with regard to their Legislatures than the Central Government was with regard to its own Legislature. The fact that since 1909 there was no majority of official members in the Provincial Legislature as there was in the Central Legislature was a matter of no moment so far as its practical consequences to the Executive were concerned ; for it is to be remembered that in practice the difference between nominated members from among the non-officials and the official members was only superficial. Both had their mandate from the Government who gave them their seats in the Legislature, and as nominees of the Government they voted for the Government, so that, though not in theory, in practice the Provincial Government had as much a standing majority in Legislatures as the Central Government had in theory as well as in practice. Nor did the budget procedure of the Provincial Government mark any decided improvement over that adopted in the Central Government in the matter of giving greater control to the Legislature over the Executive. In both cases the aim was to give the members of the Legislature the privilege of discussing *beforehand* the question of such alteration with reference to the necessities of the Budget, only in the case of the Provincial Budget this privilege was allowed to be exercised at an earlier stage than in the case of the Imperial Budget. But in view of the fact that the Resolutions of the Legislature on the Provincial Budget, as those of the Central Legislature on the Imperial, were only recommendations to their respective Executives, this difference between the Budget procedure of the two

Governments did not impose any greater control over the one Executive than it did on the other. Again, the provision that a committee of the Provincial Legislature had been allowed the privilege of framing the non-obligatory portion of the Provincial Budget did not give the Legislature any appreciable control over the Executive. First of all, the Provincial Government could always restrict the scope of this Budget Committee by transferring any head from the class of non-obligatory expenditure to the class of obligatory expenditure. Besides this, the operation of certain other rules of Budget procedure based upon general principles of public finance tended directly to restrict the powers of the committee to put forth schemes of alternative or additional expenditure. It was rightly provided that schemes involving recurring expenditure could only be proposed with due regard to the rate of growth of recurring revenues and recurring expenditure. Owing to this rule, the committee had to drop proposals which involved recurring expenditure, but which were desirable from its standpoint. On the other hand, similar proposals made by the Executive could be easily carried through by the device freely adopted of obtaining previous sanction of the Government of India. The consequence was that in all the Provincial Budgets presented under the new rules the amount of this "unallotted" fund left to the discretion of the committee bore too insignificant a proportion to the total expenditure in the budget to make the Provincial Executive in any real degree amenable to the Provincial Legislature.

No really responsible government could, however, be introduced in the Provinces without first of all making a complete change in the mutual relations between the Central Government and the different Provincial Governments in India. The relation between the two which existed before the passing of the Act of 1919 was one of complete subordination of Provincial Governments to the Central Government.[1] In this bond of subordination we can discern three strands —legislative, financial, and administrative. Of these three

[1] Report on Indian Constitutional Reforms, Cd. 9109 of 1918, Ch. V.

we have seen how tight was the financial strand. The Government of India's control over revenues and expenditure was derived from Parliamentary Statutes which treated the revenues of India as one and applied them to the purposes of the Government of India as a whole. It is true that this provision was not so strictly construed as absolutely to prevent the appropriation of particular sources of income to specific purposes all-India or provincial. Or else the development of the provincial system of finance would have been impossible. But it certainly had the effect of denying to Provincial Governments any inherent legal right to the revenues which they raised. The Government of India completely controlled taxation imposed in British India, apart from the local taxes which were raised by local bodies. Taxation could only be levied by law,[1] but the law had forbidden a Provincial Legislature, without the previous sanction of the Government of India, to consider

"any law affecting the public debt of India or the customs duties or any other tax or duty for the time being in force and imposed by the authority of the Governor-General in Council for the general purposes of the Government of India."

This is the natural corollary of the statutory hypothecation of all-India revenues to all-India needs. The law would not inhibit a provincial legislature from exploiting for provincial purposes any new source of taxation which it had the ingenuity to discover. But even in that case the project would, before being translated into action, have to secure the assent of the Finance Department of the Government of India, which would not give its sanction without considering closely if it trespassed on the Central Government's sources of taxation. Again, the provision of the law which required that

[1] There is, however, a glaring exception. The land revenue in India has been raised without any legislative sanction. The exclusion of land revenue from the province of the Legislature practically removed between 40 and 50 per cent. of the net public revenue from any sort of control.

"no governor or governor in council (of a province) shall have the power of creating any new office or granting any salary, gratuity or allowance without the previous sanction of the Governor General of India in Council"

had given the Government of India a right of control over expenditure in the Provinces which was exercised through the instrumentality of a series of codes of instructions, such as the Civil Service Regulations, the Civil Account Code, the Public Works Code and the like. These codes partly dealt with the mechanism of finance such as the maintenance of a uniform system of audit and accounts, the custody of public money, remittances, economy, and such matters; but they also imposed definite restraints upon the powers of Provincial Governments, to create new appointments or raise emoluments and other matter such as recruitment, promotions, leave, foreign service and pensions upon which the codes really constitute a digest of the case-law laid down from time to time by the Government of India which the Provincial Governments must strictly obey. If their powers of taxation and expenditure were strictly controlled the power of borrowing was never conceded to the provinces. It will be recalled that Port Trusts and Municipalities might raise loans within defined limits, but because the revenues of India were legally one and indivisible and were liable for all debts incurred for the purposes of the Government of India, Provincial Governments possessed no separate resources on the security of which they could borrow.

Even within the prescribed limits of Provincial Finance the Provincial Governments were not free from the control of the Central Government. Because the provincial settlements were based not on provincial revenues but on provincial needs, a central control was inevitable. The Government of India could not allow a Province to go bankrupt. But if the Government of India were responsible for provincial solvency they must be in a position to control provincial expenditure. Again, as regards revenues, so long as the Government of India took a share in the proceeds they had a strong motive not only in interfering in the Budget estimates of the provinces, but also in interfering in details of administration. Their interest in land revenue, for example, inevitably led them to close supervision over revenue settlements, and the control tended to become tighter in cases where expansion and development of a source of revenue, such as irrigation, depended on capital outlay.

The legislative powers of the Provincial Governments had in the same manner been made subject to statutory restrictions. There was no doubt an extensive field in which, so far as the substantive provisions of the Statute were concerned, the legislative competence of the Provincial Legislatures was legally unfettered. Actually, however, the power of the local legislatures was curtailed in two ways. In the first place, owing to the fact that in their existence all the Provincial Legislatures were younger, and most of them much younger, institutions than the Central Legislature of the Governor-General, a great part of the field that would have otherwise been open to them was covered by acts of that body, which had always retained a concurrent power of legislation for the country at large. But the field yet remaining open for Provincial Governments in the matter of legislation was further restricted by the fact that the power of the Secretary of State and Parliament to control all-Indian legislation was made operative by means of executive directions, which had made it incumbent on Provincial Governments to submit for the previous sanction of the Government of India and the Secretary of State all their projects for legislation before introduction. It is true that these directions did not apply to private members' Bills ; but inasmuch as a Bill could only be introduced with the leave of the Legislature, and the Provincial Government was in most cases in a position if it chose to do so to oppose such a motion successfully, the Government of India by directions to the Provincial Governments were in a position to control all private provincial legislation almost as effectively as the Provincial Government's Bills.

In carrying on the actual work of administration every Provincial Government was by law required to obey the orders of the Government of India and keep that Government constantly and diligently informed of its proceedings and of all matters which ought, in its opinion, to be reported to that Government, or as to which that Government required information. That was because in law every Provincial Government was placed under the superintendence, direction and control in all matters relating to the Government of its Province. This administrative control of the Government of India was exercised by that Government in the interest of uniformity. It is obvious that in many respects India is one single and undivided country, in which much work had to be carried on on uniform lines. The Civil servants who executed the orders of Provincial Governments having been recruited from England on terms guaranteed by the Secretary of State, many questions affecting them could not be determined by any Provincial Government. Again, the development of trade, industry and science throughout India similarly favoured the formulation and pursuit of uniform policies by the Government of India. Even with one law for the whole of India business and industry might have been left to their discretion to administer such matters as statistics, patents, copyright, insurance, income tax, explosives and mining, etc. Not only were the Provincial Governments subordinated to the Central Government to follow established lines in the matters of administration, but they were not free to initiate any new policy. It was the Government of India which regarded itself as distinctly charged with the duty of framing policy and inspiring reforms for the whole of India by issuing new orders. To make them effective these orders were often accompanied by handsome grants to Provincial Governments strictly earmarked for the purpose of pushing on some particular feature of the new policy. Not seldom did the Government of India appoint new advising or inspecting officers whose task it was to see that the new energy suddenly infused into the system was well maintained and well directed to the chosen ends.

So long as the Provincial Governments continued to be bound by such strands to the Government of India there could be no responsible government in the Provinces. No government can be made to serve two masters at one and the same time. To keep the Provincial Governments subordinate to [1] the Government of India and also to make them responsible to popular Legislature would have been inconsistent in theory and vicious in practice. It is quite conceivable that under such a double government the wishes of the Provincial Legislature on certain matters may not coincide with those of the Government of India. On such occasions a Provincial Government may not know whom to obey. If it deferred to the wishes of the Legislature it would be failing in its duty towards the Government of India. Indeed there is on record a case of such a conflict.[2] There was an occasion during the currency of the Morley-Minto Reforms when the Government of Bombay were unsuccessful in their endeavours to persuade the Government of India to sanction certain charges affecting the educational staff. The proposals were locally popular and were again put forward for adoption in a resolution moved in the Bombay Legislature by an elected member. The Bombay Government thereupon accepted the resolution which was carried unanimously, and once more put forward their proposals to the Government of India on the ground that they had the Legislature's entire support. But the Government of India and the Secretary of State held that these tactics were out of order and that it was

> "the duty of the Local Government in dealing with the resolutions to uphold with all their authority the decision of the Government of India,"

i.e. to have opposed the resolution even if it agreed with the Legislature in the principle thereof.

The strong ties of subordination which bound the Provinces to the Central Government were therefore the chief obstacles in the path of Provincial autonomy. In order that the Provincial Government be made subject to Provincial Legislatures, the first thing to do was to curtail the powers which the Government of India possessed of inter-

[1] The degree of subordination it should be noted varied with the status of the Provinces, for which see Joint Report, pp. 37–45.

[2] Joint Report, pp. 75–6.

ference in provincial finance, provincial legislation, and provincial administration. As was well observed by the authors of the Report [1] on Constitutional Reforms:

"We have to demolish the existing structure, at least in part, before we can build the new. Our business is one of devolution, of drawing lines of demarcation, of cutting long-standing ties. The Government of India must give and the Provinces must receive; for only so can the growing organism of self-government in the Provinces draw air into its lungs and live."

The path to provincial independence therefore lay through a satisfactory division of functions and finances between the Provincial and Central Governments. Of the two, the task of dividing the functions was comparatively an easier one. For facilitating the necessary division of functions the following principles were laid down by the Government of India.[2]

"7. There are certain subjects which are at present under the direct administration of the Government of India. The Government of India maintain separate staffs for their administration and the Provincial Governments have no share in it. The category is easily recognizable, and for the most part there will not be much room for doubt as to the subjects to be included in it. At the other end of the line are matters of predominantly local interest which, however much conditions must vary between Provinces, will, generally speaking be recognized as proper subjects for provincialization.

"8. Between these extreme categories, however, lies a large indeterminable field which requires further examination before the principles determining its classification can be settled. It comprises all the matters in which the Government of India at present retain ultimate control, legislative and administrative, but in practice share the actual administration in varying degrees with the Provincial Governments. In many cases the extent of delega-

[1] Joint Report, p. 101.

[2] Memorandum for the Functions Committee by the Government of India, Annexture II to the Report of the Committee. Cmd. 103 of 1919.

tion practised is already very wide. The criterion which the Government of India apply to these is whether in any given case the Provincial Governments are to be strictly the agents of the Government of India, or are to have (subject to what is said below as to the reservation of powers of intervention) acknowledged authority of their own. In applying this criterion the main determining factor will be not the degree of delegation already practised, which may depend on mere convenience, but the consideration whether the interests of India as a whole (or at all events interests larger than those of one Province), or on the other hand the interests of the Province essentially preponderate.

"The point is that delegation to an agent may be already extensive, but that circumstance should not obscure the fact of agency or lead to the agent being regarded as having inherent powers of his own."

These principles, in which it was stated that "where extra-provincial interests predominate the subject should be treated as central," while

"all subjects in which the interests of the provinces essentially predominate should be provincial, and in respect of (which) the Provincial Governments (to) have acknowledged authority of their own,"

were accepted by the Functions Committee appointed to make a division between all-India and Provincial subjects. The recommendations made by the Committee were with minor amendments embodied in what are called Devolution Rules under section 45A of the Government of India Act of 1919, which gave effect to the policy of responsible government and are made a part of the constitutional law of the land, so that the subjects thereby devolving upon the Provinces became the services over which the Provinces gained an *acknowledged authority of their own* such as they never had before 1833. According to these Devolution Rules the following were declared to be

PROVINCIAL SUBJECTS

1. **Local Self-government,** that is to say, matters relating to the constitution and powers of municipal corporations, improvement trusts, district boards, mining

boards of health and other local authorities established in a Province for the purpose of local self-government, exclusive of matters arising under the Cantonments Act, 1910; subject to legislation by the Indian Legislature as regards—

(*a*) The powers of such authorities to borrow otherwise than from a Provincial Government, and

(*b*) the levying by such authorities of taxation not included in schedule II to the scheduled Taxes Rules.

2. **Medical administration**, including hospitals, dispensaries and asylums, and provision for medical education.

3. **Public Health and Sanitation and Vital Statistics**; subject to legislation by the Indian Legislature in respect of infectious and contagious diseases to such extent as may be declared by any Act of the Indian Legislature.

4. **Pilgrims within British India.**

5. **Education**, provided that—

(*a*) The following subjects shall be excluded, viz.:

(i) The Benares Hindu University, and Aligarh Muslim University, and such other universities constituted after the commencement of these rules, as may be declared by the Governor-General in Council to be Central subjects, and

(ii) Chiefs' Colleges and any institution maintained by the Governor-General in Council for the benefit of members of His Majesty's Forces or of other public servants or of the children of such members or servants; and

(*b*) the following subjects shall be subject to legislation by the Indian Legislature, namely:

(i) The control of the establishment, and the regulation of the constitutions and functions, of universities constituted after the commencement of these rules; and

(ii) The definition of the jurisdiction of any university outside the Province in which it is situated, and

(iii) For a period of five years from the date of the commencement of these rules, the Calcutta University, and the control and organization of secondary education in the presidency of Bengal.

6. **Public Works** included under the following heads, namely:

(*a*) Construction and maintenance of provincial buildings used or intended for any purpose in connection with the administration of the Province; and care of historical monuments, with the exception of ancient monuments as defined in Section 2 (i) of the Ancient Monuments Preservation Act, 1904, which are for the time being declared to be protected monuments under Section 3 (i) of that Act; provided that the Governor-General in Council may by notification in the *Gazette of India*, remove any such monuments from the operation of this exception;

(*b*) roads, bridges, ferries, tunnels, ropeways, and causeways, and other means of communication, subject to such conditions as regards control over construction and maintenance of means of communication declared by the Governor-General in Council to be of military importance, and as regards incidence of special expenditure connected therewith, as the Governor-General in Council may prescribe;

(*c*) tramways within municipal areas; and

(*d*) light and feeder railways and extra-municipal tramways in so far as provision for their construction and management is made by provincial legislation; subject to legislation by the Indian Legislature in the case of any such railway or tramway which is in physical connection with a main line or is built on the same gauge as an adjacent main line.

7. **Water supplies,** irrigation and canals, drainage and embankments, water storage and water power; subject to

legislation by the Indian Legislature with regard to matters of inter-provincial concern or affecting the relations of a Province with any other territory.

8. **Land Revenue administration,** as described under the following heads, namely:

(*a*) Assessment and collection of land revenue;

(*b*) Maintenance of land records, survey for revenue purposes, records of right;

(*c*) Laws regarding land tenures, relations of landlords and tenants, collection of rents;

(*d*) Courts of wards, incumbered and attached estates;

(*e*) Land improvement and agricultural loans;

(*f*) Colonization and disposal of Crown lands and alienation of land revenue; and

(*g*) Management of Government estates.

9. **Famine relief.**

10. **Agriculture,** including research institutes, experimental and demonstration farms, introduction of improved methods, provision for agricultural education, protection against destructive insects and pests and prevention of plant diseases; subject to legislation by the Indian Legislature in respect of destructive insects and pests and plant diseases, to such extent as may be declared by any Act of the Indian Legislature.

11. **Civil Veterinary Department,** including provision for veterinary training, improvement of stock, and prevention of animal diseases; subject to legislation by the Indian Legislature in respect to animal diseases to such extent as may be declared by any Act of the Indian Legislature.

12. **Fisheries.**

13. **Co-operative Societies.**

14. **Forests,** including preservation of game therein; subject to legislation by the Indian Legislature as regards disforestation of reserved forests.

15. **Land acquisition**; subject to legislation by the Indian Legislature.

16. **Excise**, that is to say, the control of production, manufacture, possession, transport, purchase and sale of

alcoholic liquor and intoxicating drugs, and the levying of Excise duties and licence fees on or in relation to such articles, but excluding in the case of opium, control of cultivation, manufacture and sale for export.

17. **Administration of Justice**, including constitution, powers, maintenance and organization of courts of civil and criminal jurisdiction within the Province; subject to legislation by the Indian Legislature as regards High Courts, Chief Courts, and Courts of Judicial Commissioners, and any courts of criminal jurisdiction.

18. **Provincial Law Reports.**

19. **Administrators-General and Official Trustees**; subject to legislation by the Indian Legislature.

20. **Non-Judicial Stamps**, subject to legislation by the Indian Legislature, and **Judicial Stamps**, subject to legislation by the Indian Legislature as regards amount of court fees levied in relation to suits and proceedings in the High Courts under their original jurisdiction.

21. **Registration of deeds and documents**; subject to legislation by the Indian Legislature.

22. **Registration of births, deaths, and marriages**; subject to legislation by the Indian Legislature for such classes as the Indian Legislature may determine.

23. **Religious and Charitable Endowments.**

24. **Development of Mineral resources which are Government property**; subject to rules made or sanctioned by the Secretary of State, but not including the regulation of mines.

25. **Development of industries**, including industrial research and technical education.

26. **Industrial matters** included under the following heads, namely :—

(*a*) Factories;
(*b*) Settlement of labour disputes;
(*c*) Electricity;
(*d*) Boilers;
(*e*) Gas;
(*f*) Smoke nuisance; and

(*g*) Welfare of labour, including provident funds, industrial insurance (general health and accident) and housing;

subject as to heads (*a*), (*b*), (*c*), (*d*), and (*g*) to legislation by the Indian Legislature.

27. **Stores and Stationery**; subject in the case of imported stores and stationery to such rules as may be prescribed by the Secretary of State in Council.

28. **Adulteration of food-stuffs and other articles**; subject to legislation by the Indian Legislature as regards import and export trade.

29. **Weights and Measures**; subject to legislation by the Indian Legislature as regards standard.

30. **Ports**, except such ports as may be declared by rule made by the Governor-General in Council or by or under Indian legislation to be major ports.

31. **Inland Waterways**, including shipping and navigation thereon so far as not declared by the Governor-General in Council to be Central subjects, but subject as regards inland steam-vessels to legislation by the Indian Legislature.

32. **Police**, including railway police; subject in the case of railway police to such conditions as regards limits of jurisdiction and railway contributions to cost of maintenance as the Governor-General in Council may determine:

(*a*) Regulation of betting and gambling;

(*b*) prevention of cruelty to animals;

(*c*) protection of wild birds and animals;

(*d*) control of poisons, subject to legislation by the Indian Legislature;

(*e*) control of motor vehicles, subject to legislation by the Indian Legislature as regards licences valid throughout British India; and

(*f*) control of dramatic performances and cinematographs, subject to legislation by the Indian Legislature in regard to sanction of films for exhibition.

34. **Control of Newspapers, Books, and Printing Presses**; subject to legislation by the Indian Legislature.

35. **Coroners.**

36. **Excluded Areas.**

37. **Criminal tribes**; subject to legislation by the Indian Legislature.

38. **European vagrancy**; subject to legislation by the Indian Legislature.

39. **Prisons,** prisoners (except State prisoners) and reformatories; subject to legislation by the Indian Legislature.

40. **Pounds** and prevention of cattle trespass.

41. **Treasure Trove.**

42. **Libraries** (except the Imperial Library) and **Museums** (except the Indian Museum, the Imperial War Museum and the Victoria Memorial, Calcutta) and **Zoological Gardens.**

43. **Provincial Government Presses.**

44. **Elections** for Indian and provincial legislature, subject to rules framed under sections 64 (i) and 72 A (4) of the Act.

45. **Regulations of medical and other professional qualifications and standards**; subject to legislation by the Indian Legislature.

46. **Local Fund audit,** that is to say, the audit by Government agency of income and expenditure controlled by local bodies.

47. **Control** as defined by rule 10, **of members of all-India and Provincial Services** serving within the Province, and control, subject to legislation by the Indian Legislature, of public services within the province, other than all-India services.

48. **Sources of Provincial revenue,** not included under previous heads, whether—

(*a*) Taxes included in the schedules to the scheduled taxes Rules, or

(*b*) Taxes, not included in those schedules, which are imposed by or under provincial legislation which has received the previous sanction of the Governor-General.

49. **Borrowing of money** on the sole credit of the Province, subject to the provisions of the Local Government (Borrowing) Rules.

50. **Imposition** by legislation of punishment by **fine, penalty, or imprisonment,** for enforcing any law of the Province relating to any provincial subject; subject to legislation by the Indian Legislature in the case of any subject in respect of which such a limitation is imposed under these rules.

51. **Any matter** which, though falling within a Central subject, is **declared by the Governor-General in Council to be of a merely local or private nature within the province.**

52. **Matters pertaining to a Central subject in respect of which powers have been conferred by or under any law upon a Local Government.**

The second task that of allocating the revenue resources between the Central and Provincial Governments was a comparatively difficult one. As the problem was conceived in the main as one of making the Provinces independent of the Government of India in matters in which it was proposed that they should acquire an authority of their own acknowledged by law it was natural for the authors of the Report on Constitutional Reforms to hold that

"Our first aim . . . has been to find some means of entirely separating the resources of the Central Government from those of the Provinces."

The first step in that direction was therefore to abolish the system of "divided heads" or budget by shared revenues, for there was a concensus of opinion that this coparcenary system, in so far as it gave a handle to the Central Government to interfere in the domestic affairs of the Provinces, was a source of friction and was incompatible with provincial independence. But such a system of complete separation was fraught with two main difficulties. The first difficulty was in connection with the disposal of divided heads. To whom should they be handed over? At the time the scheme of complete separation was contemplated the heads of revenue which were divided in all or some of the Provinces were land revenue, stamps, excise, income tax and irrigation. The authors of the Report on Constitutional Reforms proposed [1]

"... that the revenue from stamp duty should be discriminated under the already well-marked sub-heads *General* and *Judicial*; and that the former should be made an Indian and the latter a provincial receipt. This arrangement will preserve uniformity in the case of commercial stamps where it is obviously desirable to avoid discrepancies of rates; and it will also give the provinces a free hand in dealing with court-fee stamps and thus provide them with an additional means of augmenting their resources. Excise is at present entirely a provincial head in Bombay, Bengal, and Assam, and we see no valid reason why it should not now be made provincial throughout India. . . . Land revenue, which is far the biggest head of all, is at present equally shared between the Indian and all the provincial Governments, except that Burma gets rather more than one-half and the United Provinces get rather less. . . . Now land revenue assessment and collection is so intimately concerned with the whole administration in rural areas that the advantages of making it a provincial receipt are obvious. . . . Moreover, famine expenditure and expenditure on major irrigation works are for obvious reasons closely connected with land revenue, and if the receipts from that head are made provincial it logically follows that the Provinces should take over the very heavy liability for famine relief and protective works. . . . We were told that in the days of dawning popular government in the Provinces it would be well that the provincial government should be able to fall back on the support of the Government of India (as, if the head were still divided, it would be able to do) when its land revenue policy was attacked.[2] But it is just because

[1] Report, pp. 165–7.

[2] The land revenue policy of the Government has always been looked upon by the popular leaders, rightly or wrongly, with a certain degree of suspicion, and is always in danger of being attacked. For fear that the policy may be subverted under a popular Provincial Legislature to whose control land revenue as a provincial subject

divided heads are not regarded as merely a financial expedient but are, and so long as they survive will be, viewed as a means of going behind the provincial government to the Government of India, that we feel sure that they should be abolished. We propose therefore to make land revenue together with irrigation wholly provincial receipts. It follows that the Provinces will become entirely liable for expenditure on famine relief and protective irrigation works. . . . The one remaining head is income tax. We see two very strong reasons for making this an Indian receipt. First, there is the necessity of maintaining a uniform rate throughout the country. The inconveniences, particularly to the commercial world, of having different rates in different Provinces are manifest. Secondly, in the case of ramifying enterprises with their business centre in some big city, the Province in which the tax is paid is not necessarily the Province in which income is earned. We have indeed been told that income tax is merely the industrial or professional complement of the land revenue; and that to provincialize the latter, while Indianizing the former, means giving those provinces whose wealth is more prominently agricultural, such as the United Provinces and Madras, an initial advantage over a Province like Bombay, which has very large commercial and industrial interests. Another very practical argument is

was subjected it provided by the Reservation of Bills Rules under Section 12 (1) of the Government of India Act, 1919, that—The Governor of any Governor's province *shall* reserve for the consideration of the Governor-General any Bill, not having been previously sanctioned by the Governor-General, which has been passed by the Legislative Council of the Province and is presented to the Governor for his assent, if the Bill appears to the Governor to contain provisions—

(e) affecting the land revenue of a Province either so as to

(i) prescribe a period or periods within which any temporary settled estate or estates may not be re-assessed to land revenue, or

(ii) limit the extent to which the assessment to land revenue of such an estate or estates may be made or enhanced, or

(iii) modify materially the general principles upon which land revenue has hitherto been assessed, if such prescription, limitation or modification appears to the Governor to be likely seriously to affect the public revenues of the province.

that the tax is collected by provincial agency and that if Provincial Governments are given no inducement, such as a share of the receipts or a commission on the collections which is only such a share in disguise, there will be a tendency to slackness in collection and a consequent falling off in receipts. We admit that these arguments have force; but we are not prepared to let them stand in the way of a complete separation of revenues. Equality of treatment as between one Province and another must be reached so far as it is possible in the settlements as a whole, and it is not possible to extend the principle of equality to individual heads of revenue. If it should be found that receipts fall off, it may be necessary to create an all-India agency for the collection of the tax, but this we should clearly prefer to retaining it as a divided head. To sum up: we propose to retain the Indian and Provincial heads as at present, but to add to the former income tax and general stamps, and to the latter land revenue, irrigation, excise and judicial stamps. No head will then remain divided."

However, when all the existing sources of revenue were completely distributed between the Central and Provincial Governments as proposed, it was inevitable that there should be a deficit in the Budget of the Government of India. How to make up this deficit was therefore the second difficulty that was involved in replacing the system of divided heads by a system of separate heads of revenue. The authors of the Report on Constitutional Reforms were presented with many a plan for the solution of this knotty problem. In the course of their survey they observed: [1]

" One way of meeting it would be to maintain the basis of the present settlements, but to allot to the Government of India a certain proportion of growing revenue instead of its share of the divided heads. But this device would stereotype all the existing inequalities between the Provinces which by reason of the permanent settlement in some of them are considerable; while it would also introduce an

[1] Report, p. 168.

element of great uncertainty into the Indian Government's finance. A second was that we should take an all-round contribution on a *per capita* basis. But this expedient also would not obviate very undesirable variations between Provinces in the rate of levy owing to the inequality of provincial resources and of provincial needs. A third plan was to take an all-round percentage contribution based on gross provincial revenue. This is open, *inter alia*, to the objection that it would leave several of the Provinces with large deficits. Fourthly, we considered but rejected the proposal that Provinces which had a surplus should temporarily help others as being cumbrous and impracticable."

The plan recommended by the authors of the Report was [1]

"to assess the contribution from each Province to the Government of India as a percentage of the difference between the gross provincial revenue and the gross provincial expenditure";

in other words, a levy on the surplus of the estimated gross revenue of the Province when all divided heads are separately allotted over its estimated normal expenditure, including expenditure on famine relief and protective irrigation. On the basis of the Budget figures for 1917–18 it was found that it would require a levy of 87 per cent.[2] on the provincial surpluses to make up the deficit of Rs. 1363 lakhs in the Budget of the Government of India found likely to be caused by the abolition of the system of divided heads.[3]

[1] Report, p. 169.

[2] The suggested imposition of an equal rate of levy is somewhat strange, for the authors of the Report had in para. 206 protested that "equality of contribution was impracticable," etc. Para. 206 of the Joint Report makes a confusion. It protests against equality of contributions, which is what it adopts in the plan it recommends.

[3] The way in which the proposed plan would have worked out in practice can be gathered from the following figures given in the

In making these recommendations the authors of the Report were careful to observe:[1]

"One caveat we are bound to make. Emergencies may arise which cannot be provided for by immediate raising Government of India taxation; and in that case it must be open to the Central Government to make a special supplementary levy upon the provisions. We must add that inasmuch as our proposals are based on war figures they should be open to revision hereafter, but not subject to change for a period of say six years, and to avoid intermediate discussion the scheme should in the meantime be regarded as part of the constitutional agreement with the Provinces. It should also be one of the duties of the periodic commission which we propose should be appointed to examine the development of constitutional changes after ten years' experience of their working or of some similar body at that time, to re-investigate the question of the provincial contributions to the Government of India."

Report, Cal. Ed. (p. 134), and based on the Budget figures for 1917–18:—

(*In Lakhs or Rupees.*)

Province.	Gross Prov Revenue	Gross Prov Expenditure.	Gross Prov Surplus.	Contribution (87 per cent of col 4)	Net Prov Surplus.
1	2	3	4	5	6
Madras	13,31	8,40	4,91	4,28	63
Bombay	10,01	9,00	1,01	88	13
Bengal	7,54	6,75	79	69	10
United Provinces	11,22	7,47	3,75	3,27	48
Punjab	8,64	6,14	2,50	2,18	32
Burma	7,69	6,08	1,61	1,40	21
Bihar and Orissa	4,04	3,59	45	39	6
Central Provinces	4,12	3,71	41	36	5
Assam	1,71	1,50	21	18	3
Total	68,28	52,64	15,64	13,63	2,01

N.B.—The Punjab figures in column 5 should be reduced and those in column 6 raised by 3½ lakhs in each case to allow for the continued compensation which the province is entitled to receive for the cession of a crore of its balances to the Government of India in 1914.

[1] Report, p. 170.

These proposals were put before the Provincial Governments, for their opinion. The objections to a plan which appeared to make some Provinces bear a greater burden of the cost of the Central Government than others readily suggested themselves. Madras and the United Provinces seemed to pay 47·4 per cent. and 41·1 per cent. of their surpluses to the Government of India, while Bombay and Bengal appeared to escape with a sacrifice of no more than 9·6 per cent. and 10·1 per cent. of their respective surpluses. The inequity of this treatment seemed to be so very apparent that the Provinces against which a greater burden was set down raised loud protests. So impressed was the Government of India with the justice of this clamour that in its letter [1] to the Secretary of State it observed:

"We recommend that the initial contributions should be recognized as temporary and provisional, and that steps should be taken as soon as possible to fix a standard and equitable scale of contributions. . . . The whole question . . . requires skilled investigation; (the difficulty of the position was foreseen in the Report and investigation by the first statutory commission was promised, but) we propose that a Committee on Financial Relations be appointed, either by you or by us, to advise fully upon the subject, so that each province may know exactly how it stands before the new regime starts."

And this recommendation was endorsed [2] by the Joint Select Committee of Parliament which sat on the Reform Bill. Accordingly the Secretary of State appointed a Committee under the chairmanship of Lord Meston to advise on:

(*a*) The contributions to be paid by the various provinces to the Central Government for the financial year 1921–22;

[1] Dated March 5, 1919 (para. 61), on the questions raised in the Report on Indian Constitutional Reforms, pp. Cmd. 123 of 1919.

[2] Report of the Joint Select Committee on the Government of India Bill (part V, clause 41, para. 9)—House of Commons Return 203 of 1919, p. 12.

(*b*) The modifications to be made in the provincial contributions thereafter with a view to their equitable distribution until there ceases to be an all-India deficit ;

(*c*) The future financing of the provincial loan accounts ; and

(*d*) Whether the Government of Bombay should retain any share of the revenue derived from income tax.

After about seven weeks of investigation the Committee produced its Report.[1] In advising on clause (*a*) of its terms of reference the Committee expressed its dissatisfaction of the plan set forth in the Joint Report of taking from the Provinces a fixed uniform proportion of their respective surpluses as their contributions to the Central Exchequer. The principal objection urged against the plan was that in some Provinces it left no surplus and in others no adequate surplus after the payment of their respective quotas of contributions. The Committee held, and rightly too, that

" in no case may a contribution be such as would force the province to embark on new taxation *ad hoc*, which to our minds would be an unthinkable sequel to a purely administrative rearrangement of abundant general resources."

The Committee felt itself bound by a limiting consideration in providing the contribution, as a result of which it felt itself obliged " to leave each Province with a reasonable working surplus "—a surplus which it preferred " to calculate, so far as possible, with some relation to the general financial position of the Province and the more imminent claims upon its resources."

" To be able to comply with the requirements of leaving each Province with a surplus, and of inaugurating the new Councils without the necessity of resort to fresh taxation,"

the Committee deemed that the most equitable plan to be

[1] Report of the Committee appointed by the Secretary of State for India to advise on the question of the Financial Relations between the Central and Provincial Governments in India, pp. Cmd. 724 of 1919, Ch. III.

to take, not *equal* contributions as the Joint Report advised,[1] but *unequal* contributions from the surpluses of the Provinces liable to make them.

For the consummation of its plan the Committee held that the augmentation of Provincial Surpluses was an essential step. Without it, it deemed its task to be futile. The only way to augment the provincial surplus was to allocate some other source of Imperial revenue in addition to those already provincialized. To the provincialization of the income tax, a matter which was included in clause (*d*) of its terms of reference so far as Bombay was concerned, the Committee being impressed by the reasonings of the Joint Report, felt bound to oppose. As an alternative it recommended that *General Stamps* should be provincialized, as means of augmenting provincial surpluses, along with *Judicial Stamps*. The effect of this transfer of *General Stamps* from the all-India list to the provincial list was to increase the provincial resources and diminish those of the Central Government. That deficit the Committee accepted as amounting in the year 1921–2 to ten crore, composed of six crores previously estimated by the Government of

[1] The Report of the Financial Repations Committee seems to argue that the difference between its plan of levying contributions and that suggested in the Joint Report is a difference in the *basis* of the contributions: its basis being that of "increased spending power," while that of the Joint Report was "gross provincial surplus." The Financial Repations Committee pointedly criticized the method proposed in the Joint Report to assess the contribution from each province "as a percentage of difference between the gross provincial revenue and the gross provincial expenditure." There does not seem to be much difference between that scheme and the scheme of the Committee consisting of a percentage levy on what is called increased spending power of the provinces under the new distribution of the revenues between the Central and Provincial Governments. That these two are different bases of assessment seems to be the general impression (cf. the speech of the Hon. Rai Bahadur Bakshi Sohan Lal on the Resolution *re* Provincial Contributions to the Central Exchequer, Legislative Assembly Debates, Vol. III, No. 8, p. 508). This of course is an error; for spending power is simply another name for gross surplus. The change made by the Committee was in proposing unequal contribution in place of equal contribution. It kept unchanged the basis of the assessment.

India[1] *plus* four crores for the loss of *General Stamps*, the revenue from which the Committee gave to the Provinces. This amount subject to certain adjustments,[2] which when made resulted in a clear deficit of 9,83·06 lakhs net. In strict adherence to the limiting consideration which it felt bound to respect, the Committee proceeded to fix the following ratios in which each of the nine Provinces were to contribute to make up this amount of 9,83 lakhs in the year 1921–2:—

INITIAL CONTRIBUTIONS (in lakhs of rupees)

Provinces	Increased spending power under new distribution of Revenue	Contributions as recommended by the Committee.	Increased spending power left after Contributions are paid.
Madras	5,76	3,48	2,28
Bombay	93	56	37
Bengal	1,04	63	41
United Provinces	3,97	2,40	1,57
Punjab	2,89	1,75	1,14
Burma	2,46	64	1,82
Bihar and Orissa	51	*nil*	51
Central Provinces	52	22	30
Assam	42	15	27
Total	18,50	9,83	8,67

This ratio of initial contributions was not intended in any manner by the Committee " to represent the ideal scale on which the Provinces should have in equity to be called upon to contribute." Indeed in making its recommendations as to initial contributions the Committee paid less attention to equity of contributions and more to

" established programmes of taxation and expenditure and legislative and administrative expectations and habits, that cannot without serious mischief be suddenly adjusted to a

[1] Recommendations of the Government of India regarding the Demarcation between Central and Provincial Revenues, Cmd. 334 of 1919, Statement III.

[2] These adjustments were, with regard to the Military Police Force in Burma, the payment of pensions and leave allowances. Cf. Report of the Financial Relations Committee, para. 10.

new and more equitable ratio of contributions widely different (as an equitable ratio must admittedly be) from that of the past. It is accordingly inevitable, if such mischief is to be avoided, that the ratio for initial contributions should bear little relation to that which would be ideally equitable." But the Committee also recognized that "an initial ratio of this nature can only be defended as a measure of transition. It is necessary, but it is necessary only in order to give time to the provinces to adjust their budgets to a new state of affairs; and we are clearly of opinion that no scheme of contribution can be satisfactory that does not provide for a more equitable distribution of the burden of the deficit within a reasonable time."

The Committee therefore proceeded next to consider the question of *standard* contributions as distinguished from *initial* contributions, which were only transitional. As to what should be the ideal basis for such an equitable distribution of the burden the Committee felt quite certain; for it stated that

"to do equity between the provinces it is necessary that the total contribution of each to the purse of the Government of India should be proportionate to its capacity to contribute."

Two questions were involved in translating this principle into practice. What is the *total* contribution of a province to the purse of the Government of India? Secondly, what is the measure of the capacity of a Province to contribute? With regard to the first the Committee observed that

"the total contribution of a Province to the purse of the Government of India will consist in future of its direct contributions towards the deficit, together with its indirect contribution (as at present) through the channels of customs, income tax, duties on salt, etc.";

in other words, the pressure of the taxes from within its jurisdiction for the benefit of the Central Government. With regard to the second the Committee held that

"the capacity of a Province to contribute is its taxable capacity, which is the sum of the incomes of its taxpayers, or the average income of its taxpayers multiplied by their number."

The Committee was frank in its avowal of the fact that the data available was not sufficient for a direct quantitative evaluation either of the total net contribution which a Province made to the Government of India or of its capacity to contribute, and held that it was

"useless to attempt to state a formula, to serve as a basis for a standard ratio of contributions, capable of automatic application from year to year by reference to ascertained statistics."

None the less the Committee did not abandon the ideal basis it had selected for fixing the standard contributions. For it observed:

"We are able, after surveying such figures as are available and after close inquiry into the circumstances of each Province, to recommend a fixed ratio of contributions which in our opinion represents a standard and equitable distribution of the burden of any deficit. In arriving at this ratio we have taken into consideration the indirect contributions of the Provinces to the purse of the Government of India, and in particular the incidence of customs duties and of income tax. We have inquired into the relative taxable capacities of the Provinces, in the light of their agricultural and industrial wealth and of all other relevant incidents of their economic positions, including particularly their liability to famine. It should be observed that we have considered their taxable capacities not only as they are at the present time, or as they will be in the immediate future, but from the point of view also of the capacity of each Province for expansion and development agriculturally and industrially, and in respect of imperfectly developed assets such as minerals and forests. We have also given consideration to the elasticity of the existing heads of revenue which will be secured to each Province, and to the availability of its wealth for taxation."

After estimating, to the best of its ability, the weight which should be given to each of these circumstances, the Committee recommended the following fixed ratio as representing an equitable basis for the relative contributions of the Provinces to meet the deficit in the Budget of the Government of India :—

STANDARD CONTRIBUTIONS

Province.	Per cent. Contribution to Deficit.
Madras	17
Bombay	13
Bengal	19
United Provinces	18
Punjab	9
Burma	6½
Bihar and Orissa	10
Central Provinces	5
Assam	2½
Total	100

The Committee agreed that there should be an interval of time sufficient to enable the Provinces to adjust their budgets to the new conditions before they should in equity be called upon to contribute according to this standard ratio.[1] But the Committee thought that the interval allowed for adjustment should not be unduly prolonged.

"The initial ratio which," the Committee said, "we have proposed is a practical necessity, but the Provinces which will be called upon to pay thereunder more than they should pay in equity, ought not to be required to bear that burden for a longer period or to a greater extent than is required to prevent dislocation of the provincial budgets."

The Committee therefore proposed

"that contributions should be made on the standard ratio to any deficit that there may be in the seventh year of contribution, and that the process of transition from the initial to the standard ratio should be continuous, beginning

[1] For a good piece of criticism of the basis *adopted* by the Financial Relations Committee in arriving at the standard ratio, see para. 12 of a rather splenetic letter from Rai Bahadur K. V. Raddi to the Reforms Commissioner, Simla, pp. Cmd. 974 of 1920, p. 58.

in the second year of contribution, and proceeding in six equal annual steps."

The following table shows the initial, intermediate, and ultimate ratios of contributions for the seven years in accordance with the recommendations of the Committee:—

PER CENT. CONTRIBUTIONS TO DEFICIT IN SEVEN CONSECUTIVE YEARS, BEGINNING WITH THE FIRST YEAR OF CONTRIBUTION (rounded off to even halves)

Province.	1st Year	2nd Year.	3rd Year	4th Year	5th Year	6th Year	7th Year.
Madras	35½	32½	29½	26½	23	20	17
Bombay	5½	7	8	9½	10½	12	13
Bengal	6½	8½	10½	12½	15	17	19
United Provinces	24½	23½	22½	21	20	19	18
Punjab	18	16½	15	13½	12	10½	9
Burma	6½	6½	6½	6½	6½	6½	6½
Bihar and Orissa	*nil*	1½	3	5	7	8½	10
Central Provinces	2	2½	3	3½	4	4½	5
Assam	1½	1½	2	2	2	2	2½
Total	100%	100%	100%	100%	100%	100%	100%

These recommendations were accepted by the Government of India and the Secretary of State. But when the rules in which they were embodied came before the Joint Select Committee of Parliament appointed to revise the draft rules made under the Government of India Act, for consideration, the Committee made some important alterations in the allocation of revenues and contributions from the Provinces. In its Report [1] the Joint Committee recognized

"the intricacy of the problem with which the Financial Relations Committee had to deal, and the difficulty, amounting almost to impossibility, of arriving at any solution which was likely to be acceptable to all Local Governments. . . .

[1] Second Report of the Joint Committee appointed to revise the draft rules made under the Government of India Act, pp. 172 of 1920, pp. 2–3.

They believe that such dissatisfaction as the proposals have aroused is inevitable in distributing resources between a Central and Provincial Governments, and that the impossibility of removing by a stroke of the pen inequalities which are the result of long-standing and historical causes have been overlooked." "None the less," the Committee desired, "on grounds of policy, to alleviate the disappointment caused by the restraints which the system of contribution laid on the employment by the provinces of their revenues. As a means of alleviating the burden the Committee suggested :

"(1) That there should be granted to all provinces some share in the growth of revenue from taxation on incomes so far as that growth is attributable to an increase in the amount of income assessed.

"(2) That in no case should the initial contribution payable by any province be increased, but that the gradual reduction of the aggregate contribution should be the sole means of attaining the theoretical standards recommended by the Financial Relations Committee."

Accordingly it is provided in the Devolution Rules that :

(15) There shall be allocated to each Local Government a share in the income tax collected under the Indian Income Tax Act, 1918, within its jurisdiction. The share so allocated shall be three pies on each rupee brought under assessment under the said Act, in respect of which the income tax assessed has been collected. The number of pies to be specified shall be so calculated as to yield at the outset to the Local Governments collectively a sum amounting as near as may be to 400 lakhs.[1]

and that

[1] This arrangement was subject to the following provision attached to Devolution Rule 15 :—

(2) In consideration of this allocation, each Local Government shall make to the Governor-General in Council a fixed annual assignment of a sum to be determined by the Governor-General in Council as the equivalent of the amount which would have accrued to the Local Government in the year 1920–21 (after deducting the provincial share of the cost of special income tax establishments

(17) In the financial year 1921–2 contributions shall be paid to the Governor-General in Council by the Local Governments mentioned below according to the following scale :—

Name of the Province.	Contributions (in lakhs of rupees.)
Madras	3,48
Bombay	56
Bengal	63
United Provinces	2,40
Punjab	1,75
Burma	64
Central Provinces and Berar	22
Assam	15

(18) From the financial year 1922–3 onwards a total contribution of 9,83 lakhs, or such smaller sum as may be determined by the Governor-General in Council, shall be paid to the Governor-General in Council by the Local Governments mentioned in the preceding rule. When for any year the Governor-General in Council determines as the total amount of the contribution a smaller sum than that payable for the preceding year, a reduction shall be made in the contributions of those Local Governments only whose last previous annual contribution exceeds the proportion specified below of the smaller sum so determined as the total contribution; and any reduction so made shall be proportionate to such excess :

in that year) had the pie-rate fixed under sub-rule (1) been applied in that year, due allowance being made for any abnormal delays in the collection of the tax.

(3) The cost of special income tax establishments employed within a province shall be borne by the Local Government and the Governor-General in Council in the proportions of 25 per cent. and 75 per cent. respectively.

(4) If in any financial year the total amount payable by a Local Government under sub-rules (2) and (3) in respect of the fixed assignment and the cost of special income tax establishments exceeds the amount of the share of income tax allocated to it under sub-rule (1), the fixed assignment for that year shall be deemed to have been reduced by the amount of such excess.

Madras	$\frac{17}{90}$ths
Bombay	$\frac{13}{90}$ths
Bengal	$\frac{19}{90}$ths
United Provinces	$\frac{18}{90}$ths
Punjab	$\frac{9}{90}$ths
Burma	$\frac{6\frac{1}{2}}{90}$ths
Central Provinces and Berar . .	$\frac{5}{90}$ths
Assam	$\frac{2\frac{1}{2}}{90}$ths

(19) In cases of emergency the Local Government of any Province may be required by the Governor-General in Council, with the sanction of the Secretary of State, to pay to the Governor-General in Council a contribution for any financial year in excess of the amount required by the preceding rules in the case of that year.

Two more matters had to be settled in order to make the separation between Provincial and Central Finance as complete as possible. Both were connected with capital transactions. One was the question of the Provincial Loan Account. This Account represented the fund from which a Provincial Government advanced agricultural loans, loans to indebted landholders, to municipalities and other local bodies, etc. The capital was provided by the Government of India as required and was returned to it as it was repaid. The province paid the Government of India interest on the average capital outstanding in each year, recouping itself by higher rates of interest which were supposed to compensate it for bad debts. It was commonly agreed that it was the natural result of the Reforms Scheme that the Provinces should for the future finance their own loan transactions, and that joint accounts of this nature between them and the Government of India should be wound up as quickly as possible. The matter was referred to the Financial Relations Committee and on the basis of its recommendations in that behalf it was provided by Rule 23 of the Devolution Rules that:

> "Any moneys which, on the 1st day of April 1921, are owed to the Governor-General in Council on account of advances made from the provincial loan account of any Province shall be treated as an advance to the Local Government from the revenues of India, and shall carry interest at a rate calculated on the average rate carried by the total amount owed to the Governor-General in Council on this account on the 31st March 1921. The interest shall be payable upon such dates as the Governor-General in Council may fix. In addition, the Local Government shall pay to the Governor-General in Council in each year an instalment in repayment of the principal amount of the advance, and this instalment shall be so fixed that the total advance shall except where for special reasons the Governor-General in Council may otherwise direct, be repaid before the expiry of twelve years. It shall be open to any Local Government to repay in any year an amount in excess to the fixed instalment."

The other was the question of responsibility for capital expenditure on irrigation works. In this as in the matter of Provincial Loan Account it was agreed that it would be incompatible with the scheme of complete separation of Provincial Finance to hand over to the former the control of irrigation works and to make the latter responsible for the capital transaction incurred thereon. Hence the rule[1] that:

(1) The capital sums spent by the Governor-General in Council upon the construction in the various Provinces of productive and protective irrigation works and of such other works financed from loan funds as may from time to time be handed over to the management of Local Governments shall be treated as

[1] Devolution Rule 24.

advances made to the Local Governments from the revenues of India. Such advances shall carry interest at the following rates, namely:

(*a*) In the case of outlay up to the end of the financial year 1916–17, at the rate of 3·3252 *per centum*.

(*b*) In the case of outlay incurred after the financial year 1916–17, at the average rate of interest paid by the Governor-General in Council on loans raised in the open market since the end of that year.

(2) The interest shall be payable upon such dates as the Governor-General in Council may fix.

Thus was broken the financial and administrative strand which tied the Provincial Governments to the Central Government and prevented the introduction into them of responsible government. As the Provinces thereby acquired "an acknowledged authority of their own" over the services and sources allocated to them it followed that they should have the freedom to borrow in their own name, which was denied to them heretofore. Consequently the Local Government Borrowing Rules [1] made under the Reforms Act provided that subject to certain conditions: [2]

"A Local Government may raise loans on the security of the revenues allocated to it for any of the following purposes, namely:

(*a*) To meet capital expenditure on the construction or acquisition (including the acquisition of land, maintenance during construction and equipment) of any work or permanent asset of a material character in

[1] Rules under Section 2 (2) of the Government of India Act, 1919.

[2] The rules required that:

(1) No loan shall be raised by a Local Government without the sanction (in the case of loans to be raised in India) of the Governor-General in Council, or (in the case of loans to be raised outside India) of the Secretary of State in Council, and in sanctioning the raising of a loan the Governor-General in Council or the Secretary of State in Council, as the case may be, may specify the amount of the issue and any or all of the conditions under which the loan shall be raised.

(2) Every application for the sanction of Secretary of State . . . shall be transmitted through the Governor-General in Council.

connection with a project of lasting public utility, provided that:

(i) the proposed expenditure is so large that it cannot reasonably be met from current revenues, and

(ii) if the project appears to the Governor-General in Council unlikely to yield a return of not less than such percentage as he may from time to time by order prescribe, arrangements are made for the amortization of the debt;

(*b*) to meet any classes of expenditure on irrigation which have under rules in force before the passing of the Act been met from loan funds;

(*c*) for the giving of relief and the establishment and maintenance of relief works in times of famine or scarcity;

(*d*) for the financing of the Provincial Loan Account; and

(*e*) for the repayment or consolidation of loans raised in accordance with these rules or the repayment of advance made by the Governor-General in Council."

With the cutting off of the financial and administrative strand there remained only the legislative strand which had so far debarred the growth of provincial autonomy. This legislative strand, as was pointed out before, operated through the principle of requiring previous sanction and subsequent assent of the Government of India. By the rules made under the Reforms Act a field has been marked off for the free exercise of the Legislative powers of the Provinces in which that principle has been dispensed with. So far as the field of tax legislation was concerned it was provided [1] that:

"The Legislative Council of a Province may, without the previous sanction of the Governor-General, make and take into consideration any law for imposing for the purposes of the Local Government any tax included in Schedule I."

This schedule comprises the following heads of taxation:—

1. A tax on land put to uses other than agricultural.

[1] Rules under Section 10 (3) (*a*) of the Government of India Act, 1919, Schedule Taxes Rules.

2. A tax on succession or acquisition by survivorship in a joint family.
3. A tax on any form of betting or gambling permitted by law.
4. A tax on advertisements.
5. A tax on amusements.
6. A tax on any specified luxury.
7. A registration fee.
8. A stamp-duty other than duties of which the amount is fixed by Indian legislation.

In the matter of non-tax legislation the procedure adopted by the rules has been slightly different. In tax legislation the rules stated in what cases previous sanction was not necessary. In non-tax legislation the rules required in what cases previous sanction was necessary. The effect of this difference in the requirements of the rules of previous sanction [1] was that while in matters of tax legislation a Provincial Government could only levy certain named taxes, in the matter of non-tax legislation it could do anything provided it did not infringe certain laws. The reasons for this difference are obvious. A widening of the basis of provincial taxation means a narrowing field for imperial taxation. Such a detrimental effect could not flow to the Government in the matter of non-tax legislation, be the non-tax legislative powers of the Provinces howsoever large. The taxing power to be granted to the Provinces had therefore to be more strictly circumscribed than the grant of legislative power. None the less it cannot be denied that the rules regarding previous sanction sufficiently loosened the Legislative strand as to permit

[1] Rules under section 10 (3) (L) of the Government of India Act, 1919, Local Legislature Previous Sanction Rules. It should, however, be noted that if a Provincial Bill is such that it does not require previous sanction it does not follow that it can become law under the above rules because it has been assented to by the Provincial Legislation. For, by virtue of another set of Rules made under section 12 (1) of the Government of India Act, 1919, called Reservation of Bills Rules, it is provided that the Governor of a Province *must* reserve some and may reserve other Bills for the subsequent assent of the Governor-General before declaring them law even if the Bills be such as to require no previous sanction.

of the Provinces being autonomous in theory as well as in practice.

This autonomy is well reflected in the new Budget Procedure in the Provinces. Under the old regime the Provincial Budgets had to be passed by the Finance Department of the Government of India, the Provincial Accounts to be supervised by the Accountant-General and audited by the Controller and Auditor-General of the Government of India and appropriation reports submitted to the Finance Department of the Government of India. All this is changed under the new regime. The Provincial Budget, instead of being passed by the Finance Department of the Government of India, is framed by the Finance Department constituted in each Province under the Reforms Act,[1] and is voted item by item by the Provincial Legislature.[2] The accounts of the Provinces still continue [3] to be supervised and audited by the officers of the Government of India, but the important point under the new regime which is the hall-mark of provincial independence is that the appropriation reports, instead of being sent to the Government of India for action, are now sent to the Committee of Public Accounts constituted from amongst the members of the Provincial Legislature which sanctioned the Budget for report that the money voted by the Legislature was spent within the scope of the grants made by the Legislature.

Thus is effected the demarcation of the field for the governance of India into Central and Provincial. Such a demarcation of administrative and financial matters was the dream of many an Indian politician and statesman. It was urged before the Royal Commission on Decentralization and was also urged by the late Mr. Gokhale in his political testament which he left before he died. But all

[1] For the constitution and functions of the Finance Department of the Provinces, see Part III of Devolution rules made under Section I of the Government of India Act, 1919.

[2] See Rules 25 to 32 of the Rules of Business for Provincial Legislative Councils made under Section 11 (5) of the Government of India Act, 1919.

[3] Rules framed under Section 96 D (1) of the Government of India Act.

these projects were ill timed and could not be given effect to until the law of the Indian constitution had been altered. Now that such an alteration has been made the ideal of Provincial autonomy bids fair to become real. But before closing this study it may be useful to evaluate the changes of its successful working.

CHAPTER XII

A CRITIQUE OF THE CHANGE

It is obvious that good administration depends upon good finance; for finance is "the fuel of the whole administrative machine." No aspect of the scheme of Reforms therefore demands a closer and more anxious study than the financial arrangements with which the new system of administration starts. The necessity for such an examination is all the greater because this aspect of the Reforms Scheme has received comparatively little intelligent criticism at the hands either of the public or the expert.

The first question to consider is, can the new financial arrangements be said to be *administratively* workable? To make administrative polities independent by requiring them to finance themselves entirely out of their own respective resources without having to depend upon one another must always be regarded as a very important end to be kept in view in devising a new financial arrangement. It is true that it is not always possible to realize this end, and it may in some cases be actually helpful to their working that the polities should be made mutually dependent; for interdependence, at least in matters of public finance, instead of being an impediment might conceivably furnish a basis for co-operation and strength. None the less independence in finance for each administrative policy is to be sought for wherever possible. There can be no doubt that from this standpoint the system of contributions is better than the system of divided heads. This is not to condemn the system of divided heads. The existence of several concurrent or overlapping tax jurisdictions must always be a source of difficulty whenever an attempt is to be made to distribute the different sources of revenue among the competing tax jurisdictions so as to allow each a sufficiency of funds. The reason is that this distribution of the sources of revenue must not only be governed by considerations of adequacy, but must also be governed by considerations of suitability. "The problem of efficiency of taxation," as Prof. Seligman observes,[1]

"is naturally of vital importance. No matter how well intentioned a scheme may be, or how completely it may harmonize with the abstract principles of justice, if the tax does not work administratively it is doomed to failure."

Whether among the sources of revenue to be partitioned there are any which are naturally more suitable for utilization by one tax jurisdiction rather than by another depends upon what is the basis of the tax. If the basis of the tax is narrow then the argument in favour of its utilization by a narrower tax jurisdiction will be correspondingly stronger. If its basis is wide then the scales would weigh in favour of its utilization by the broader tax jurisdiction. But as a result of following the dictates of suitability it is not always possible to make a partition such as to give each administrative polity revenues adequate for its purposes. For it may happen that a particular tax is suitable for one jurisdiction while its yield, instead of being necessary for that jurisdiction, may be required for another jurisdiction which is unfit to levy it, or may be partially necessary for both. In such a case, how are the ends of adequacy to be subserved? Two remedies suggest themselves. One is the adoption of the system of divided heads, and the second is to apportion the deficiency among the several component states and require them to make a definite contribution towards meeting it.[2]

The system of divided heads was by no means peculiar to the Indian fiscal system. It has been adopted in some

[1] *Essays in Taxation* (8th edition, 1913), Chapter XII, "The Relations of State and Federal Finance."

[2] It will be noted that although the new Indian system is largely a system of contributions it is not without an admixture of the system of divided heads so far as the Income tax is concerned.

form or other by many other countries. In England, for instance, the inheritance tax is assessed by the Central Government, but a part of the proceeds is allotted to the Local Government. The same is true of some other taxes in England. In Germany, under the Empire, the proceeds of certain indirect taxes were divided between the federal and state governments. In Canada it is well known that a large part of the provincial revenues is derived from proceeds of taxes that are levied by the federal government.

The prejudice in India against the system of divided heads of revenue is particularly regrettable because it is founded on the view that it is opposed to the principle of separation of revenues. People who opposed it said [1] that it involved divided heads of expenditure which fettered the spending powers of the Provinces and enabled the Government of India directly to interfere in their Budget estimates and "to have its finger in every pie" of theirs. The system of divided heads was no doubt characterized by these objectionable features. But division of expenditure is not a necessary accompaniment of division of revenue. Nor is it a necessary incident of it that a polity which shared in the yield of a tax but did not administer it should interfere in calculating the estimates of the yield. Chipped of its evil features, the system of divided heads of revenue is simply another name for what Prof. Seligman calls [2] the system of segregation of source and the division of the yield. The essence of the system consists in the exclusive assessment of a particular source of revenue by one tax jurisdiction, coupled, however, with an apportionment of a part of the proceeds to another tax jurisdiction. The system of divided heads of revenue does not cease to be a system of separation of sources merely because there is the division of the yield. In such a system of divided heads there is a separation because the assessment of the tax is segregated—which is the essence of separation—exclusively

[1] *R.C.D.*, Mit. of Evid., Vol. VI, Q. 25017–25020 ; Vol. VIII, Q. 35531, 35225–29.

[2] *Op. cit.*, Chapter XI, "Separation of State and Local Revenues," particularly pp. 365–6.

in the hands of one tax jurisdiction, and the division of the yield can be so regulated that it need not be incompatible with real separation.

The system of contributions does what the system of divided heads aims to do. Like the system of divided heads it answers the tests of suitability as well as of adequacy by allowing the tax to be administered by the jurisdiction most competent to do it, and also of adequacy by making the taxing jurisdiction hand over a sum to the non-taxing jurisdiction. Essentially the system of divided heads and the system of contributions are alike. The only difference between the two is that so far as the apportionment of proceeds are concerned the one is an itemized arrangement while the other is a lump-sum arrangement. There is therefore really nothing much to choose between them. But this is not altogether a case of merely giving a different name to a discredited system in the hope that it might smell more sweet. For the system of contributions has one real point of superiority as compared with the system of divided heads. It does not merely permit of separation of assessment, but it also makes for a greater separation than does the system of divided heads. Under the system of divided heads the receiving party has still an anxious concern in the assessment and collection of the tax for any laxity in the administration of a divided head of revenues is bound to affect its interests adversely, and may therefore claim a hand in the administration of the tax. But under the system of contributions there is no room for such a possibility. Its quota being assured it is out of the business of assessing and collecting the tax. There is thus a greater separation under the system of contributions than there can be under the system of divided heads.

When we come to analyse the equity of the new financial arrangements we find that great objections are raised to the system of contributions. But many of these objections are misconceived. It will be recalled that the contributions from the Provinces to the Central Government in India are regulated according to their spending powers.

In other words, it is the apportionment by expenditure method of dealing with the deficit. That the method subserves the ends of adequacy is of course obvious. But what does not seem to be so obvious, but which all the same is a great virtue of the system of contributions, is that it promotes economy in the giving as well as in the receiving tax jurisdiction; for extravagance in the contributing tax jurisdiction immediately increases its burden, while extravagance in the receiving tax jurisdiction is directly reflected in enhancing the contributions. None the less, the contributions, it is protested, are inequitous, for they are held to be based not on population, nor on area, nor on wealth, nor on the capacity of the Provinces. It is also complained that the system of contributions according to spending powers is unwise, for it tends to check desirable expenditures in the more progressive Provinces. The latter is, of course, a real objection to the apportionment by expenditure method of contributions in its general form. But it may be said, on the other hand, that in the first place if a jurisdiction is willing to undertake the burdens of a larger expenditure for desirable aims, it will scarcely be deterred by the slight additional burden which might result from the increase in the contribution. Secondly, if it were found that the contribution did produce such a result it would be possible to obviate it by adopting the simple expedient of exempting certain kinds of expenditure which might be deemed to be necessary. What these expenditures should be would be a matter of adjustment, which might differ in different provinces. The virtues of the system of apportionment by expenditure method of levying contributions would still be conserved intact, and its automatic features would work equally well if certain expenditures only, instead of all expenditures, were selected as the basis of calculations.

This objection cannot, however, be urged against the Indian system of contributions. In the first place, the contribution is not a varying sum as is the case in the financial systems of other countries. Because the Provinces are made contributory towards the deficit of the Central Government it is to be remembered that they are not liable to the whole of the central deficit whatsoever it may be from year to year. On the other hand, in ordinary years the Provinces are only liable to make contributions towards meeting what is called the Standard Central Deficit of Rs. 9,83 lakhs. That being the case the contributions do not form an element of uncertainty in the Provincial Budgets. Secondly, the contributions are not a permanent feature of the financial arrangements between the Central and Provincial Governments. The levy of the contributions is contemplated to be only transitional, to allow the Government of India to work out its financial salvation, and the Government of India has promised that they will adopt such a policy as to bring about the extinction of the contributions in as short a time as possible. Lastly, the ratio of the contributions to the standard revenues or expenditure of any of the Provinces is not so great as to place a heavy incubus on their financial system, and not being a varying quantity cannot be said to check useful expenditures by Provinces which propose to incur them.

As a matter of fact whatever may be said against the flaws in the apportionment by expenditure method of levying contributions it would be difficult to deny that the system eminently answers the requirements of equity. It certainly brings about a more equitable [1] distribution of the burden than is possible under other systems. For it may fairly be assumed that expenditures very nearly correspond to the actual abilities of the communities concerned more than do population [2] or area. Not only is the principle equitable in itself, but care has been taken to do equity in its application as between the different Provinces. For we know that the contributions are so regulated as to leave to the Provinces, rich as well as poor, a reserve of spending power in order to enable them to meet such of their pressing needs as may not have been covered by the figure for standard expendi-

[1] Cf. Seligman, *op. cit.*, p. 360.

[2] In Germany under the Empire the contributions from the states were apportioned according to population. The same is the case in Switzerland.

ture. The main purpose of rejecting equal in favour of unequal contributions was to see that the burden of the contributions did not prevent any of the Provinces from meeting such extra expenditure as may be absolutely necessary. Indeed, no system of contributions can be said to be calculated to produce greater equity than the Indian system.

So far we have examined whether the new financial arrangement is administratively workable and equitable. What we have now to see is: Has the arrangement proved

(*In Thousands of Rupees.*)

Province.		Standard Figures.	Revised 1921–2	Budget 1922–3
Madras	Revenue	14,98,02	15,58,59	16,76,50
	Expenditure	14,07,20	17,15,93	17,18,55
	Surplus and Deficit	90,82	– 1,57,34	– 42,05
Bombay	Revenue	12,09,70	13,67,13	14,93,06
	Expenditure	11,55,03	16,52,80	15,42,17
	Surplus and Deficit	54,67	– 2,85,67	– 50,11
Bengal	Revenue	8,55,28	8,86,53	10,55,86
	Expenditure	8,61,13	11,10,60	10,36,90
	Surplus and Deficit	– 5,85	– 2,24,07	18,96
United Provinces	Revenue	12,29,88	13,34,31	13,58,67
	Expenditure	12,06,56	14,59,87	13,85,65
	Surplus and Deficit	1,23,32	– 1,25,56	– 26,98
Punjab	Revenue	9,73,51	10,73,76	11,38,26
	Expenditure	9,10,69	12,23,24	12,68,44
	Surplus and Deficit	62,82	– 1,49,48	– 1,30,18
Burma	Revenue	8,24,28	9,99,33	10,00,57
	Expenditure	7,84,78	10,27,51	11,90,70
	Surplus and Deficit	39,50	– 28,18	– 1,90,13
Bihar and Orissa	Revenue	4,30,39	4,46,15	4,62,65
	Expenditure	4,20,70	4,85,97	5,13,80
	Surplus and Deficit	90,69	– 39,82	– 51,15
Central Provinces	Revenue	4,35,37	5.14,80	5,35,23
	Expenditure	4,38,80	5,41,76	5,72,17
	Surplus and Deficit	– 3,43	– 26,96	– 36,94
Assam	Revenue	1,81,46	2,01,12	2,08,06
	Expenditure	1,78,25	2,19,45	2,22,58
	Surplus and Deficit	3,21	– 18,33	– 14,52

itself to be financially adequate? It will be recalled that the Financial Relations Committee held that the general resources of the country were abundant, and that it required only a wise plan of distribution in order to leave each Province with a sufficiently large "spending power" or surplus. That the plan recommended by the Committee was calculated to bring about such a result must of course be taken for granted. But when we analyse the Budgets of the different Provinces since the introduction of the Reforms the result appears to be entirely disappointing (*see* Table, p. 256).

Thus, taking the estimated revenue and expenditure of the nine Provinces for 1922–3, equilibrium between current revenue and expenditure is only to be found in two of them, Burma and Bengal, and in the latter this result could not have been attained but for the temporary remission [1] of its annual contribution to the Central Government, and a programme of taxation calculated to bring in Rs. 140 lakhs. In the rest of the Provinces the deficits of the year aggregated to the large figure of Rs. 7,74 lakhs. This huge deficit was financed by new [2] taxation to the extent of Rs. 3,52 lakhs, and for the rest by drawing on balances and by raising loans from the public and from the Central Government. But as the Secretary of State in his despatch [3] pointed out, this

> "process of financing provincial deficits in part from the accumulated revenue balances of the past will now practically come to an end, as such balances will be generally exhausted by the end of the current financial year. . . . If the financial stability of the Provinces is not to be undermined, with ultimate jeopardy to the Government of India itself, it is impossible to contemplate the continuance of a series of Provincial deficits financed by borrowing either direct from the public or from the Central Government."

What is to be the remedy? At the Conference held in Simla in April, 1922, "to consider various matters connected

[1] *Legislative Assembly Debates*, Vol. III, No. 8.

[2] Cf. the letter of the Government of India, Finance Department, No. 13 of July 13, 1922, to the Secretary of State.

[3] Cf. the despatch in reply to the above by the Secretary of State (Financial), No. 17, of November 9, 1922.

with the financial arrangements between the Central Government and the Provinces," it was disclosed [1] that the Government of India and the Provinces were divided as to the proper solution for the rehabilitation of Provincial Finance on a stable and secure footing. The Provinces proposed an increase in their resources by revising the financial arrangements made by the Reforms Act. On the other hand, the Secretary of State as a mouthpiece of the Government of India urged that

> " Equilibrium can only be achieved by reduction of expenditure and the adoption of measures which will lead to an increase of revenue." [2]

The Provinces were not, however, unanimous in the suggestions they made for the revision of the arrangements effected by the Act. Some like the Government of Bombay suggested a return to the system of " divided heads " while others were opposed to it. But the majority was for securing relief through the abolition of contributions. This attitude of the Provinces towards the new financial arrangements is on the face of it a very unreasonable attitude. They are opposed both to the system of divided heads and the system of contributions as well. This is to have things both ways, and they could certainly have had it if the existing resources of the country had been properly husbanded. Inadequacy of finance is not always the result of a paucity of revenue resources. National prosperity may be great and growing and the increase of national wealth may be proceeding unchecked. If under such circumstances enough revenue is not obtained the fault does not lie with the social income. Rather it is a fault of the government which must be said to have failed to organize and marshal the national resources for fiscal purposes. The same is to some extent true of the Indian Government.

Surveying the national resources of the country, it becomes evident that there are two sources which the Government

[1] For a summary of the result of this Conference, see Letter of the Government of India, *supra*, p. 257.

[2] The despatch of the Secretary of State, *supra*, p. 257.

has not been able to marshal properly. One is the land revenue. It is notorious that land revenue has been the biggest resource to the Government of India. In the collection of the land revenue every landholder is laid under contribution, but the rate of assessment is not periodically enhanced for every one of them. On the other hand, in Bengal and in other parts of India the rate of assessment is permanently settled. Consequently in such parts of India which by the long period of settled government enjoyed by them, and by the consequent influx of capital, have attained to a greater advance in prosperity than any others, the land revenue yields practically no increase; the land-owners, with enormously increased incomes, contribute nothing to the increase in the financial burdens of the State. Permanent Settlement has ever since the days of Lord Canning been suggested as a panacea for improving the financial condition of the people. After the severe famine of 1860, Lord Canning, then Viceroy and Governor-General of India, recommended the extension of the Permanent Settlement to all parts of India. Sir John (afterwards Lord) Lawrence supported the recommendation, and the two Secretaries of State for India, Sir Charles Wood and Sir Stafford Northcote, approved of the proposal. Fortunately for the country the proposal for making the Permanent Settlement universal was finally rejected in 1883. Some no doubt regarded the decision as unfortunate, and continued the agitation in favour of the Permanent Settlement long after. But the real force, if there was any in the agitation, was derived from the motive of putting a limit on the financial resources of an alien and an irresponsible bureaucracy. Those who then agitated in favour of the Permanent Settlement probably did not realize that some day this irresponsible bureaucracy would give place to a responsible government of the people and the Permanent Settlement which it was desired to be instituted as a curb on the unchartered licence of a bureaucracy would result in placing a fetter on the freedom of a popular government to enter upon the path of orderly progress. A bad government may abuse its financial powers; but a government cannot be a good government if there is a serious limitation on its financial powers. It was therefore a good thing that this evil of a permanent settlement was not allowed to spread to the whole of India. But it would have been better if the new financial arrangements had contrived to replace the permanent settlement system of land revenue by a periodical settlement system. That was one important way of augmenting the general resources of the country and thereby giving adequacy to all the governments concerned. Instead of this the financial arrangements were so conceived as not to

"subject the permanently settled provinces to financial pressure which would have the practical result of forcing them to reconsider the permanent settlement."[1]

If this had been done it would have augmented the general resources to the benefit of all. As it was, not only provision was made favouring the retention of the Permanent Settlement, but the Bengal Government, which has the largest number of permanently settled holders of land, was later on exempted from contributing to the Government of India which was compelled to meet its deficit in other ways.

Land Revenue therefore is one source which the Government could have marshalled in the interest of giving adequacy to the new financial arrangements. The other source which the Government refuses to tap is the customs revenue. The kind of fiscal policy that was adopted during the pre-Mutiny days, was, as we know it to be, of a suicidal character. The same is true of the post-Mutiny fiscal policy. From the Mutiny up to the present time, the Government of India has never looked upon the customs revenue as a resource to be used to meet the exigencies of the State, and when it has used it, it is only very reluctantly, and never to the fullest, not to mention the circumstances when it has actually reduced its revenue from this source in spite of the crying needs of the exchequer.[2] While the

[1] Joint Report, p. 171.
[2] Financial Statement for 1880–81, para. 74.

ostensible reason given in favour of such a fiscal policy is that the customs revenue is wrong in principle, everybody knows that the customs revenue is not raised in India because it is feared that under it Indian industries would be protected against English industries. That the whole policy of India has been dictated by the interests of English manufactures is beyond dispute, and the reason for it is not far to seek. The Secretary of State for India, the supreme executive for India, is directly amenable to the English voters, whose primary concern has been to see that their markets are not closed against them. Whether a protectionist policy is good or bad is another question. For the present it is sufficient to note that the Government of India has been subjected to a pernicious kind of limitation on its fiscal powers which prevents it from using a source of revenue which has everywhere else proved to be most elastic and abundant of financial resources. If these limitations were not there the present financial inadequacy in all probability might not have ensued at all, and there would have been no necessity either for adopting the system of divided heads or for imposing contributions. As it is, owing to these limitations on the taxable resources of the country, a deficit in the Budget of the Central Government is inevitable. Given this fact, the adoption of some method of meeting that deficit was imperative, and there is no doubt that the system adopted is better than the system it replaced. In the present circumstances of the finances of the Central Government, contributions must be taken as a settled issue. Nor can it be said that the abolition of contributions would restore stability to Provincial Finance. Such no doubt is the prevalent view of the Provincial Governments and also of non-official politicians. The Resolution moved in the Indian Legislative Assembly on the 14th September, 1922, rested on the same view that if the Government of India were only to dispense with the contributions it would immediately restore equilibrium in the financial position of the Provinces. This belief was strengthened by the assumption that the aggregate estimated deficit of all the Provinces disclosed itself to be 352 lakhs of rupees for the financial year 1922–3; and as the total contribution to the Imperial Government by the Provinces aggregated to the sum of 983 lakhs, a remission of this amount would more than wipe off the deficit in the Provincial Budgets. It must, however, be said that the deficit of 352 lakhs of rupees does not disclose the true position of the Provinces as derived from the financial arrangements made by the Act. If we are to deduce the true position of the Provinces as following from the new arrangement we must take note of the new taxation imposed and of the gain to Bengal through the remission of its contribution to the Imperial exchequer. Making adjustments for these, the position of the Provinces as it would have been without contributions may be seen from the following:—

FINANCIAL POSITION OF THE PROVINCES 1922–3
(in thousands of rupees)

Provinces.	Revenue	Expenditure	Surplus or Deficit
	Rs	Rs	Rs
Madras	15,99,00	17,18,55	−1,19,55
Bombay	14,32,06	15,42,17	−1,10,11
Bengal	9,15,86	10,99,90	−1,84,04
U.P.	13,58,67	13,85,65	− 26,98
Punjab	11,38,26	12,68,44	−1,30,18
Burma	10,00,57	11,90,70	−1,90,13
Bihar and Orissa	4,62,65	5,13,80	− 51,15
Central Provinces	5,35,23	5,72,17	− 36,94
Assam	2,05,06	2,22,58	− 17,52
Total deficit			−8,66,60

According to this calculation the aggregate deficit of the Provinces would have been about 867 lakhs. But we must make some further adjustments to this account. It has not been possible to deduct from the revenues of the Central Provinces the sum derived from the enhancement of the Excise duty in the Provinces. Secondly, the revenues of the Central Provinces for the year 1922–3 include collections of suspended revenue of previous years. If these adjustments were made the aggregate deficit of the Provinces would give rise to a figure which would be barely covered by the remission of contributions. We must therefore conclude that remission of contributions would have at best been a very inadequate measure for removing the financial stringency of the Provinces, even if the problem of financing the extra deficit caused by such remission in the budget of the Central Government were to be ignored.

But if remission of contributions cannot improve the difficult situation that has arisen with regard to Provincial Finance, we must go to the root of the matter and inquire what are the causes which have brought on that situation. Is it due to the normal expenditure of the Provinces being underrated ? Or is it due to the normal revenues of the Provinces being over-estimated ? For this purpose we must first ascertain whether the resources allocated to the Provinces were really inadequate to their normal needs. The following table compares the standard receipts and expenditure and shows the margin left between them for covering a probable advance in expenditure.

STANDARD REVENUE AND STANDARD EXPENDITURE

Provinces	Standard Revenue	Standard Expenditure.	Excess or Defect of Standard Revenue over Standard Expenditure.
Madras	14,98,02	14,07,20	90,82
Bombay	12,09,70	11,55,03	54,67
Bengal	8,55,28	8,61,13	— 5,85
U.P.	12,29,88	11,06,56	1,23,32
Punjab	9,73,51	9,10,69	62,82
Burma	8,24,28	7,84,78	39,50
Bihar and Orissa	4,30,39	4,20,70	9,69
C.P.	4,35,37	4,38,80	— 3,43
Assam	1,81,46	1,78,25	3,21

From this it is obvious that except in the case of two Provinces the standard revenue has left a sufficient margin over standard expenditure. Only in Bengal and Central Provinces there was no margin, owing to the fact that the standard expenditure was slightly in excess of the standard revenue. But this defect was more than remedied in the case of Bengal by the remission of the contributions to the Central Government, and the excess of standard expenditure over standard revenue in the case of Central Provinces was indeed very small. Barring this, in the rest of the Provinces the margin allowed was substantial. Let us now turn to the actual figures and compare them with the standard figures. First of all, let us take the revenue side of the Provincial Budgets. Has the realized revenue fallen short of the standard revenue ? The following table compares the realized receipts of the Provinces with the standard figure assumed to be the normal in the financial allocation made under the new Act :—

PROVINCIAL REVENUES [1]

Provinces	Standard Revenues	+ Increase over Standard — Decrease from Standard	
		For 1921–2.	For 1922–3
Madras	14,98,02	60,57	40,41
Bombay	12,09,70	1,57,47	2,22,36
Bengal	8,55,28	31,25	60,58
U.P.	12,29,88	1,04,43	1,28,79
Punjab	9,73,51	1,00,15	1,64,75
Burma	8,24,28	1,75,05	1,76,29
Bihar and Orissa	4,30,39	15,76	32,26
C.P.	4,35,37	79,43	99,86
Assam	1,81,46	22,60	23,60

The above table brings out very clearly the fact, not readily admitted, namely that the realized revenue has in no case fallen short of the standard revenue. It may, however, be asked : Has the increase in the realized revenue been equal to the margin allowed under the allocation between the standard revenue and the standard expenditure of the Provinces ? As throwing some light on that aspect of the question the following table is interesting :—

[1] Exclusive of new taxation.

Expansion of Provincial Revenues

Provinces	Standard Margin.	Excess or Defect of Realized Margin over Standard Margin.	
		For 1921-2.	For 1922-3.
Madras	90,82	— 30,25	— 50,41
Bombay	54,67	1,02,80	1,68,19
Bengal	— 5,85	25,40	54,73
U.P.	1,23,32	— 18,89	5,47
Punjab	62,82	37,33	1,01,93
Burma	39,50	1,35,55	1,36,79
Bihar and Orissa	9,69	6,07	22,57
C.P.	3,43	76,00	96,43
Assam	3,21	19,39	20,39

From these figures it is obvious that except in the case of Madras the realized margin has in no case fallen below the standard margin. The excess of the realized over the standard margin is enormous. It cannot, therefore, be said that the financial deficit in the Provinces is due to provincial revenue having failed to reach the assumed normal. On the other hand, the revenues were more than necessary to cover the normal expenditure of the Provinces. The only conclusion that can fairly be drawn from the facts of the case is that the provincial deficits are due to an extraordinary increase [1] in the expenditure of the Provinces. The following figures furnish enough evidence in support of this view :—

Provinces	Standard Expenditure.	+Increase over Standard — Decrease from Standard.	
		For 1921-2	For 1922-3
Madras	14,07,20	3,08,73	3,11,35
Bombay	11,55,03	2,97,77	3,87,14
Bengal	8,61,13	2,49,47	1,75,77
U.P.	11,06,56	3,43,31	2,79,09
Punjab	9,10,69	3,12,55	3,57,75
Burma	7,8 78	2,42,73	4,05,92
and Orissa	4,20,70	65,27	93,10
C.P.	4,38,80	1,02,96	1,23,37
Assam	1,78,25	41,20	44,33

[1] For a brief review of this fact see the summary of it in the letter of the Government of India, *op. cit.*

We are, therefore, led to the view held by the Secretary of State that reduction of expenditure and increase of taxation is the only remedy for placing provincial finance on a sound footing.

What chances are there that the Provinces will undertake the reduction of expenditure and increase of taxation so very necessary for their safety ? In this connection it is well to recall the dictum of that great financier, Mr. James Wilson, who once said:

> "Finance is not mere arithmetic; finance is a great policy. Without sound finance no sound government is possible: without sound government no sound finance is possible."

If there is any truth in this, then whether or not the Provincial Governments will undertake economy or face increase of taxation depends upon whether or not the system of government established in the Provinces by the Reforms Act is a sound system. Now, what is the nature of the government that is established in the Provinces under the Reforms Act ? In common parlance the system is known as dyarchy. Under it the Executive of the Province, instead of being composed of the Governor in Council as before, is now divided into the Governor in Council and the Governor in Ministry. Under it the subjects marked off as Provincial from the Central are further divided into "Reserved" and "Transferred" subjects. The former are in charge of the Governor in Council, and the latter in that of the Governor in Ministry. Of these parts of the Provincial Executive the Council in charge of the "reserved" subjects still remains as before irresponsible to the Provincial Legislature, is unremovable by it, and in that sense is a non-parliamentary executive. The other part of the Provincial Executive, namely the Ministry in charge of the "transferred" subjects, is recruited from the elected members of the Provincial Legislature, is made responsible to the Provincial Legislature which is based on a more or less popular franchise, and is removable by it, and in that sense is a Parliamentary Executive.

The Provincial Legislature is supreme with regard to both the parts of the Provincial Executive. It has not only full powers of legislation, but has also full and unfettered powers of interpellation. Its powers of sanctioning and voting upon the Provincial Budget are complete, although provision is made in the Reforms Act,[1] which allows that

"the Local Government shall have power in relation to any such demand (for a money grant) to act as if it had been assented to, notwithstanding the withholding of such assent or the reduction of the amount therein referred to (by the Provincial Legislature), if the demand relates to a reserved subject (which is assigned to the charge of the Governor in Council) and the Governor certified that the Expenditure provided for by the demand is essential to the discharge of his responsibility for the subject."

Can such a government tackle the problems of sound finance? It is obvious that of the two parts of this dyarchical Executive, one, i.e. the Governor in Council, need have very little anxiety for reduction of expenditure or for the increase of taxation. It derives its mandate from Parliament, and as such is free to adopt any policy—backed up as it is by the certification power of the Governor without any regard for the best interests of the taxpayer. The authors of the Joint Report had seen that this certifying power to override the wishes of the Legislature might lead to irresponsible extravagance on the part of the Governor in Council, and had proposed to endow the Governor in Ministry with a countervailing power which was to act as a curb on the former. That power was to have consisted in the Proviso which laid down that no taxation even in the interests of the "reserved" subjects should be imposed in any Province without the consent of the ministry.[2] The Extremists—a class of politicians in India who were bent upon minimizing the reforms as being inadequate—disliked the proviso as calculated to make scapegoats of ministers and to bring them into discredit with the people. But their rivals, the "Moderates," now calling themselves "Liberals"—

[1] Government of India Act, 1919, sect. II (2) (a).
[2] Joint Report, para. 256.

one does not know why—saw clearly what the proviso meant. If this had materialized, there can be no doubt that the ministry would not have been a mere outsider tendering advice to the Council which might be accepted or rejected, but would have obtained a powerful voice in the settlement of the budget. Having regard to the fact that no minister unless he was in a position to justify the budget proposals, including even those which pertained to the reserved subjects, would have hoped to persuade the Legislature to agree to a proposal of new taxation, the influence of the ministry on the "reserved" subjects, i.e. on the Council, would have inevitably been in the direction of thrift and retrenchment. The moderates were entirely right in their interpretation of the proviso and also in their insistence upon acquiring power, even at the cost of burdening the country with new taxation.[1] But in the heat of the controversy and their desire to convince the public of the substantiality of the Reforms, they drew some very amusing pictures of how the ministers working under the ægis of the proviso would be able to hold the Council at bay. This alarmed the bureaucracy, which raised the cry that it was dangerous to leave the provison for the "reserved" subjects to the tender mercy of ministers who bore no responsibility for the consequences of refusing adequate Budget provision for those subjects. The authors of the Joint Report[2] had realized the force of this argument, and had confessed that the success of the arrangements depended upon their being worked by reasonable men who would conduct themselves in a reasonable manner. They were probably right in refusing to assume that the ministers would not co-operate, either by reducing their own claims or by imposing taxation, in order to meet expenditure which the Council considered essential for the proper administration of the "reserved" subjects. But the bureaucracy, which had been frightened by the tactless jubilations of the

[1] Vineberg, *Separation of State and Local Revenues in Canada*, p. 13, for an instance where military power was bought in Canada by volunteering to pay for the cost of it.

[2] Joint Report, para. 257.

Moderates, insisted that even reasonable men would at times, in all good faith, differ vitally from other reasonable men when it was a question of providing supply for work which one party was responsible for safeguarding and developing, while the other was only concerned in getting a share of the money. In its opinion circumstances could well be imagined in which reasonableness might not prevail. Let us suppose, it was argued, that the Governor in Council finds new and heavy expenditure imperative on some reserved subject, but that he cannot induce ministers to consent to accept less for their subjects or impose taxation for it. The Governor then, under his exceptional powers, insists on the expenditure being provided for in the next budget, and the result is to leave ministers with inadequate funds for their transferred subjects. What is to happen? Are ministers to be compelled to raise a tax which is apparently for their own need, but a need which has been created against their will by the Council refusing to curtail their demands? Such a procedure, it was pointed out, would be tortuous, provocative, and indefensible. Again, let us suppose that ministers consented to raise the necessary money, but the legislature refused to pass their revenue measures. Are the ministers to resign as having lost its confidence? The bureaucracy placed another dilemma before the authors of the Joint Report. Ministers have raised a new tax for some purpose of their own. In the next budget the Governor finds himself compelled to add substantially to the reserved provision for some new necessity, and thus to curtail the provision for "transferred" subjects. Ministers virtually see their new taxation receipts going to finance some development for which they are not responsible, and of which indeed they may disapprove. What are they to do? To avoid these difficulties the proviso was dropped and in its place the following changes were made in the Devolution Rules :—

Taxation and Borrowing

30. All proposals for raising taxation or for the borrowing of money on the revenues of a Province shall in the case

of a Governor's Province be considered by the Governor with his Executive Council and ministers sitting together, but the decision shall thereafter be arrived at by the Governor in Council, or by the Governor and Minister or Ministers, according as the proposal originates with the Governor in Council or the Governor and Ministers.

Allocation of Revenues for the Administration of Transferred Subjects

31. Expenditure for the purpose of the administration of both reserved and transferred subjects shall, in the first instance, be a charge on the general revenues and balances of each Province, and the framing of proposals for expenditure in regard to transferred and reserved subjects will be a matter for agreement between that part of the government which is responsible for the administration of transferred subjects and that part of the government which is responsible for the administration of reserved subjects.

Procedure in Event of Failure to Agree

32. (1) If at the time of the preparation of the budget the Governor is satisfied that there is no hope of agreement within a reasonable time between the members of his Executive Council on the one hand and Ministers on the other as to the apportionment of funds between reserved and transferred departments respectively, he may, by order in writing, allocate the revenue and balances of the Province between reserved and transferred subjects, by specifying the fractional proportions of the revenues and balances which shall be assigned to each class of subjects.

(2) An order of allocation under this rule may be made by the Governor either in accordance with his own discretion or in accordance with the report of an authority to be appointed by the Governor-General in this behalf on the application of the Governor.

Period of Order of Allocation

33. Every such order shall (unless it is sooner revoked) remain in force for a period to be specified in the order, which shall be not less than the duration of the then existing Legislative Council, and shall not exceed by more than one year the duration thereof :

Provided that the Governor may at any time, if his Executive Council and Ministers so desire, revoke an order of allocation or make such other allocation as has been agreed upon by them :

Provided, further, that if the order which it is proposed to revoke was passed in accordance with the report of an authority appointed by the Governor-General, the Governor shall obtain the consent of the Governor-General before revoking the same.

Condition of Order of Allocation

34. Every order of allocation made under these rules shall provide that, if any increase of revenue accrues during the period of the order on account of the imposition of fresh taxation that increase, unless the legislature otherwise directs, shall be allocated in aid of that part of the Government by which the taxation is initiated.

Preparation of Budget in Default of Agreement of Order of Allocation

35. If at the time of the preparation of any budget no agreement or allocation such as is contemplated by these rules has been arrived at, the budget shall be prepared on the basis of the aggregate grants respectively provided for the reserved and transferred subjects in the budget of the year about to expire.

Thus rather than depend too implicitly on reasonableness when circumstances must often be provocative effective precaution is taken by these rules against the ministry disapproving the allocation of funds to the "reserved" subjects by allowing the Governor to make such an allocation which is to be binding on both parts of the executive and also by arming him with the power of veto over the Provincial Legislature by allowing the Governor, should he deem it necessary, to restore a Budget grant on a reserved subject if it were refused or reduced by the Provincial Legislature which has the right to determine the Provincial Budget, and thirdly by allowing the Governor in Council equally with the Governor in Ministry to raise new taxation or new loans for the development of the subjects in its own charge. The result is that one part of this dyarchical Executive, namely the Governor in Council, can have little reason to be interested in economy or be over-weighed by considerations of taxation. Its supply being assured its concern in the stability of provincial finance must be deemed to be somewhat remote. The whole burden of meeting the problem of restoring sound finance, therefore, falls upon the Governor in Ministry in charge of the "transferred" subjects. For, under the distribution and certification powers it is the "transferred" subjects which must go without the funds they need, and it is those in charge of them, namely the Ministers, who must bear the brunt of economy or resort to new taxation to bring about an equilibrium in the finances of the Provinces. For it is doubtful that the Governor in Council will choose the onerous task of raising new taxes or practise economy when there are open to them other ways of amply providing themselves for the subjects they have under their control. Will the other half of the Government, namely the Governor in Ministry, consent to practise economy, or if need be undertake the burden of new taxation ? That obviously depends upon the temper of the Legislature.

At the outset it is to be noted that the Legislature will not readily favour projects of increased taxation. It is true, as Burke remarks,[1] that

> "To tell the people that they are relieved by the dilapidation of their public estate, is a cruel and insolent imposition. Statesmen, before they valued themselves on the relief given to the people by the destruction of their revenue, ought first to have carefully attended to the solution of the problem: Whether it be more advantageous to the people to pay considerably, and to gain in proportion; or to gain little or nothing, and to be disburthened of all contribution ?"

Whatever may be the philosophers' answer to this question, there can be no doubt that in a poor country like India with a very low capacity for bearing the burden of

[1] *Reflections on the Revolution in France.*

taxation, it is always very unpleasant, if not cruel, to propose an augmentation of that burden. Besides, any proposals for extra taxation would be shunned as likely to prejudice the chances of the legislators at the polls. So long as nomination was the general mode of obtaining a seat in the Legislature it was unnecessary to mind the prejudices of the electors. But when a seat is in the gift of the elector a candidate to the Legislature who proposes to touch his pocket has a small chance of success, even though the new taxes are to result in more than proportionate benefit. Besides, a political party which has won power from a bureaucracy by accusing it of heavy taxation cannot easily consent to disgrace itself by continuing the same policy. This innate aversion to taxation on the part of the Legislature is strengthened by the peculiar attitude of the Legislature towards the "reserved" and "transferred" subjects. The reserved subjects are those which mostly pertain to peace and order, while the transferred subjects are those which largely pertain to progress. But as has already been pointed out, the policy of the bureaucracy before the Reforms was calculated to sacrifice progress to order. It is therefore obvious that under the revised constitution the popular Legislatures should aim at turning the scales in favour of subjects tending towards progress. Their aversion to increase of taxation and their partiality for the transferred subjects will favour them to welcome proposals on the part of ministers making drastic reduction in the funds allotted to the reserved subjects. Their attitude towards the ministers will be largely governed by the amount of economy they will be able to effect in the reserved subjects for the benefit of the transferred subjects. Thus in the absence of any very large chances of increase of revenue the two halves of the Executive, the Governor in Council backed by the distribution and certification power and the Governor in Ministry backed by the general Budget powers of a popular Legislature, will compete in the matter of developing their subjects by forcing economy on each other. The Legislature being unwilling to tax, the Governor in Council being in a position to resist retrenchment and the Governor in Ministry anxious to expand, the chances of an early equilibrium in Provincial finance are very small.

It is, therefore, evident that if there is no sound finance in the Provinces it is because dyarchy is not a good form of government. Now, why is dyarchy not a good form of government? The answer to this question is very simple. Dyarchy is a bad form of government because it is opposed to the principle of collective responsibility. An administrative machine must work smoothly and harmoniously. But in order that it may do so it must recognize the principle of impartibility of governmental work and a collective responsibility of the administrators in the execution thereof. That the work of government is by its nature impartible may not seem to accord with facts: for, in practice the functions of government can be and commonly are partitioned, as they are between local bodies and between departments. Nevertheless it is true that a common thread runs through them all: that no function of government acts *in vacuo*; that each reacts on some other function, and that the various functions cannot act at all to produce orderly progress unless there is some force to harmonize them. Otherwise a policy enunciated in one department may fail to fructify for want of helpful action on behalf of other departments. That harmonizing force can only be found in the principle of collective responsibility. This is so because under it, as Hearn points out:[1]

> "Each minister acts in his own department as the recognized agent of his colleagues in that particular department, subject, however, to inquiry and control by the whole body. But in all cases on which any difficulty is likely to arise each minister, from motives not merely of prudence but of honour, takes the opinion of the Cabinet. When the precaution is taken the measure becomes the common act of the Ministry."

Right or wrong there is a common co-ordinated policy which guides a unified government based on collective responsibility. But having made a partition of governmental

[1] *The Government of England*, p. 204.

work, dyarchy must be said to have introduced an element of divided responsibility in the Executive. It is true that the partition is not horizontal but vertical. It is also true that in setting the two parts to work it has not been provided that there should be two separate Legislatures for two separate executives; or that each should make its own laws, control its own finance, frame its own budget, impose its own taxation, and raise its own loans; or that each should have its separate staff for the administration of subjects allotted to it and have its own methods of recruitment, pay and pension for its services; so that the two authorities might in fact have clearly defined spheres of their own exclusively within them. The Government of India had indeed suggested that some, if not all, of these concomitants of a typically dual executive should also be made a part of the dyarchical system adopted to carry on the government of the Provinces. Fortunately for the country the framers of the new constitution held [1]

"that wisdom lies not in equipping each of the different elements with a complete paraphernalia of its own, and trusting to their orbits lying sufficiently apart for collisions to be avoided; but in taking every opportunity of bringing the two elements into contact so as to induce the habits of joint action." "It is our intention," wrote the authors of the Joint Report,[2] "that the Government thus composed and with this distinction of functions shall discharge them as one Government," and that "the Provincial budget should be framed by the Executive Government as a whole." [3]

It was no doubt well to have modified the working of dyarchy by subjecting it to the interplay of two principles, one of division in order to give as clear a definition as possible of the several responsibilities of the two parts of the government and of union, in order to get association in aims and policy between those parts. For to have equipped each part of the Executive with a separate paraphernalia would have been nothing short of a calamity. But because there is an understanding that when ministers will act in matters

[1] Joint Report, p. 199. [2] *Ibid.*, p. 180. [3] *Ibid.*, p. 207.

of transferred subjects the councillors will advise them, and that when councillors will act in matters of reserved subjects the ministers will advise them, it does not alter the fact that dyarchy is a system of divided responsibility. It is not a system which ensures the work of government being conducted in harmony and in accordance with a common policy. On the other hand, it is a system fraught with organized quarrel. The dividing line between dyarchy and anarchy is very narrow. If such a system is not rent in practice it is because of two transient circumstances. One such circumstance consists in the Provincial Legislature being a weakling sapped of its vitality by political dissensions. The other consists in the tenure of the Ministers not being at the will of the Legislature, but for the duration of the Legislature's existence, and are to hold office during the pleasure of the governor. To allow a governor to choose ministers from among the elected members of the Legislature instead of requiring him to accept ministers who are elected by the Legislature is a grave derogation from the principle of responsible government which was avowedly the object of the Reforms Act. A minister who has the confidence of the governor, and a minister who has the confidence of the Legislature, are two entirely different things. How great is the difference between the two in so far as good government is concerned is writ large in the pages of English political history of the eighteenth and the nineteenth centuries. That such a system should have been adopted against which the whole English constitutional history is a grand protest cannot of course be without some reason. The ostensible reason advanced[1] is that the Legislature

"had had no experience of the power of dismissing Ministers, or the results attending the exercise of such power. Nobody in India is yet familiar with the obligations imposed by tenure of office at the will of a representative assembly. It is only by actual experience that these lessons can be learned. . . . By the device of appointing the ministers from the elected members of the (Legislature) and making their tenure of office conditional on the retention of their

[1] Joint Report, p. 181.

seats (there is) established at once some measure of responsibility, in the form of responsibility to their constituents and thus (is) put an end to the condition of affairs in which those entrusted with the administration are wholly irresponsible to the constituents who elect the (Legislature)."

It is difficult to believe in the cogency of this piece of reasoning. To argue that nothing can be learned without experience is simply absurd. What is necessary for a proper conduct on the part of an individual or a group is to understand the meanings and values of things. For that it is unnecessary to undergo actual trial. A Legislature composed of responsible persons may be trusted to know the consequences of dismissing a Minister at the start without having to wait to learn it by experience. Again, to argue that the system is not the less responsible because ministers are responsible to their constituents is a shallow piece of pedantry. It was no doubt argued by Austin,[1] in connection with the English Constitution, that the House of Commons was "merely trustee for the body by which they are elected and appointed." It is true that in a political sense the electors are the most important part of, we may even say, are actually, the Sovereign power, since their will is under every representative system of government sure to obtain ultimate obedience. But as Prof. Dicey points out,[2]

"any expressions which attribute to Parliamentary electors a legal part in the process of law-making are quite inconsistent with the view taken by the law of the position of an elector. The sole legal right of electors under the English constitution (and the same is true under the Indian constitution) is to elect members of Parliament. Electors have no legal means of initiating, of sanctioning, or of repealing the legislation of Parliament. No court will consider for a moment the argument that a law is invalid as being opposed to the opinion of the electorate":

and this exactly defines the status of the Indian electors. To make the minister responsible to such a nonentity is

[1] *Jurisprudence*, Vol. I, 4th Ed., p. 253.
[2] *Law of the Constitution*, 8th Ed., 1915, p. 57.

to make him virtually irresponsible. That the framers of the constitution were not alive to these considerations in suggesting this particular mode of appointing Ministers it is hard to believe. What is more probable is that this particular mode of appointing ministers was adopted because it permitted to select a man who was more likely to co-operate with those in charge of the reserved subjects and who being irremovable by the Legislature would be less swayed by its wishes. But the Ministers cannot remain altogether immune from the axe of the Legislature. The dangers of the position of a minister who has cultivated friendship with the councillor and has failed to ingratiate himself into the favour of the Legislature, cannot fail to come home to him on budget occasions. The proposals of the minister as embodied in the budget will be liable to be reversed by a vote of the majority of the Legislature, but neither he himself nor the governor will be able to intervene. The minister's only remedy will be to resign.

Anyhow these circumstances which have, so to say, saved dyarchy from failure are only transitory. The political dissensions may be no more than a passing phase, and the ministers from the second term of the reformed Legislature will become amenable to it: so that before long the forces may be organized better than they are, when dyarchy is sure to fail.

Hybrid executives, divided responsibility, division of functions, reservation of powers, cannot make for a good system of government, and where there is no good system of government there can be little hope for a sound system of finance. The primary solution is that there should be an undivided government with a collective responsibility. That, however, can be achieved only when the whole of government derives its mandate from a common source. That such a consummation should take place as early as possible is devoutly to be wished. In that behalf it is encouraging to know that dyarchy is but a transitional system. The only question is how long and protracted will the period of transition be. The justification for introducing a dyarchical form of government rests on the supposition that India is at present ill-prepared to sustain a system of responsible government in anything like completeness, for owing to the lack of education and political experience, the Indian electorate will for some time be unable either to formulate their requirements intelligently or effectively impose a mandate upon their representatives, and that owing to the inveterate social prejudices of the educated classes there is a great danger of their abusing the political power to exploit the masses. This cardinal fact, it was held, must differentiate the degree and the kind of responsibility which can be introduced at the outset from that which will be the eventual resultant of the new system, and must impose the obligation of ensuring that the forces which now hold the people together are not completely withdrawn before satisfactory substitutes are ready to take their place. On the other hand, it has been urged [1] that there is no necessity to wait till the cardinal fact disappears; for

> "in all countries responsibility in the beginning has been entrusted to a very small section of the people, and government has been in the hands of a small educated minority, who have naturally cared for the interests of the uneducated masses pending the spread of education and the consequent extension of the franchise."

This is of course a familiar line of argument which is usually put forth in India by the political radicals and social tories. If we put aside the painful story of the harsh, cruel and inhuman treatment which the classes in India have accorded to the masses, truth is on their side, for in every country there have been downtrodden communities suffering from social oppression and social injustice, and yet no country has had to be without political power on that account. But those who use this argument forget that if other countries like America with her negroes and Japan with her Hitas are in possession of political power without having first destroyed social inequality, it is due

[1] Cf. the evidence of the Hon. V. J. Patel and Mr. Madhava Rao before the Joint Select Committee on the Government of India Bill. House of Commons Return 203 of 1919, p. 106.

to the fact of their having been in possession of military power. Military force and moral force are the two chief means to political freedom, and a country which cannot generate the former must cultivate the latter. Thus in India the political problem is entirely a social problem, and a postponement of its solution virtually postpones the day when India can have a free government subject to the mandate of none but her own people.

INDEX